Charisma and Leadership in Organizations

D1484367

Charisma and Leadership in Organizations

Alan Bryman

SAGE Publications
London • Newbury • New Delhi

SAGE Publications Ltd
6 Bonhill Street
London EC2A 4PU

SAGE Publications Inc
2455 Teller Road
Newbury Park, California 91320

SAGE Publications India Pvt Ltd
32, M-Block Market
Greater Kailash – I
New Delhi 110 048

British Library Cataloguing in Publication Data

Bryman, Alan
Charisma and Leadership in Organizations
I. Title
303.3

ISBN 0-8039-8317-4
ISBN 0-8039-8318-2 (Pbk)

Librrary of Congress catalog card number 91-051216

Typeset by Contour Typesetters, Southall, London
Printed in Great Britain by Biddles Ltd., Guildford, Surrey

Contents

For Sue and Sarah

Glossary of Abbreviations

AA	Alcoholics Anonymous
AL	achievement-oriented leadership
CEO	chief executive officer
DSO	direct selling organization
ES	*Economy and Society*
GE	General Electric
IBM	International Business Machines
ICI	Imperial Chemical Industries
IL	instrumental leadership
LBDQ	Leader Behavior Description Questionnaire
LPI	Leadership Practices Inventory
MLQ	Multifactor Leadership Questionnaire
NCA	National Council on Alcoholism
PL	participative leadership
RLS	Romance of Leadership Scale
SL	supportive leadership
VDL	Vertical Dyad Linkage

Preface

Leadership has become in recent years a major focus for a variety of writers concerned with organizations. It has always been an important area of enquiry among academic researchers concerned with organizations, as the voluminous literature on the subject testifies, but since the early 1980s the amount of interest seems to have escalated, and at the time of writing there seems to be no sign of this tendency abating. Book after book has appeared extolling the virtues of an understanding of leadership, implying that leaders hold the key to organizational effectiveness. This surge of interest has occurred at the same time that popular interest in prominent leaders has grown. There seems to be an insatiable appetite for stories about the heroic exploits of individuals whose leadership has made a dramatic impact, whether as leaders of new organizations that grow into major corporations or as leaders of ailing firms which are brought back from the brink of disaster. Like Aesop's fables, their stories are meant to contain morals for countless other leaders.

Moreover, much of the emerging literature began to focus on a number of fairly congruent themes. I have dubbed this literature 'the New Leadership'. It is always risky to call any intellectual approach 'new', since today's new rapidly becomes tomorrow's old. However, to anticipate somewhat one of the later themes in this book, a variety of terms have been employed to describe the ideas that emerged in the 1980s, and rather than add to the profusion of names or arbitrarily choose one to stand for the rest, the expedient of writing about the New Leadership has been adopted. One of the chief aims of this book is to summarize some of these themes and to provide an evaluation of their strengths and weaknesses. As such, the book essentially starts where my previous book on the subject, *Leadership and Organizations* (1986), left off. However, so that the present book can be treated as a critical assessment of leadership theory and research in its own right, Chapter 1 contains a presentation and evaluation of central themes in the 'old leadership'. Obviously, this discussion is somewhat selective, but it is hoped that it will serve as a helpful background to the presentation of the New Leadership ideas. A number of passages in this chapter have been taken from *Leadership and Organizations*, but have been revised.

One focus of the New Leadership has been a resurgence of interest among some writers in the concept of charismatic leadership. Not only do many of the contributors to the New Leadership write about charismatic leadership, but also a lot of the themes associated with the New Leadership overlap with conceptions of charismatic leadership. As a result, charisma and charismatic leadership are, as the book's title implies, prominent areas in the discussion that follows. Indeed, Chapters 2, 3 and 4 are specifically concerned to elaborate the nature of charismatic leadership and its empirical manifestations. These chapters will entail excursions into areas that are far removed from the modern complex organization with which New Leadership writers are concerned. However, in order to appreciate what charisma is and what its effects are, such a discussion provides an important backcloth to the later chapters. Chapter 5 examines the emergence of charisma as a theme in the literature on modern organizational settings, with an emphasis on business organizations, as well as an introduction to other strands within the New Leadership. Chapter 6 explores research findings on charismatic leadership and other aspects of New Leadership writing.

What has been missing from much of the emergent literature on the New Leadership (including charismatic leadership) is critical reflection. As congruent themes in the New Leadership literature have emerged, a new orthodoxy has built up. It is timely to take stock of this emergent literature. This is especially important in view of the heavily normative approach that many writers within the New Leadership genre exhibit and the rather strident style that much of the writing reveals. Therefore, Chapter 7 provides a critical examination of the literature on charismatic leadership in business settings and the New Leadership generally.

A number of people have read all or parts of the book. I should like to thank Peter Baehr, Mike Bresnen, Steve Bruce, Mike Gane, Peter B. Smith and my wife, Sue, for their helpful and perceptive comments. I have tried to accommodate their suggestions wherever I can, but they are not responsible for any deficiencies in the book. I also wish to thank Sue Jones of Sage for her encouragement in getting this book under way and for her editorial comments on the product, and Hamleys for permission to reproduce the job advertisement that appears in Chapter 3. As usual, Sue and Sarah have put up with my writing by providing a supportive environment, with only the occasional suggestion that perhaps I should be doing something else. As with everything I do, this book is for them.

Alan Bryman

1
Leadership Theory and Research

The purpose of this chapter is to summarize the central approaches to the study of leadership in organizations up to the early 1980s to provide a backcloth to the later chapters. In essence, the aim will be to examine material that was explored in *Leadership and Organizations* (Bryman, 1986). Since it is clearly impossible to cover the ground dealt with by a book in a single chapter, the present exposition will have two chief foci. The broad definition of leadership that is typically employed by the approaches to be examined in this chapter will be briefly outlined. Then, the three main approaches to the study of leadership prior to the 1980s – the 'trait', 'style' and 'contingency' approaches – will be examined. Their respective periods and core themes are outlined in Table 1.1, along with the 'New Leadership' approach which will be explored in later chapters. In examining the trait, style and contingency approaches, it will only be possible to discuss a representative of each. It should be recognized that the dates in Table 1.1 have to be treated in a fairly circumspect way, in that they represent rough indications of the junctures at which shifts of emphasis appeared. Moreover, each new stage does not herald the demise of its predecessor; rather, a change in emphasis is indicated.

Table 1.1   *Trends in leadership theory and research*

Period	Approach	Core theme
Up to late 1940s	Trait approach	Leadership ability is innate
Late 1940s to late 1960s	Style approach	Leadership effectiveness is to do with how the leader behaves
Late 1960s to early 1980s	Contingency approach	It all depends; effective leadership is affected by the situation
Since early 1980s	New Leadership approach (includes charismatic leadership)	Leaders need vision

Before embarking upon an examination of the three approaches that provide the chief focus for this chapter, some consideration of the definition of leadership is required. Researchers concerned with leadership have tended to emphasize three main elements in their definitions: influence, group and goal. First, leaders are perceived as individuals who *influence* the behaviour of others, who are often referred to as subordinates. Second, the leader is examined in relation to a *group* – usually, in the context of research on leadership in organizations, a work group. Accordingly, the vast literature on leadership is replete with studies of foremen and their subordinates, sergeants and their combat units, managers and their teams, and so on. To some extent, this level of analysis has led to the accusation that leadership research is relatively small-scale in focus and that it therefore tends to neglect the leadership of organizations as such. However, the New Leadership has gone quite a long way towards countering this trend. Third, leadership research tends to place considerable emphasis upon a group *goal* that has to be accomplished. Thus, leadership is typically defined in terms of a process of social influence whereby a leader steers members of a group towards a goal. This broad definition captures fairly well the essence of most of the definitions that underpin the approaches examined below.

The trait approach

The trait approach emphasizes the personal qualities of leaders and implies that leaders are born rather than made. The bulk of research on leadership traits has sought to establish the personal features of leaders which distinguish them from non-leaders or followers. It might be argued that such a question is of only limited use in the context of the study of leadership in organizations where one would hope to identify the characteristics of effective, as against less effective, leaders. This latter issue, however, was addressed only in a relatively small number of studies. Unfortunately, reviews of the literature on leadership traits often fail to distinguish the two issues.

There are three broad types of trait which the literature has addressed. First, there are physical factors such as height, weight, physique, appearance and age. Second, researchers have examined ability characteristics such as intelligence, fluency of speech, scholarship and knowledge. Third, a wide range of personality features have been examined. These have included conservatism, introversion–extroversion, dominance, personal adjustment, self-confidence, interpersonal sensitivity and emotional control.

An influential review by Stogdill (1948) of trait research cast doubt on the evidence. His was not the only assessment that had sounded a negative note, but it was the most influential. Stogdill failed to find consistent evidence to suggest that personal factors played a part in who became a leader. At best, he was able to conclude that the personal factors associated with leadership are substantially affected by the requirements of the situation from which the leader emerges. This suggests that the personal factors associated with leadership are situation specific. Stogdill carried out a subsequent review of the literature up to 1970 which was published along with his 1948 article in his *Handbook of Leadership* (1974). Both of these reviews, along with yet a further update, were published in Bass's (1981; 1990a) revised and expanded edition of the *Handbook*, published after Stogdill's death in 1978. These 'editions' of the review of research on leadership traits, along with other useful assessments such as Gibb's (1947; 1969) and Mann's (1959), provide a comprehensive account of the trait approach, upon which the author will borrow heavily. All references to Stogdill's (1948; 1974) work will be cited in terms of Bass (1990a).

Stogdill's 1948 review is often cited as a major cause, albeit in conjunction with reviews by other writers, of disillusionment with research into leadership traits. Even Stogdill recognized in 1974 that they 'sounded the seeming deathknell of a purely traits approach to the study of leadership' (Bass, 1990a: 78). It is true that the reviews were a contributory factor to a surge of interest in leadership styles and behaviour (see next section) but they certainly did not kill off trait research. Stogdill's review of the 1949–70 literature was able to uncover 163 studies, hardly evidence of a moribund field. In particular, research into the traits of effective managers seems to have thrived during this period. Of particular interest is that, on the basis of his second review, Stogdill (Bass, 1990a) asserted that his own and others' reviews had overemphasized the situational element and underemphasized the universal traits which leaders seem to exhibit. This assertion was consistent with a review by Mann (1959) of personality factors alone and their relationship with leadership. Mann's review indicated that leaders tend to be more intelligent, extrovert, dominant, masculine, conservative and better adjusted than non-leaders. Mann found contradictory evidence in respect of all of these variables, as well as a very large number of findings which did not attain acceptable levels of statistical significance. However, the general tenor of his review was much more positive about the potential of personality variables to discriminate between leaders and others. Similarly, in contrast to the 1948 review, Stogdill's second survey resulted in a somewhat less tentative conclusion:

> The leader is characterized by a strong drive for responsibility and task completion, vigor and persistence in the pursuit of goals, venturesomeness and originality in problem solving, drive to exercise initiative in social situations, self-confidence and sense of personal identity, willingness to accept the consequences of his or her decisions and actions, readiness to absorb interpersonal stress, willingness to tolerate frustration and delay, ability to influence other people's behavior, and the capacity to structure social interaction systems to the purpose at hand. (Bass, 1990a: 87)

Stogdill retained his views about the importance of the situation in the study of leadership traits, but sought to attach greater significance to traits as such than in his earlier work.

There is some evidence, then, to suggest that the loss of confidence in the trait approach from the late 1940s may have been unwarranted. A further indication of this possibility is suggested by an analysis by Lord et al. (1986) of the studies from which Mann (1959) drew his conclusions. The authors used a technique called 'meta-analysis' which pools the results of studies in a domain to provide an overall estimate of the impact of one or more independent variables. Lord et al. found that their procedures suggested stronger evidence for the role of the six traits which Mann emphasized in his review in differentiating leaders from non-leaders. Kirkpatrick and Locke (1991) have also reviewed evidence that portrays the trait approach in a more favourable light. Unlike many other writers, they do not view traits purely in terms of special qualities with which leaders (and especially effective leaders) are naturally endowed. They argue that trait theorists have never seen traits purely as the products of natural endowment; instead, traits were simply personal characteristics in terms of which leaders differed from non-leaders. This may be true, but exponents of the trait approach have usually emphasized personal characteristics which are innate and not generally amenable to change. There is a danger that the term 'trait' becomes so stretched that it applies to any variable on which leaders differ from non-leaders, including even the kinds of behaviour pattern examined in the next section. Kirkpatrick and Locke's review suggests that the following traits distinguish leaders from others: drive (including ambition, energy, tenacity); strong desire to lead; honesty and integrity; self-confidence (including emotional stability); cognitive ability (that is, the ability to marshal and interpret a wide variety of information); and knowledge of the business. These authors also differ from many other writers on traits when they assert that traits in any case only tell part of the story, since there is much more to being an effective leader than the possession of this collection of traits.[1]

There appear to be signs of a resurgence of interest in the trait approach, albeit in a somewhat transformed state. However, what was crucial about reviews like Stogdill's was that they led to a belief in the relative unimportance of traits in relation to leadership. This disillusionment played an important role in generating a search for an alternative approach out of which the next phase of leadership research emerged.

The style approach

From the late 1940s, the study of leadership in organizations moved increasingly towards the understanding of leadership style or behaviour, the two terms being employed interchangeably to describe what leaders do. Researchers were particularly concerned to identify the kinds of leader behaviour that enhanced the effectiveness of subordinates. This shift in emphasis was also significant in relation to the practical implications of leadership research. The implication of trait research was that leaders with the right qualities need to be selected, since the traits of good leaders are largely innate and hence not amenable to substantial change. By contrast, most leadership style researchers believed that once the behaviour that makes for effective leadership is known, leaders can be trained to exhibit that behaviour, so that they can become better leaders. The research associated with Ohio State University was one of the first manifestations of the style approach and is used as an illustration since it exemplifies the approach.

The Ohio research generally entails taking focal leaders who occupy formal leadership positions and administering questionnaires to their subordinates. The questionnaires ask about the frequency with which the focal leader engages in certain kinds of behaviour. In the original Leader Behavior Description Questionnaire (LBDQ) there were 130 such questions. The idea is then to look for clustering among the answers to the questions. The early research, which was mainly conducted on military leaders, suggested that there was some 'bunching' of the descriptions that subordinates gave of their leaders. Two clusters of questions were especially significant in the early research and have continued to prove the main focus for many studies. These two clusters suggest that leaders can be described in terms of how far they exhibit consideration and initiating structure. Consideration relates to the extent to which leaders promote camaraderie, mutual trust, liking and respect in the relationship between themselves and their subordinates. Initiating structure denotes the degree to which leaders organize work tightly, structure the work context, provide clear-cut definitions of role responsibility and generally play a very active part in getting the work at hand fully scheduled. Leaders' scores for consideration and initiating structure are then related to various outcomes, such as subordinate job satisfaction, group productivity and assessments by each leader's superior of his or her performance. The LBDQ has undergone a number of changes and the most frequently used version is the one devised by Stogdill (1963) and known as LBDQ-Form XII (LBDQ-XII).

The Ohio State researchers conceived of consideration and initiating structure as separate dimensions and not as opposite ends of a continuum. Each leader can therefore be depicted as having a 'profile' in terms of his or her level of both consideration and initiating structure. The initial analyses of the data (e.g. Halpin, 1957; Halpin and Winer, 1957; Fleishman et al., 1955) suggested a tension between consideration and initiating structure. Research initially suggested that considerate leaders provide a pleasant work environment for their subordinates, but are regarded as less effective. Leaders who emphasize structuring work activities often reduce the levels of job satisfaction experienced by the work group, but are regarded as more effective by their superiors. However, Halpin's (1957) research on aircraft commanders suggested that leaders who emerge with high scores on both dimensions are regarded as more effective by their own supervisors *and* have subordinates who experience job satisfaction. This finding led Halpin (1957: 64) to conclude that the optimal leader behaviour is that which achieves high scores on both dimensions, and not that which involves a trade-off between the two. In later years, the sobriquet of the 'hi-hi leader' was employed to describe the leader who exhibits high scores on both dimensions.

This summary cannot do full justice to the wide range of studies which have employed the Ohio framework. Indeed, many of the studies conducted under the auspices of path-goal theory (see next section) made considerable use of the Ohio measuring instruments. However, the Ohio research encountered criticisms, many of which it shares with other examples of the style approach. Six problem areas are identified.

Inconsistent findings

A detailed analysis of early findings by Korman (1966) revealed that the magnitude and direction of correlations between consideration and initiating structure and various outcome measures were highly variable. Also, many correlations failed to achieve statistical significance. Among LBDQ studies which use subordinate ratings of outcomes (such as morale and satisfaction), correlations with consideration range from –0.52 to +0.84, and with initiating structure from –0.19 to +0.68. Not only is the fact of divergent findings disconcerting, but the small correlations that are frequently found call into question the extent to which leadership (or leadership as measured by the Ohio researchers) is a genuinely important predictor of the various outcome measures which have been examined. A meta-analysis of post-1968 studies by Fisher and Edwards (1988; see Bass, 1990a: 533–5) found that the adjusted mean correlation between job performance and both consideration and initiating structure was 0.45 and 0.47 respectively for the LBDQ and 0.27 and 0.22 for the LBDQ-XII. When job satisfaction was the outcome variable, the parallel correlations were 0.65 and 0.51 for the LBDQ and 0.70 and 0.46 for the LBDQ-XII. This pattern implies fairly high levels of correlation overall, though it also reveals a tendency for results to vary according to the Ohio measurement instrument employed and for correlation coefficients to be larger when an outcome like job satisfaction is assessed rather than performance. Although the levels of correlation revealed by this meta-analysis are reassuring, they almost certainly belie substantial variation of the kind depicted by Korman.

The assertion that it is high levels of *both* consideration and initiating structure that promote work group effectiveness, job satisfaction, morale and the like has been found empirically wanting by some studies. Research by both Larson et al. (1976) and Nystrom (1978) strongly suggests that combining a leader's consideration and initiating structure scores does not add a great deal to the singular effects of either dimension on subordinate satisfaction and performance. These researchers tend to prefer a more parsimonious model which examines the effects of consideration and initiating structure singly rather than together. A similar conclusion about the hi-hi combination was reached by Fisher and Edwards's (1988) meta-analysis.

Absence of situational analysis

Korman (1966) took many of the Ohio studies to task for failing to include in their research situational variables, that is, variables which moderate the relationship between leader behaviour and various outcomes. The failure to take situational factors into account may in part have contributed to the previously mentioned inconsistent findings.

Kerr et al. (1974) sought to instil a situational interpretation into many of the Ohio studies. It is only possible to deal with two instances. They point to research which suggests that pressure on the work group (for example, due to time urgency or external threat) moderates the relationship between initiating structure and both satisfaction and performance. The latter was confirmed in a study of a social services organization using the LBDQ-XII (Schriesheim and Murphy, 1976), in that when jobs are stressful greater initiating structure enhances subordinate performance, but when they are not stressful it reduces performance. These researchers also found that job stress moderated the effects of consideration. In high-stress conditions the correlations with both performance and job satisfaction were negative; in low-stress conditions they were positive. Failure to take into account this variable may in part be the reason for some contradictory findings. The Kerr et al. (1974) review points to intrinsic task satisfaction as a moderating variable, in that higher levels of intrinsic satisfaction reduce the positive relationships between consideration and both job satisfaction and performance, and render less negative the relationship between job satisfaction and initiating structure.

An increasing number of writers have become conscious of the need to take into account situational factors when employing the Ohio approach (for example, Katz, 1977; Schriesheim, 1980). The outcome of this tendency is a loss of the neatness of the early Ohio research and a necessity for more complex ways of handling the data. Also, there is often little theoretical (or even practical) justification for the various situational factors examined by various researchers. To some extent, the path-goal approach (see below) mitigates this tendency, but it too has a tendency for atheoretical investigations of particular moderating variables. Any notion of a grand synthesis of work in the Ohio tradition becomes more difficult to envisage while researchers proceed with their investigations in this manner.

The problem of causality

Like the two criticisms developed thus far, the problem of causality applies equally to other approaches to the study of leadership style (and 'traits' too), and by no means solely to the output of researchers in the Ohio tradition. The assumption in such research tends to be that style of leadership influences various outcomes, so that the direction of casual influence is as follows:

leadership style $\longrightarrow$ group performance, job satisfaction, morale etc.

However, the bulk of research mentioned thus far is cross-sectional, that is, data for both the presumed causal variable (leadership style) and the dependent variable (such as job satisfaction) are collected more or less simultaneously. The notion that leadership style constitutes the independent variable is an assumption rather than the consequence of investigations designed to establish such a view. It is extremely risky to deduce a cause–effect relationship from the correlation of two variables. Indeed, such a deduction has quite a strong prima facie set of reasons for being incorrect, for it would not seem in the least unlikely to suppose that leaders adjust their styles in response to group performance or job satisfaction:

group performance, job satisfaction, morale etc. $\longrightarrow$ leadership style

It is not possible to choose between these competing explanations of a correlation between two variables from a cross-sectional study.

The possibility that the causal relationship between leadership style and outcomes can be complex is suggested by a laboratory experiment by Lowin and Craig (1968) in which subordinate competence and quality of work were experimentally created. The question was: did the people who were allocated the role of leader in the study vary their leadership style in response to good or poor performance? The results suggest that, when faced with subordinates who perform poorly, leaders exhibit greater initiating structure and closeness of supervision but less consideration. Evidence such as this is important for two reasons. First, it points to the likelihood that a leader's style is not inert, but can react to the circumstances of his or her subordinates. Second, it challenges the 'leadership style causes outcome' interpretation, by pointing to the possibility of causation being the other way around. Of course, it does not disprove the interpretation, for performance may also be responsive to leadership style (and almost certainly is).

A longitudinal investigation of first-line managers from a number of firms by Greene (1975) provides confirmation of the experimental findings. Data were collected at three one-month intervals to allow for 'lagged' effects of leader behaviour. The research suggests that higher consideration leads to greater subordinate satisfaction, a causal interpretation very much in line with conventional reasoning. Greene also found that subordinate performance (both quantity and quality as rated by each subordinate's peers) affected initiating structure; poor subordinate performance led to more structuring behaviour on the part of leaders. This finding strongly suggests that initiating structure is best thought of as a response to subordinate performance levels rather than a cause of them. However, Greene also found that consideration moderated the direction of the relationship. Among highly considerate leaders, greater structure makes for better performance; when they are low in consideration, performance is the causal variable in that better performance leads to a lesser emphasis on structure. These findings confirm that the causal direction is often not of the 'leadership style influences outcome' kind, but in the other direction.

The problem of the group

The predominant focus in leadership theory and research is the leader in relation to the group, and the Ohio tradition exemplifies this tendency. There has been a growing recognition that the group-level emphasis imposes something of a dilemma on leadership researchers. The Ohio approach, and that of a number of other researchers, involves averaging individual subordinates' descriptions of their leader (when instruments such as the LBDQ are used) to form a group-level description of their leader. But leaders often behave in different ways to different group members, so that the procedure of averaging individual descriptions may mask important divergences in the style(s) of a leader in respect of particular subordinates. In a series of papers advocating a vertical dyad linkage (VDL) approach to the study of leadership, the averaging approach has been criticized by Graen and Cashman (1975) and Danserau et al. (1975). Their approach involves much closer attention to the exchange and negotiation practices and processes which underpin the formation of leader–subordinate dyads. It is the leader in relation to the subordinate, not to a work group or unit, which is the focus of their attention.

Cummings (1975) has suggested that the VDL approach exaggerates the variability in leader–subordinate dyads within a group. For example, he points out that the need to behave equitably to subordinates, so as not to discriminate or display preferences, constrains leaders to limit the variability of their behaviour in respect of subordinates. Against such a view are some of the findings deriving from the VDL approach, such as a study of managers (Danserau et al., 1973) which found that whereas averaged LBDQ measures were virtually unrelated to turnover, individual-level scores were related to this variable.

A survey of commanders, sergeants and their respective subordinates in the US Army National Guard by Katerberg and Hom (1981) permitted an examination of whether average army unit depictions of leader behaviour or individual accounts were more strongly related to various outcomes. Katerberg and Hom found that variations in leader behaviour using the LBDQ-XII analysed at the individual level tended to display strong relationships with various measures of satisfaction, as well as role clarity and conflict. This was the case more or less irrespective of whether the leader was a commander or a first sergeant. Some evidence was also found to suggest that averaged depictions of leaders by their subordinates also had an impact – albeit a lesser one – on various measures, particularly those associated with satisfaction. An overview of such research by Dienesch and Liden (1986) confirms that it is necessary to encapsulate both group-level and individual-level descriptions of leader behaviour in investigations, since each accounts for some of the variation in outcomes. In conclusion, while the case for the VDL approach is by no means clear-cut, it is evident that the Ohio measuring instruments neglect differences between subordinates in their descriptions of leader behaviour.

Informal leadership

The literature on leadership in organizations addresses the question of informal leadership surprisingly rarely. The vast majority of studies employing the Ohio instruments direct their questioning to designated leaders, that is, people in positions of leadership, and the focus of empirical enquiry is upon their behaviour and its effects. Yet social scientists have long been aware that individuals often assume, or are ascribed, leadership even when the group in question does not have a formal structure. Whyte's (1943) classic study of a street corner gang in the USA provides an example of such a process. In an apparently egalitarian group, Whyte was able to show how leaders emerged, how individuals became leaders, and how leaders retained their position. If the emergence of leadership can be demonstrated in a context such as this, it may be hypothesized that informal leadership can arise outside a formal system within work organizations. Indeed, there is every reason to expect the emergence of informal leaders in work groups in view of the recognition of the importance of the so-called 'informal organization' which arises in the context of the formal structure. This term refers to a cluster of unofficial practices and structures which, it is often suggested, arise in all work environments (Selznick, 1943). Informal leaders may well emerge as part of the phenomenon of informal organization, such that a group of peers have their own, rather than a bureaucratically conferred, leader.

Informal leadership may occur in either of two main ways. First, the subordinate may be influenced by an individual in a leadership position other than the person to whom he or she is formally responsible. Second, informal leadership may arise among peers. The problem with the failure to include informal leadership is that when the Ohio State instruments are administered, the questions may not relate to the most appropriate person. Also, the behaviour patterns of formal and informal leaders may differ. Experimental evidence suggests that elected as against appointed leaders perceive themselves differently, and are so perceived by followers. Also, they differ in the amount of influence they have over their followers (Hollander and Julian, 1978a; 1978b). While the appointed/elected distinction differs from formal/informal, they do share some common ingredients, so that the suggestion that the impact of informal leadership needs to be taken into account receives some reinforcement from these findings.

Measurement problems

Although the Ohio State measures of consideration and initiating structure are internally consistent (Schriesheim and Kerr, 1974), a number of measurement problems have been identified. For example, consideration seems to be vulnerable to leniency effects, that is, a tendency to describe a leader in a favourable but probably untrue manner (Schriesheim et al., 1979; Tracy, 1987). A further complication is that ratings of leaders are contaminated by subordinates' implicit leadership theories. In a study by Rush et al. (1977), undergraduates were initially given a brief description of a person in a supervisory position. The description was varied slightly to convey different impressions of the supervisor's level of performance, level of accomplishment, and sex. No account was provided of the person's behaviour *qua* leader. The LBDQ-XII was administered to the experimental subjects in a slightly altered form to reflect the fact that the LBDQ statements would refer to leaders for whom they had had little information. Rush et al. found the LBDQ descriptions provided were broadly similar to those which were typically provided in descriptions of actual leaders whose behaviour was being rated by real subordinates. The authors then assessed the effects of the manipulated performance cues (that is, high, average or low departmental performance).

The evidence suggests that respondents downgrade their assessments of both consideration and initiating structure of a leader when the cue indicates poor performance. When provided with cues indicative of good performance, leaders tended to be evaluated in hi-hi terms, suggesting that people carry around with them implicit theories about the nature of leadership and its effects which correspond closely to the central conceptual categories of leadership theorists. Such findings raise questions about whether questionnaire approaches like that of the Ohio tradition are based on subordinates' depictions of a particular leader or whether they reflect broad, implicit categorizations. A number of studies have confirmed the role of implicit leadership theories (for example, Lord et al., 1978; Bryman, 1987). Research by Gioia and Sims (1985) suggests that the problem with the LBDQ may lie in the use of general statements about leader behaviour to which subordinates respond. When questionnaire items relate to leaders' specific behaviour patterns, the distorting effects of implicit leadership theories are less pronounced. Indeed, a general problem with research instruments like the LBDQ is that they are based on perceptions by subordinates of their leaders' behaviour, and are therefore not based on the behaviour of leaders as such.

The Ohio research has been treated here as exemplifying the emphasis on leadership style that became prominent after trait research. Other approaches include: the Michigan studies (for example, Kahn and Katz, 1953); the four-factor theory (for example, Bowers and Seashore, 1966); research on participative leadership; studies of leader reward behaviour (for example, Podsakoff et al., 1984); and Oldham's (1976) research on leaders' motivational strategies. These strands of research exhibit many of the features identified in relation to the Ohio studies, while suffering from many similar limitations.

The contingency approach

The contingency approach to the study of leadership proposes that the effectiveness of a leadership style is situationally contingent. This means that a particular style or pattern of behaviour will be effective in some circumstances (such as when a task is intrinsically satisfying, or when the personalities of subordinates predispose them to a particular style) but not others. Contingency theorists explicitly draw attention to the notion that there are no universally appropriate styles of leadership; particular styles have an impact on various outcomes in some situations but not in others. Situational factors were considered by researchers working within the leadership style tradition, but, as was seen in the previous section, they were not given great prominence and were even somewhat residual elements. The traditions associated with the contingency approach placed situational factors at the forefront of concern and provided a theoretical framework within which they could operate in conjunction with the examination of leadership *per se*.

The path-goal theory of leadership, which is largely associated with the work of House (1973; House and Mitchell, 1974), is a good example of a contingency approach. In large part, it represents an application of the 'expectancy theory' of work motivation. Expectancy theorists propose that people choose levels of effort at which they are prepared to work. The choice of a high level of effort is contingent upon their assessment of whether it leads to good performance and the value (called 'valence' in the language of expectancy theory) of good performance to them. While expectancy theory has been subjected to considerable criticism and the research which stems from it is fraught with methodological difficulties (Mitchell, 1979), it was adapted by House to the context of the leader's ability to motivate his or her subordinates.

The early formulation supplied by House (1973) was rapidly revised (House and Dessler, 1974; House and Mitchell, 1974) and it is upon the more recent versions that the following explication draws. According to this formulation:

> The motivational functions of the leader consist of increasing personal payoffs to subordinates for work goal attainment, and making the path to these payoffs easier to travel by clarifying it, reducing roadblocks and pitfalls, and increasing the opportunities for personal satisfaction *en route*. (House and Dessler, 1974: 31)

In other words, leaders are an important source of motivation in so far as their behaviour can enhance the desirability of good performance in the eyes of their subordinates and facilitate goal attainment for them. If subordinates believe that a high level of effort and hence good performance lead to desirable outcomes, they will work harder. Desirable outcomes might involve greater pay or prestige. If the perceived outcomes are undesirable or unclear, the subordinate will not be motivated to work hard. Undesirable outcomes might include loss of prestige, or greater personal risk. Later formulations of the approach (House and Mitchell, 1974; Filley et al., 1976) examined four kinds of leader behaviour which may have an impact upon the motivational processes which the theory emphasizes:

1   Instrumental leadership (sometimes called 'directive'). This form of leader behaviour entails a systematic clarification of what is expected of subordinates, how work should be accomplished, each person's role and the like.
2   Supportive leadership. Such behaviour entails a concern on the leader's part for his or her subordinates' well-being and status. The supportive leader tends to be friendly and approachable.
3   Participative leadership. This notion denotes a consultative approach in which the leader seeks to involve subordinates in decision-making.
4   Achievement-oriented leadership. This involves setting high performance goals and exhibiting confidence in subordinates' ability to attain lofty standards.

According to path-goal theory, the extent to which each of these categories of leader behaviour will have a beneficial impact upon subordinate performance and job satisfaction is contingent upon two broad classes of situational factor. The first of these is the personal characteristics of subordinates. According to

House and Mitchell, subordinates' characteristics are likely to affect their perception of whether the leader's behaviour is 'an immediate source of satisfaction or . . . instrumental to future satisfaction' (1974: 85). Attributes such as their level of authoritarianism, or whether they are 'externals' or 'internals' in terms of the Locus of Control Scale (Rotter, 1966), or their perceptions of their task-related abilities, have been investigated as potential moderators of the effects of types of leader behaviour. The second broad class of situational factors is 'environmental' and comprises: the nature of subordinates' tasks, the formal authority system of the organization, and the primary work group. It may be, for example, that the subordinates' task is highly structured, so that it is clear to them what needs to be done, as well as how and when. Instrumental leadership may lead to excessive control of subordinate behaviour, and so occasion resentment and dissatisfaction. When the task is unstructured, subordinates may experience confusion and role ambiguity, so that their ability to recognize how their effort will lead to better performance is jeopardized. When such a condition exists, it is necessary to clarify the task and the procedures for task accomplishment, implying that instrumental leadership is likely to be preferable.

The bulk of the research deriving from the path-goal tradition has focused upon instrumental and supportive leader behaviour. Initially, the Ohio scales of initiating structure and consideration were used as surrogate measures for these ideas, but later researchers tended to develop their own instruments or derivatives of the Ohio scales. A number of outcome measures have been examined, including job satisfaction and subordinate performance. Among the environmental group of situational factors, the degree of task structure and the subordinate's hierarchical level have been prominent areas of attention. The early studies generated by the theory tended to use static correlational research designs, but some later researchers employed longitudinal designs in their investigations. The procedure adopted by other writers (for example, House and Mitchell, 1974; Filley et al., 1976; Indvik, 1986) of summarizing the research evidence under each of the four categories of leader behaviour identified earlier will be followed.

Instrumental leadership (IL)

Since IL is supposed to involve the imposition by the leader of a high level of structure on the task at hand, when the latter is highly structured this form of leadership may be unnecessary. This proposition would suggest that the level of task structure will moderate the effects of IL. However, path-goal theorists have also proposed that IL enhances subordinate performance irrespective of task structure or of other aspects of the structure of the subordinate's work environment (for example, Fiedler and House, 1988). When structure is at a low level, IL compensates by increasing role clarity; when it is high, IL 'prevents low motivation from decreasing performance' (1988: 85). One might also anticipate that the subordinate's level in the hierarchy will moderate its effects in a similar fashion, as higher-level jobs tend to be less routine and more ambiguous. One of the first tests of these ideas was a study by House and Dessler (1974) of employees at a range of hierarchical levels in each of two companies. The researchers examined the impact of a derivative of the Ohio initiating structure measure (as a surrogate for IL) on perceived role clarity, on intrinsic and extrinsic satisfaction, and on subordinates' expectations of the extent to which their effort has an impact on their task performance and of the likelihood of good performance being rewarded. These two expectations are referred to in the research literature as Expectancy I and Expectancy II respectively. IL was found to be negatively correlated with subordinate satisfaction when tasks were highly structured; when there was little structure, the relationship became positive. There was also some evidence to suggest that when task structure is fairly high the impact of IL on the two notions of expectancy is negative, but when it is low the relationship is positive. The relationship of IL with role clarity failed to follow any clear pattern when degrees of task structure were investigated as potential moderators. This is surprising because the theory suggests that when task structure is low, IL compensates for the ensuing role ambiguity that is inherent in such circumstances by clarifying what the subordinate is supposed to be doing. This in turn clarifies the expectancies held by subordinates who are better able to perceive how their effort can relate to their performance and the implications of their performance for likely rewards. As a result, they are likely to be more satisfied and their performance will be enhanced. Quite apart from the difficulties inherent in inferring a sequence of events such as this from a static study, the apparently indeterminate effects of IL on role clarity (the obverse of role ambiguity) under varying degrees of task structure pose a difficulty for the theory. Nonetheless, the House and Dessler study was one of a number of investigations which, according to House and Mitchell (1974), provided support for the path-goal theory's hypothesis about the effects of IL on satisfaction.

A number of studies have failed to provide support for these ideas, however, as House and Mitchell (1974) recognized in their review. A study by Stinson and Johnson (1975), drawing on data on military officers, civil service personnel and project engineers, found that the amount of both task structure and task repetitiveness moderated the effects of initiating structure on subordinate satisfaction, but in a manner opposite to that which path-goal theory would lead one to anticipate. In other words, there was a strong positive correlation between initiating structure and subordinate satisfaction among these subordinates with higher levels of task structure and task repetitiveness. Among those with low scores on these two task attributes, the correlations between initiating structure and satisfaction were either negative or weakly positive. House and Mitchell (1974) sought to come to terms with the pattern of mixed results by suggesting that the personal characteristics of subordinates may moderate the effects of IL. They point to an unpublished study which indicated that the level of authoritarianism exhibited by subordinates is an important moderating variable. Among workers in a manufacturing firm doing routine repetitive work, IL was preferred by authoritarian, closed-minded individuals, but non-instrumental leadership was preferred by those who exhibited little authoritarianism. However, this study also found that when faced with non-routine, ambiguous tasks, IL was preferred irrespective of levels of authoritarianism. A finding such as this may go some way towards explaining the discrepant findings. A study of employees in research and development organizations by R. T. Keller (1989) suggests that subordinates' need for clarity moderates the relationship between IL and their performance and job satisfaction. Among those with a high need for clarity, there was a strong relationship between IL and both performance (in one of the organizations) and job satisfaction. This finding confirms the possible importance of personal factors as situational moderators. In a study of non-academic university employees, Indvik (1988) found that subordinates' need for achievement moderated the relationship between IL and satisfaction.

Other recent research reveals a similar pattern of mixed findings. Dessler and Valenzi's (1977) research in a manufacturing company found that among those workers performing structured tasks, initiating structure (standing as a surrogate for IL) and intrinsic satisfaction were positively correlated. Among those doing less routine work, the effect of initiating structure was negligible. These findings are in direct contrast to the path-goal theory notion that people doing unstructured tasks will welcome IL, whereas those involved in routine work will react against it. Research by Schriesheim and Schriesheim (1980) on managerial and clerical workers in a US public utility found that levels of task structure did not moderate the effects of IL on a variety of job satisfaction measures. R. T. Keller's (1989) study also failed to confirm the moderating effect of task structure. Indvik's (1988) research also failed largely to confirm the moderating effects of task structure on the relationship between IL and various aspects of satisfaction, though she was able to confirm that the impact of IL on performance is not moderated by task structure. By contrast, a study of bank and manufacturing employees by Schriesheim and DeNisi (1981) found that the amount of task variety (implying a lack of task structure) moderated the effects of IL on subordinate satisfaction with supervision in a manner congruent with path-goal theory.

Clearly, then, the evidence is mixed, although there is a fair degree of support for the tenets of path-goal theory. While the effects of IL on satisfaction measures have been emphasized in this section, it should be borne in mind that when performance has been the dependent variable, the results have been less favourable to path-goal theory (Mitchell, 1979). A meta-analysis of forty-eight path-goal studies by Indvik (1986) confirmed that when task structure is low, IL generates greater subordinate job satisfaction, satisfaction with the leader and intrinsic motivation; under conditions of greater structure, these relationships tend to be smaller. When task structure is low, IL is unrelated to subordinate performance, which is inconsistent with path-goal theory. Where possible, the studies reported in this section will be used in discussing the three other categories of leader behaviour.

Supportive leadership (SL)

According to path-goal theory, SL 'will have its most positive effect on subordinate satisfaction for subordinates who work on stressful, frustrating or dissatisfying tasks' (House and Mitchell, 1974: 91). When work exhibits such characteristics, SL goes some way towards anaesthetizing its effects by making it more bearable. When tasks are not stressful, frustrating or dissatisfying it is assumed that SL will not make a great deal of difference to subordinate satisfaction or the amount of effort someone is prepared to expend. When tasks are stressful, by contrast, SL may enhance subordinates' confidence and underline the important contribution they make so that they may more readily perceive the relationship between their effort and goal attainment. House and Dessler (1974) proposed that the level of task structure would moderate the effects of SL. They argued that unstructured tasks are complex and varied, and hence more intrinsically satisfying, thereby rendering SL redundant. When tasks are highly structured, SL will be positively related to satisfaction and the 'expectancies' because 'supportive leadership is assumed to reduce frustration resulting from highly structured dissatisfying tasks' (House and Dessler, 1974: 41). This suggestion received some support in their research in that SL seems to have a stronger positive impact on intrinsic satisfaction when task structure is high. The same was only true in respect of the relationship with extrinsic satisfaction for one of their two samples. The evidence was only partially supportive of the view that task structure would moderate the effects of SL on the 'expectancy' notions. In the Stinson and Johnson (1975) study, leader consideration seems to have had a more pronounced impact on satisfaction measures when task structure and repetitiveness were high, thereby providing some confirmation of path-goal hypotheses.

   In their review of the relevant research, House and Mitchell (1974) felt that the predictions of path-goal theory regarding the effects of SL had received a great deal of confirmation. By the time of Schriesheim and von Glinow's (1977) later review there seemed to be more evidence which was not supportive, though Mitchell (1979) is probably correct in his view that the balance of evidence is less mixed than for IL. Later research by Schriesheim and Schriesheim (1980) found that SL had a very strong impact on a range of aspects of satisfaction (with work, pay, supervision etc.) and job clarity, but that task structure levels did not moderate the relationships to any substantial degree. This finding suggests that, contrary to what path-goal theory would lead one to expect, SL is strongly related to a number of dependent variables, but that the relationships are in large part not situationally contingent. On the other hand, Indvik's (1986) meta-analysis suggests that SL does enhance satisfaction and performance in highly structured work settings. However, Indvik's (1988) study found that the moderating effects of task structure on SL–satisfaction relationships were minimal, but that organizational formalization (another indicator of environmental structure) did act as a moderator, though not always in the manner that would be expected from path-goal theory. In formalized contexts, SL was found to enhance intrinsic and general satisfaction, but to reduce satisfaction with the superior and performance.

The overall balance of the evidence is fairly supportive of the predictions derived from path-goal theory regarding this dimension of leader behaviour. Nonetheless, the number of studies which have failed to provide confirmation is slightly disconcerting.

Participative leadership (PL)

Path-goal theory provides a particular formulation of the reasons for the potential impact of PL on an individual's productivity. Mitchell (1973) provides four possible reasons for believing that PL enhances subordinate motivation. First, in a participative climate people are likely to be better informed, so that they will have a more complete understanding of the relationships between the amount of effort they expend and goal attainment. They will also better understand which task-related patterns of behaviour are rewarded and which are not. Participation, then, clarifies the relationships between paths and goals. Second, Mitchell suggests that subordinates are more likely to be able to select goals whose attainment directly reflects the amount of effort they are prepared to expend. Third, subordinates in a participative environment are likely to select goals to which they are more personally attached, so that the motivation to perform well may be generated by the subordinate's 'ego involvement' in the task. Finally, Mitchell points out that participation enhances the individual's control over his or her work and suggests that people are more likely to work harder under such circumstances, since they will recognize that the consequences of their effort depend more upon themselves than upon others or external factors.

The evidence which has been accumulated on the impact of situational factors on the PL–outcome relationship within the path-goal tradition has pointed to the need to take into account environmental and subordinate characteristics simultaneously. An exploratory investigation of the role of task structure as a moderator in the House and Dessler (1974) study failed to find a clear pattern of relationships in both samples. Further, in their review of the relevant literature, House and Mitchell (1974) recognized that sub-ordinates' personal characteristics, such as authoritarianism, do not always moderate the effects of PL. An investigation of employees at a range of hierarchical levels in a manufacturing firm by Schuler (1976) points to the need to take into account environmental and personal characteristics simultaneously. It seems that people are more interested in work which is unstructured because of the variety and challenge it involves. When tasks are unstructured the impact of PL on job satisfaction is unaffected by subordinates' personal characteristics. However, when the task is highly structured, PL leads to job satisfaction only for subordinates who exhibit high scores on a scale of authoritarianism. Thus, it seems that among people with a strong drive for independence and self-direction, PL leads to job satisfaction. People's preferences about self-control in their activities have an impact on the relationship between PL and job satisfaction only when tasks are routine. When the task is unstructured and ego involving, PL enhances job satisfaction regardless of their personal characteristics. Overall, Indvik's (1986) meta-analysis suggests that PL engenders greater satisfaction for subordinates who experience low levels of task structure. However, Indvik's (1988) research found only limited support for some of these notions.

Achievement-oriented leadership (AL)

According to path-goal theory, AL 'will cause subordinates to strive for higher standards of performance and to have more confidence in the ability to meet challenging goals' (House and Mitchell, 1974: 91). As such, AL enhances the subordinate's expectation that difficult goals can be achieved through greater effort. Very little research has been conducted in relation to AL but an unpublished investigation suggests that when subordinates are performing ambiguous, non-repetitive tasks, AL is more likely to enhance their confidence that their effort would yield effective performance (reported in House and Mitchell, 1974: 91). When tasks are only moderately ambiguous, AL has little effect on subordinate expectations. Indvik (1988) found AL to have no impact on subordinates with low levels of need for achievement. She also found that when need for achievement and task structure are high, AL enhances intrinsic satisfaction, but has an adverse effect on extrinsic satisfaction and performance.

General problems with path-goal theory

The path-goal approach shares many of the same problems that were identified in relation to the Ohio tradition. To some extent, this is not surprising in view of the heavy reliance on Ohio measures that pervades a good deal of the research within the path-goal tradition. The problem of inconsistent findings, the frequent employment of group average methods of describing leaders, the near absence of the investigation of informal leadership, and potential measurement problems are all evident in the studies deriving from the theory. The criticism levelled at the Ohio studies of insufficient attention devoted to situational factors is obviously not appropriate. The problem of causality, however, is very pertinent, since many of the investigations summarized were static, cross-sectional studies. A longitudinal investigation by Greene (1979) provides evidence of the problems of assuming causal direction from cross-sectional studies with a particular focus on path-goal ideas. Greene studied sixty leader–subordinate dyads drawn from the financial and marketing divisions of a firm. Measures of IL and SL were developed from the Ohio initiating structure and consideration subscales of the LBDQ-XII. Measures of both leader behaviour and a number of dependent variables were gleaned on two occasions three months apart. Some of Greene's findings were supportive of path-goal theory. Both IL and SL were found to enhance subordinate satisfaction under different conditions of task structure. When task structure was low, IL led to greater intrinsic work satisfaction; when task structure was high, SL led to greater satisfaction. In each case, the leadership variable was found to be the causal influence. The pattern for performance was different in that in medium and high structure conditions, subordinate performance affected levels of IL. Only in the low task structure condition was there some evidence that IL induced higher performance. Furthermore, subordinate performance was found to affect SL, almost irrespective of levels of task structure. It would seem that subordinate performance is a more important determinant of leader behaviour than vice versa.

A problem with research relating to the path-goal theory was that much of it became rather stereotyped. Research tended to focus on the IL and SL dimensions of leader behaviour, even though other aspects of what leaders do could be seen as potentially important. Similarly, in spite of House's insistence that a range of moderating variables might be examined, there was an overwhelming emphasis upon the role of task structure in this respect. Furthermore, combinations of types of leadership behaviour have rarely been examined. Indvik's (1988) study is an exception to this tendency. So too is Griffin's (1980) research on 171 manual employees in a manufacturing firm which examined all four types of leader behaviour. Further, instead of task structure, he examined the moderating effects of 'individual–task congruence' which 'refers to the extent to which the growth needs of the individual match the motivational characteristics of the task being performed' (1980: 665-6). In terms of this variable, a task may exhibit high or low levels of scope for employee growth, while the subordinate may exhibit high or low growth needs. This approach suggests a 2 x 2 scheme in which the two dichotomies present four possible individual–task combinations. It seems reasonable to assume that the extent to which an individual's 'growth needs' fit with the opportunities that the task offers for growth will affect his or her views about, for example, the likelihood that enhanced effort will lead to successful goal attainment. For example, SL may be highly desirable to subordinates with high growth needs but little scope for realizing them in their work. SL could compensate for the disenchanting effects of such an experience. This particular notion received some support in that SL led to greater overall satisfaction, and satisfaction with both the job and the supervisor, in such circumstances. Further, when people have low growth needs but high task scope, there was evidence that IL promotes satisfaction, presumably because it imposes a structure on the work of relatively unmotivated people. However, in neither case was better performance a consequence of the moderated effects of SL or IL, thereby echoing Mitchell's (1979) view that the evidence tends to be stronger when satisfaction measures, rather than performance indicators, constitute the dependent variable. This tendency is very troublesome to the path-goal approach which is ultimately seeking to explain the leadership circumstances which result in an enhanced preparedness to expend effort. This tendency can also be seen in a study of US and Saudi Arabian managers by Al-Gattan (1985) which borrowed heavily from Griffin's framework. He found that path-goal predictions worked for satisfaction measures, but not when performance was the outcome. Further, Griffin found that when individual growth needs and task scope are either high or low, there seems to be little that leaders can do to promote greater subordinate satisfaction. While the results of these studies are slightly equivocal, particularly in relation to performance, they provide an alternative to task structure as a moderating variable.

House and Baetz (1979) have suggested that future developments in path-goal research should seek to include a broader range of moderating variables. Although this is a possible way forward, the early promise of path-goal theory seems to be abating. The discrepant findings, the problem of causality, and the failure of the theory to predict performance in many studies are not encouraging. Further, the plethora of leadership styles and situational factors that the theory and research have put forward do not provide leaders with clear guidance as to how they should behave, even if the findings were less inconsistent.

The other chief representatives of the contingency approach are associated with the work of Fiedler (1967), Vroom (Vroom and Yetton, 1973; Vroom and Jago, 1988) and Hersey and Blanchard (1977). Fielder's research has been highly controversial and plagued by inconsistent results and by confusion about the meaning of its main measurement instruments. Vroom's work has received quite a lot of empirical support, but in focusing upon whether situational factors moderate the effectiveness of participative leadership, it has been viewed as limited in some quarters. Hersey and Blanchard's framework has largely failed to generate much research and has therefore suffered from a lack of empirical confirmation.

Conclusion

By the early 1980s, there was a general sense of pessimism about leadership theory and research. The enormous output of leadership researchers seemed to have yielded little that could be clung to with any certainty. Each new hope seemed to run into a wall of inconsistent findings, methodological problems, and so on. It is possible that some of this pessimism was rather misplaced. It has been seen that the trait approach has stimulated renewed interest and there is the suggestion that there are more lessons to be learned from it than the researchers who turned their backs on it in the early 1950s may have realized. The distinction between task-oriented and person-oriented leadership, which underpinned distinctions like initiating structure and instrumental leadership on the one hand and consideration and supportive leadership on the other, has had and still has wide currency in management circles and has proved to be an important and basic classification of leader behaviour. The various contingency approaches (such as path-goal theory) have brought to our attention the need to take situational factors into account when examining the effects of leader behaviour. It is clear that styles of leadership that work well in one situation will not necessarily be appropriate in another context.

Also, meta-analyses of both Ohio State research and path-goal investigations have shown the results to be more robust than a simple comparison of the results of different studies implies. Thus, higher levels of consideration and initiating structure are associated with greater job satisfaction and better job performance, while the results from path-goal theory studies suggest that situational factors like task structure generally moderate the effects of a variety of types of leader behaviour. There is also little doubt that the development of the various measures of leader behaviour and the recognition of some of their problems has greatly aided later research into leadership.

However, there *was* considerable disillusionment with leadership theory and research in the early 1980s. Out of this pessimism emerged a number of alternative approaches, which shared some common features. In the present book, these approaches are referred to collectively as the 'New Leadership', which is the fourth (and current) phase in leadership theory and research. For some of the authors with whom this phase is associated, a central focus was a concept whose origin goes back around two millennia – charisma. Before the New Leadership is examined in Chapter 5, the concept of charisma is explored. In Chapter 2, charisma is examined in relation to the main theorists who have contributed to our understanding of it. In Chapters 3 and 4, research on charisma will be examined, particularly in the context of religious and political environments. Chapter 3 will emphasize the nature of charisma and how it is created, while Chapter 4 will concentrate upon the links between charisma and organizational settings. The subsequent chapters aim to elucidate and examine the New Leadership.

Note

1 Interestingly, Kirkpatrick and Locke (1991) propose, as additional factors which are essential to leadership, activities that are themes in the New Leadership. In particular, they write that 'the core job of a leader . . . is to create a *vision*' (1991: 56; emphasis in original) and they go on to specify the activities that are necessary to implementing the vision. In their formulation, traits 'endow people with the potential for leadership' while such activities as creating a vision 'actualize this potential' (1991: 56).

2

The Concept of Charisma

Charisma is an important term in the context of the New Leadership, because it is used fairly frequently by a number of its main contributors. Also, in business and management periodicals the term is employed a great deal in the context of discussions of certain prominent figures. In such discussions, the term is often employed to describe someone who is flamboyant, who is a powerful speaker, and who can persuade others of the importance of his or her message. The non-charismatic leader, by contrast, is often depicted as a lacklustre, ineffectual individual. Such conceptions of charisma link only partly with the ways in which it has been conceptualized by social scientists, who have been the major exponents of the modern use of the term. The New Leadership writers vary in the extent to which they draw on social scientists' writings on charisma. When charisma is conceptualized as a personal trait (for example, Kirkpatrick and Locke, 1991), the approach is fairly distant from the way in which social scientists have elucidated the concept. When charisma is examined in terms of how the leader is perceived by his or her followers, New Leadership writers have been much closer to the main ingredients of the social scientific approach (for example, Conger, 1989).

In this chapter, the chief concern will be to map out the main ways in which charisma has been conceptualized by social scientists. In addition, some issues that have been raised about the notion of charisma will be examined. However, the primary focus is theoretical and it will not be until the next chapter that empirical evidence will be employed.

Weber on charisma

It is to the German sociologist, Max Weber (1864–1920), that one inevitably turns for the most influential treatment of the concept of charisma. The bulk of his writing on charisma can be found in his important work, *Economy and Society* (in German *Wirtschaft und Gesellschaft*), which in the following discussion will be referred to as *ES*, along with the relevant volume number in the English translation (Weber, 1968). Through his exposition of charisma in the context of his sociology of religion and his historically based account of the nature of modernity, Weber forged what is for many writers the starting-point for any appreciation of the concept. In large part, the introduction of the concept of charisma into both serious social scientific endeavour and popular discourse can ultimately be attributed to Weber's writings, although it has been stretched far beyond its original meaning and context in many later treatments. The ways in which charisma has been adapted will provide a later focus; in the meantime, Weber's discussion will be the main target of attention.

In fact, as will become apparent, commentators on and users of Weber's writings on charisma have invariably disagreed wildly over the meaning, content and potential of the concept. This tendency can be attributed largely to the nature of Weber's writings on the subject. They are highly diffuse, sometimes contradictory, and often more suggestive of what is interesting and important in charisma than a definitive exposition. Indeed, if there is one thing over which writers on charisma tend to agree, it is that Weber provided a highly stimulating but frustratingly abstruse discussion. One of the aims of the following exposition will be to cut a swathe through some of these problematic areas, whilst retaining the complexity of Weber's writings.

The main initial stimulus for the exposition of charisma was Weber's interest in the mechanisms by which power comes to be seen as legitimate by those to whom it is applied. When power is viewed as legitimate, a situation which can be contrasted with power that has to be enforced, those who possess power can be said to have authority. Weber recognized three types of authority, each of which represents a different claim to the legitimate exercise of power. Each of these types should be viewed as a 'pure' or 'ideal' type, that is, as an extreme delineation of the chief characteristics of the phenomena it stands for, but which may never be found in such a form in reality. The methodology of ideal types allowed the distinctive characteristics of classes of phenomena to be depicted.

The three types of authority which Weber distinguished are as follows:

Authority based on rational grounds   Here, authority stems from a belief in the legality of rules that have been created and in the right of those individuals who have been given responsibility within such a system of rules to issue commands. This type of authority was called legal authority. It is also sometimes referred to as legal-rational authority to express the close interconnectedness of the belief in the legality of the commands issued by a person and the rules on which his or her ascent to power is based. For Weber, legal authority is primarily, though not exclusively, a phenomenon of the modern world, which finds organizational expression in the spread of bureaucracy.

Authority based on traditional grounds   Traditional authority emanates from a belief in the inviolability of age-old traditions and hence in the right of power holders in such social systems to expect adherence to their commands. Individuals in a position to issue commands have usually acquired this right through an inherited status. Whereas under legal authority one finds a superior who has gained a superordinate position through rationally designed procedures (and hence resting on identifiable rules), under traditional authority those with legitimate power are masters, to whom, as in a feudal society, personal allegiance is owed.

Authority based on charismatic grounds   Charismatic authority rests on 'devotion to the exceptional sanctity, heroism or exemplary character of an individual person, and of the normative patterns or order revealed or ordained by him' (*ES* I: 215). It is this type which provides the exclusive focus for the rest of this section. The term 'charisma' itself derives initially from the New Testament where it was employed to refer to 'gift of grace', that is evidence of having received the Holy Spirit, as manifested in evidence of the capacity to prophesy, to heal or to speak in tongues. However, Weber's use of the term moves it well beyond this somewhat specific range of phenomena.

With charisma, allegiance is owed to persons who possess charisma by virtue of their unique attributes and abilities. It is these individual-specific features that result in the special allegiance shown by the followers of charismatic leaders. With traditional authority, allegiance is also owed to the individual (such as a tribal chief or elder); however, the follower's adherence arises not from a belief in special qualities that inhere in the leader, but from the leader's customary right to be obeyed by virtue of his or her position.

But what is charisma? In what must be one of the most heavily quoted passages in the social sciences, Weber defines it as follows:

> The term 'charisma' will be applied to a certain quality of an individual personality by virtue of which he is considered extraordinary and treated as endowed with supernatural, superhuman, or at least specifically exceptional powers or qualities. These are such as not to be accessible to the ordinary person, but are regarded as of divine origin or as exemplary, and on the basis of them the individual concerned is treated as a 'leader'. (*ES* I: 241)

Throughout his writings on charisma, Weber gave illustrations of the kinds of leader whose authority can invariably be said to be based upon charisma. In primitive societies, Weber saw magical powers as being particularly instrumental in the initiation of charismatic authority. But equally, in primitive societies and elsewhere, charisma may be attributed in respect of a variety of contexts: the capacity for ecstasy displayed by the shaman; the powers of revelation associated with prophets; exceptional military prowess and heroism; the ascetic regimen of the holy man; or a capacity to demonstrate exceptional therapeutic abilities or legal knowledge.

Although Weber saw charisma as a force which wanes with the onrush of modernity, he did not perceive it to be the exclusive province of the past. In general, charismatic impulses are, according to Weber, most likely to occur in times of distress – 'whether psychic, physical, economic, ethical, religious, or political' (*ES* III: 1112). This list seems to comprise causative factors that operate at the level of both large-scale processes and the individual.

A vital feature of an individual's claim to charisma is his or her mission and the subsequent preparedness of others to believe in it. Weber writes that the bearer of charisma 'seizes the task for which he is destined and demands that others obey and follow him by virtue of his mission' (*ES*: III: 1112). At another point, Weber wrote:

The bearer of charisma enjoys loyalty and authority by virtue of a mission believed to be embodied in him; this mission has not necessarily and not always been revolutionary, but in its most charismatic forms it has inverted all value hierarchies and overthrown custom, law and tradition. (*ES* III: 1117)

This mission will have an appeal to specific groups which see in it the solution to their distress. This means that the mission must be situationally relevant for the prospective charismatic leader to achieve a following: he or she must demonstrate that the mission is the answer to their needs.

In contrast to the tendency nowadays to treat charisma as a characteristic of the charismatic individual, Weber recognized the importance of its validation by the leader's followers. For example, Weber referred to the importance of 'how the individual is actually regarded by those subject to charismatic authority, by his "followers" or "disciples"' (*ES* I: 242). On other occasions, Weber referred to the importance of prospective charismatic leaders 'proving' their charisma to their followers (for example, *ES* I: 266; *ES* III: 1112). An important corollary of charismatic leaders' need for their claims to be validated is that should their powers or abilities desert them, their followers will likewise abandon them. In Weber's writings there seem to be two components to this process. First, the charismatic leader may simply lose the ability to perform miracles or magic. The second element derives from Weber's treatment of the charismatic leader as having a mission. The followers must achieve some benefit from the mission, and if they do not the leader will be abandoned. The two elements are related, in that the ability to perform supernatural feats or to exhibit exemplary standards or heroism may be a route by which the mission is achieved, but they are to a certain degree analytically distinguishable in Weber's writings. However, the chief point is that these processes mean that charisma is an unstable force. Whereas legal and traditional authority are capable of a considerable degree of continuity, charisma can easily burn itself out.

According to Weber, some of a charismatic leader's followers can share in his or her charisma. There is a sense here of a kind of religious stratification order with the charismatic leader at its apex. For example, Weber described the organized group that is subject to charismatic authority as a 'charismatic community' (*ES* I: 243), which exists in a communal state. In this respect, charisma stands in marked contrast to bureaucratic organization, a point that will be developed below. He also referred to the charismatic leader as having 'permanent helpers, who are active co-workers with the prophet in his mission and who generally also possess some charismatic qualifications' (*ES* II: 452) The notion that the charismatic leader's followers may also exhibit charismatic elements is of some significance in view of the tendency in many popular treatments of charisma for it to be regarded as a special quality of the leader only. However, the general issue was barely developed by Weber, so that it is difficult to ask fundamental questions about the differences between the charisma of leaders and that of their staff.

The routinization of charisma

Weber viewed charisma as an essentially unstable phenomenon. This instability was seen as manifesting itself in a variety of ways. First, he argued that a charismatic leader frequently 'arises from collective excitement produced by extraordinary events and from surrender to heroism of any kind' (*ES* III: 1121). However, when the specific situation that propelled the charismatic leader's emergence subsides, there is a serious possibility that the 'collective excitement' will also wane, as followers are forced to concentrate their minds on facing anew the inescapable 'workaday routines' (*ES* III: 1121) of everyday life. In order to ensure that the charismatic impulses are not allowed to dissolve, the charismatic leader's administrative staff or disciples as well as his or her subjects (and often the leader him- or herself as well) will wish to place their relationship on a more stable footing. Weber viewed this tendency as particularly motivated by a recognition among the charismatic leader's administrative staff that their ideals and material interests would be better served by a formalization of their own position. Second, Weber suggested that the anxieties of the charismatic leader's permanent helpers and followers will become more acute with the departure of the leader, for example, following his or her death. When this occurs, they must face the problem of succession.

Weber referred to the process of maintaining the charismatic relationship as the routinization of charisma. He cited a number of different ways that the problem of succession has been handled: a search may be instituted for a new charismatic leader in terms of pre-selected criteria; a choice may be made through revelation as represented by such techniques as the use of oracles; the charismatic leader may designate a successor; charisma may come to be seen as inheritable; or charisma may come to be seen as conferable through the commission of ritual as a result of which an individual can assume a charismatic position (a process referred to as 'charisma of office'). In each case, it is clear that Weber saw the character of the initial charisma as being changed in the process of routinization. One aspect of this change is that charisma is 'depersonalized'. No longer is it a characteristic that applies to a special individual; instead, it becomes a quality that can be transferred or acquired, or is attached to a position in an organizational setting. Furthermore, the charismatic leader's staff changes from a loose assemblage of devoted and enthusiastic disciples into a stable organization. In the modern world, this development largely meant the creation of a bureaucratic form of organization. Thus, Weber pointed to the creation of positions within a hierarchy, to which economic benefits accrue, as an instance of this trend. The development of charisma of office perhaps best exemplifies the way in which the character of charisma is transformed by its routinization, since it effectively means the transposition of charisma by a stable institutional structure. While many of Weber's illustrations of the process relate to the context of religious organizations, such as the apostolic succession, he regarded the development of charisma of office as something which occurs outside this sphere.

Charisma and organization

As the second half of the extended quotation on p. 25 suggests, in Weber's eyes charisma is usually a revolutionary force in that it involves a radical break with the pre-existing order, regardless of whether that order is based on traditional or legal authority. Weber wrote: 'Charismatic domination transforms all values and breaks all traditional and rational norms' (*ES* III: 1115). Indeed, he described charismatic authority as antithetical to both traditional and legal authority. This antithesis was most evident when he contrasted the social structure and internal practices of charismatic administrative arrangements with those of legal authority, and bureaucracy in particular. Since this question relates to the issue of charisma in an organizational context, which is an important focus in this book, it is worth exploring this particular facet of charisma in greater detail.

Weber depicted charisma as contrary to bureaucracy because they represent divergent positions in relation to rules. He wrote: 'Bureaucratic authority is specifically rational in the sense of being bound to intellectually analysable rules; while charismatic authority is specifically irrational in the sense of being foreign to all rules' (*ES* I: 244). However, the contrast goes further than this. The absence in charismatic authority of an administrative staff of technically trained officials stands in marked contrast to the emphasis upon qualified staff in the bureaucratic organization. Instead, members of the administrative staff demonstrate their 'charismatic qualifications' to the leader who 'calls' them to assume their positions in relation to his or her mission (*ES* I: 243; *ES* III: 1119). Also, again unlike staff in a bureaucracy, the followers of a charismatic leader do not have a 'career' as a result of their association; they do not form a hierarchy and they do not receive a salary. These contrasting features are further underscored by the contempt for everyday economic considerations among charismatic leaders and their followers. The lack of interest among the followers in the receipt of a salary is a manifestation of this tendency. Rather, in charismatic authority the provision of everyday needs is met through such mechanisms as gifts, bribery, honoraria and begging. This economic independence seems to be seen by Weber as a means of maintaining an intellectual independence, so that the mission is uncontaminated by the rigours of the outside world.

One way in which Weber pointed to the inconsistency of charisma and stable organizational forms is through his depiction of charismatic leaders as 'natural leaders'. By this he meant that charismatic leaders are not appointed leaders occupying offices deriving from their special technical expertise (*ES* III: 1111–12). For example, at one point he wrote that charismatic authority rests 'on personal devotion to, and personal authority of, "natural" leaders, in contrast to the appointed leaders of the bureaucratic order' (*ES* III: 1117). This contrast seems to forge a clear separation between the leadership that derives from an individual's occupation of a position in a hierarchy (the appointed leader) and the leadership that is associated with a particular person *qua* individual (the charismatic leader). Here again, a fairly sharp separation is drawn between charisma and permanent organizational forms.

A further feature of Weber's juxtaposition of charisma against permanent organizational contexts can be discerned in his discussion of prophets in ancient Judaism (Weber, 1952) and, indeed, of prophets as a general category (*ES* II: Chapter VI, iii). The essence of Weber's approach is that prophets were generally socially marginal individuals whose rise to religious prominence was independent of organized religion and its social structures. Thus, in contrasting the priest, as representative of organized religiosity, and the prophet, Weber wrote:

> The [priest] lays claim to authority by virtue of his service in a sacred tradition, while the prophet's claim is based on personal revelation and charisma. It is no accident that almost no prophets have emerged from the priestly class. As a rule, the Indian teachers of salvation were not Brahmins, nor were the Israelite prophets priests. (*ES* II: 440)

Here again, we can see the opposition in Weber's eyes of organization and charisma. However, it is of special interest for the present discussion that this element of Weber's work has been questioned, at least in connection with his writings on Israelite prophets. Berger (1963) has argued that Weber based his conclusion upon scholarship on ancient Judaism which has since been shown to be faulty. The later scholarship suggests that the prophets were not socially marginal; instead, they were integrally involved in the organized religion of ancient Israel. As such, these prophets exercised their charismatic authority within the context of their offices. This finding is of considerable importance, for it implies that charisma may constitute a radical force from within established institutions rather than exclusively beyond them. Berger is at pains to point out that the post-Weberian scholarship does not undermine Weber's general approach to the concept of charisma, since all the later findings mean is that charismatic authority is not inevitably inimical to stable organization structures.

In the previous section, the point was made that Weber saw charisma as transformed when it underwent routinization, especially if stable and permanent structures were created. He suggested that it was no longer a creative force when routinization occurred, although he recognized that there may be subsequent eruptions of charismatic fervour. This tendency was also evident in broad historical terms, since he saw the growing rationalization of the modern world as restricting the importance of charisma. Charisma would seem to be a significantly less important phenomenon in modern times. We begin to get a picture of the Dionysian fires of the charismatic force finding their nemesis in the Apollonian constraint of bureaucracy and legal authority in general. On the other hand, it is possible to detect in Weber's writings a recognition of the potential for charismatic leaders to arise within the context of the bureaucratic setting. This possibility is most explicit when he wrote:

> In times of great public excitement, charismatic leaders may emerge even in solidly bureaucratized parties, as was demonstrated by Roosevelt's campaign in 1912. (*ES* III: 1132)

On the other hand, Weber viewed the rise of charismatic leaders in the context of 'solidly bureaucratized' political parties as unusual because such leaders pose a threat to political managers and other functionaries. These party bureaucrats may fret about the possible loss of financial and managerial control if sponsorship were to accrue increasingly to charismatic leaders outside the formal party apparatus. Nonetheless, the case of Roosevelt (as well as Gladstone, whom he also cites as a charismatic leader within a party bureaucracy) raises the possibility that the chasm between charisma and the enduring organization setup is not as wide as some of his writings would lead one to suppose.

In his political writings Weber seems to have presented a view of the prospects of charismatic leadership within bureaucratic conditions that is less pessimistic than the one he presented in *ES*. Moreover, as Beetham (1974: 231) has observed, Weber increasingly came to the view, contrary to that expressed in *ES*, that the party bureaucracy's reservations about having charismatic leaders would be eclipsed by the advantages of having an electorally successful leader. Weber (1948) also argued that the administrative apparatus of the political party (the 'machine') is a necessary feature of the political landscape because it may assist in the promotion of charismatic leaders in modern democracies. The alternative scenario, which was an unacceptable one so far as Weber was concerned, was 'the rule of professional politicians without a calling, without the inner charismatic qualities that make a leader' (Weber, 1948: 113).

Gladstone exemplified the former process in that his rise within the Liberal Party was facilitated by a party machine controlled by a few party officials who held sway within a rigid bureaucracy and who were solidly behind him.

> In 1886 the machine was already so charismatically oriented to his person, that when the question of Home Rule was raised the whole apparat from top to bottom did not ask: do we really stand on Gladstone's ground? It simply, on his word, fell in line with him and said – right or wrong we follow him. (quoted in Beetham, 1974: 230)

Similarly, Mommsen has noted that Weber increasingly saw a need for great politicians to create a following 'on the basis of their personal charismatic qualifications' (1989: 13). Thus, modern democracy would form the framework within which charismatic political figures would arise. Such leaders would also constitute an antidote to the growing rationalization and bureaucratization of everyday life, by introducing elements of dynamic innovation and of freedom from the constraints that these broad processes imposed.

Thus, it would seem that in his political writings Weber did not present a picture in which charismatic leadership and bureaucratic organization constituted incompatible forces. The germs of this idea were apparent in *ES*, but there the prospect of the 'castration of charisma' (*ES* III: 1132) by the party organization was given greater prominence than in the more exclusively political writings where the possibility of the party bureaucracy as a mechanism which could facilitate the rise of the charismatic leader was a notable theme.

When this point is coupled with Berger's (1963) reinterpretation of Israelite prophecy, it becomes apparent that it is probably undesirable to forge a view of charisma as inherently antipathetic to permanent organization structures.

Charisma and the modern world

Is Weber's notion of charisma relevant to an understanding of leadership in the modern world? Weber clearly thought it was. As the discussion of his understanding of charisma has shown, Weber used a number of modern examples of charisma, such as Roosevelt, as well as many pre-modern illustrations. However, a number of writers have questioned the appropriateness of charisma in the context of modernity. This argumentation has assumed two guises. First, there are writers who question the degree to which Weber was correct in his view that charisma can be extended beyond the religious sphere in which it was initially formulated. Since religion is waning in many modern industrial societies, this argument would limit the application of the concept to a narrow range of purely religious phenomena, like religious sects and cults, which have indeed attracted a very large literature (see Chapter 3). The second version asserts that charisma cannot sensibly be applied to the modern world because charisma is increasingly a manufactured phenomenon, rather than the natural upsurge of the charismatic response that Weber depicted in the context of pre-modern societies. These two arguments are related to a certain degree, but in the following exposition will be kept separate.

Charisma beyond the religious sphere   Friedrich (1961) is one of the most prominent critics of the view that the application of the concept of charisma should not be allowed to stray from the purely religious domain. In coming to this conclusion, Friedrich makes much of the fact that Weber drew heavily upon Rudolph Sohm's (1882) writings on church history which possess an explicitly religious referent (see also Haley, 1980). For Sohm, charisma referred to the Christian form of organization in which individuals are called to assume leadership by virtue of evidence of charismata (gifts of grace), which are bestowed directly by God. According to Friedrich this very explicit situating of charisma within the religious domain severely limits the possibility of broadening it. Friedrich argues that when Weber was writing about charismatic leadership in non-religious contexts, he was in fact referring simply to 'inspirational leadership', that is, a form of leadership that is capable of producing strong attachments between leader and led and which incites the latter to follow the former's bidding, but which comprises no reference to a religious entity. The resistance to the use of the concept of charisma outside the religious domain often in part stems from a belief that it would be a sacrilege to extend charisma to such prominent leaders as Hitler, Stalin or Mussolini who have been described as charismatic, but who have been responsible for heinous deeds against mankind.

The issue at hand is whether it is appropriate to apply the concept beyond the religious sphere in which it was first formulated. It would seem strange to argue that one should not be able to apply ideas stemming from one area to another. Such a view would greatly restrict the intellectual deployment of metaphor. It has been suggested, for example, that scientists make frequent use of metaphors to inform the nature of the entities that they examine, because a metaphor allows the characteristics of somethng that is unfamiliar to be understood in terms of something that is familiar (Harré, 1972). In other words, the fact that the meaning of a word derives from one area does not mean that it cannot have a legitimate meaning in another. The word 'ritual' has a largely religious meaning, but this does not prevent us from employing it in other contexts where it helps to illuminate the nature of certain kinds of action. Also, the fact that Weber's concept of charisma may lump together Hitler and Jesus Christ should not be a source of anxiety, since it is consistent with his view that the term is independent of ethical considerations (*ES* I: 241–2). Further, Friedrich's observations neglect the fact that the origins of Weber's interest in charisma lay not in religion, but in politics. Baehr (1987) has noted that in his political writings Weber employed the term 'Caesarism' to denote the same kind of leadership phenomenon that he described as 'charisma' in his sociological writings, where his concern was to develop categories that could traverse spheres and epochs.[1] Whereas Caesarism was inseparable from the political sphere, charisma was a term which was little known and which did not bring with it a cluster of prior conceptions. As a result, the term gave Weber a *carte blanche* to apply his ideas to a variety of situations and contexts, and was therefore more versatile than Caesarism could be. Thus, the prospect of applying 'charisma' to diverse milieux was very much at the heart of Weber's intention.

The problem of modern charisma   The second questioning of the relevance of charisma to the modern world suggests that what we tend to call charisma in contemporary society is a fake form. True charisma is a thing of the past, which could only take root in its genuine form at a time when contacts between leaders and led were personal and therefore much less attenuated than they typically are nowadays. In particular, it is argued, most notably by Bensman and Givant (1975), that charisma is nowadays manufactured by mass communications which rationally create an image of the leader as a charismatic figure. To a certain extent, this tendency is inevitable because of the nature of modern urban, bureaucratic societies which would not allow the kind of personal relationship between leaders and followers about which Weber wrote. Instead, the semblance of personal contact must be created through television, radio and newspapers. Simultaneously, these media create a charismatic figure out of the political leaders whom they project. Charismatic leaders are the products of the artifices of media experts and advertising exponents who consciously seek to train them in the art of striking oratory and to create an aura of an extraordinary person in order to enhance the likelihood of the imputation of charisma occurring (though of course the word itself may not be used). Modern charisma, according to this view, has more to do with stage management and advertising than with the personal and spontaneous context of charismatic leadership which provided Weber's focus. Bensman and Givant use the term 'pseudocharisma' to describe the modern form. The notion of a fake charisma was to some extent anticipated by Weber, who in a rather ambiguous passage contrasted the charisma that inhered 'by virtue of natural endowment' with charisma that 'may be produced artificially in an object or person through some extraordinary means' (*ES* II: 400). However, he did not evoke a hard and fast distinction because he took the view that even in the artificial form, 'a germ' must already exist which 'some ascetic or other regimen' merely kindles.

The view of charisma as largely irrelevant to the modern world, while compelling in certain respects, is flawed in others. First, Bensman and Givant are almost exclusively concerned in their discussion with charismatic leadership in the political sphere. Ostensibly, the personal element that they see as crucial to true charisma could be said to operate wherever the focus is not upon mass audiences. Charisma would still seem relevant, in Bensman and Givant's terms, to leadership in organizations and to religious cults and sects, at least in their initial stages. Image creation probably occurs in these contexts, but are we really expected to believe that there were not elements of this in the cases of 'pure' charisma upon which Weber largely concentrated? Second, it seems excessive to argue that simply because the characteristics of the phenomena to which the concept of charisma refers have changed with the onset of modernity, *ipso facto* the concept is no longer relevant. We are faced with different forms of the concept and a consequent requirement to be sensitive to the changes that have occurred. To do otherwise runs the risk that social scientific concepts like charisma will lose their continuity. Third, what are we to make of the fact that Weber himself clearly viewed charisma as a legitimate notion in the context of the modern world, as his analysis of political charisma demonstrates? Of course, one might want to argue that Weber was misguided in his attempt to apply the notion of charisma to the likes of Roosevelt; simply because he is the major exponent of the idea of charisma does not mean that he was incapable of misapplying it. On the other hand, Weber's preparedness to employ charisma in the modern context could be taken to provide support for the previous point that the character of charisma has simply changed. Fourth, it seems disingenuous to propose (as Bensman and Givant do by inference) that the charismatic leaders of old were indifferent to the tactics and artifices of image creation. It seems quite likely that many of them and their followers knew exactly what words to utter and the required style for delivering them. They will have been aware (as Weber observed) that they must continually validate their charisma through further deeds and words, and it is difficult to believe that they were naïve about how best to present these deeds and words. The modern charismatic leader simply has a far wider range of tools with which to project an image. Finally, as Runciman (1963: 149) has observed, even if charisma in the modern world is substantially different from that which existed in earlier times, the concept may still be useful in helping us to understand how a certain kind of authority comes to be seen as legitimate.

Shils on charisma

Weber's exposition seems to restrict the manifestation of charisma to a narrow range of phenomena. This tendency is further enhanced by the way in which the reader is given the impression that it is only in its initial pristine form that charisma finds its genuine expression. Such phenomena as the charisma of office or hereditary charisma appear to constitute an inferior and rather artificial form. In the writings of Edward Shils (1958; 1965; 1968) one finds a systematic attempt to stretch the concept of charisma beyond the very specific meanings and contexts upon which Weber had concentrated.

According to Shils, the expression of charisma that was the focus of Weber's attentions is in fact merely one form of a general 'charismatic propensity' that can be found in all societies. Moreover, whereas Weber tended to view this propensity as an essentially revolutionary force, Shils proposes that it is present in the ordinary, everyday operation of society. As such charisma does not necessarily imply a tendency to disrupt the status quo. Shils departs even further from Weber in suggesting that the charismatic propensity does not reside solely in persons and how they are perceived by others, but can also inhere in a host of diverse contexts, such as social positions and organizations:

> There is, in society, a widespread disposition to attribute charismatic properties to ordinary secular roles, institutions, symbols, and strata or aggregates of persons. Charisma not only disrupts social order, it also maintains or conserves it. (Shils, 1965: 200)

Thus, whereas Weber viewed the charisma which inhered in organizational roles, and which stemmed from the routinization of charisma, as a substitute form, Shils sees no reason to regard the various manifestations of charisma as possessing different ingredients. What is common to all of the objects which are deemed to possess charismatic qualities is that they are regarded with 'awe and reverence'.

Shils argues that charisma can be viewed as varying in terms of both its intensity and its dispersion. He specifies two combinations: an intense and concentrated form and an attenuated and dispersed form. Either form can apply to a variety of objects (people, institutions, social roles etc.), but they differ in regard to the nature of the occurrence of charisma. Shils suggests that Weber was far too preoccupied with the intense and concentrated form, and that he further narrowed the range of the concept of charisma by viewing it as something that only existed in its genuine form in relation to persons. By contrast, Shils proposes that charisma can occur in the context of organizations which operate under legal-rational authority, such as bureaucratic organizations. Of course, Weber recognized the operation of such forces as the charisma of office, but Shils sees no reason to forge a view where one is designated genuine and the other as lacking this quality. This disinclination arises because of Shils's conviction that when phenomena are perceived to have attributes that conform to the notion of charisma, they share the common component of evoking awe and reverence.

But what does this sense of awe and reverence comprise? According to Shils, objects which are deemed to exhibit charismatic attributes function to help us to understand 'the condition of man in the universe and the exigencies of social life' (Shils, 1965: 203), and as such strike at the very heart of the need for order in society. In other words, those persons, roles and institutions that possess charismatic attributes embody the core or central values of the societies to which they are attached, and are therefore instrumental in helping people to understand the nature of their social condition. As Shils puts it: 'The most fundamental laws of a country, its constitution, its most unchallengeable traditions and the institutions embodying or enunciating them, call forth awe in the minds of those in contact with them' (1965: 205). Moreover, for an organization under legal-rational authority that is touched by this sense of awe, 'the charisma is not concentratedly imputed to the person occupying the central role or to the role itself, but is dispersed in a diminished but unequal intensity throughout the hierarchy of roles and rules' (1965: 205). In such a context, the charisma is both widely dispersed and of a less intense character than the form discussed by Weber.

Charisma, for Shils, is more widely dispersed in two senses. First, charisma, as we have seen, is regarded by Shils as attaching to a much wider range of objects than Weber recognized. Second, Shils views charisma as capable of adhering to whole organizations and hence to a variety of roles within them, albeit with differing degrees of intensity. The notion of dispersion was given special significance in an early article on charisma in underdeveloped countries (Shils, 1958). Here, he argued that an important role of leaders of such nations is to instil a sense of charisma as residing in their nationhood, rather than in the objects of traditional authority with which sacredness (and hence charisma) is associated. These objects are connected with the symbols of tribe and village in which charismatic qualities are deemed to reside. The leaders of underdeveloped countries create a sentiment whereby nationhood is endowed with charismatic significance. In other words, these leaders seek to transplant the charismatic attachments to traditional objects on to the nation which becomes a charismatic object. Once this sense of nationhood has been created, those persons most directly encompassed by it (rulers, civil servants etc.) are suffused with the charisma that emanates from the centre. However, Shils argues that for the country to take further steps towards development it must create an economic infrastructure. This necessity means that the charisma that now attaches to the political centre must be dispersed to the economic sphere so that the sense of sacredness with which the new political sphere is endowed (in the form of the aura of nationhood) can be expressed in economic actions. Shils seems to be suggesting here that charisma should be calculatingly dispersed into the economic sphere from the political centre.

Here, we see again the tendency in Shils's account to apply charismatic qualities to a wide range of phenomena.

Moreover, whereas Weber recognized the possibility of charisma of office, he saw it as arising out of the routinization of charisma and hence the creation of an organizational apparatus. Shils, however, proposes that the charisma that relates to an organization need not be the product of its creation by a charismatic leader. Instead, organizations which are central to the society are viewed as imbued with charisma by dint of their sheer importance.

Shils, then, argues that Weber was referring to a special form of charisma that occurs relatively infrequently. By contrast, Shils argues that 'normal charisma is an active and effective phenomenon, essential to the maintenance of the routine order of the society' (1968: 390). Shils's approach is especially noteworthy for the present book, with its particular focus upon the occurrence of charisma in organizations, since it goes much further than even Weber's later political writings in viewing charisma and organization as compatible entities.

However, it is scarcely surprising that Shils's stretching of the Weberian approach to charisma has been subjected to a number of criticisms. In particular, Bensman and Givant (1975) have subjected Shils's views to a detailed critique. They take issue with Shils's tendency to connect charisma with the central power of institutions, which are in turn the recipients of awe and reverence. They argue that one problem with this connection is that it is difficult to see how new charismatic entities can come into existence, other than with the failure of the existing social order. In fact, as we shall see below, charisma can still be acquired when persons or institutions are able to align themselves with a society's core values. The second point they raise is that many relatively powerful institutions are not held to be endowed with charisma, while some people who are regarded as charismatic are not necessarily aligned with the central values of the society. But above all, Bensman and Givant argue that Shils stretches the idea of charisma to such a degree, and in such a way, that it encompasses a host of different manifestations and becomes almost indistinguishable from the notion of legitimacy, of which charisma was only one expression according to Weber. By embracing so much, Shils's version of charisma loses its conceptual and theoretical utility.

Shils's account of charisma is not greatly helped by the way in which he writes about charisma in three different senses. First, he writes about charisma as though it is a distinctive quality of certain outstanding individuals. For example, he writes about the leaders of developing countries: 'They are themselves almost always charismatic men in the conventional sociological sense – strikingly vivid personalities and extremely sensitive' (1958: 4). It is a very moot point whether this is a truly sociological view of the nature of charisma (cf. Friedland, 1964); instead, it seems to have a closer connection with the popular view of charisma as a unique and special quality of individuals. While Weber sometimes slipped into this style of referring to charisma, the importance of the validation by followers of charisma suggests that the conception to which Shils refers is not a 'conventional sociological' one. Second, Shils writes about entities, be they persons or objects, as possessing charismatic qualities, or as having charismatic qualities attributed to them. Third, people are seen as having charismatic proclivities which are permanently available for excitement by contact with a charisma-bearing agency. He refers to 'the charismatic propensity' (1965: 203) and to great charismatic leaders as arousing 'charismatic sensibilities' (1958: 4). The three senses are to a certain degree related. The first sense could be seen as simply a special instance of the second, while both the first and second can be seen as entities which are capable of stimulating the charismatic propensities referred to as the third sense. In other words, these different ways of writing about charisma are not necessarily contradictory; on the other hand, we need to be aware that the term is used in these different ways and of the ambiguities that inhere in Shils's use of the term.

Should we reject Shils's reconceptualization of charisma, as do Bensman and Givant (1975), for overextending its breadth and hence for depriving it of conceptual sharpness? Geertz (1983) has provided an exploration of Shils's use of charisma which points to one or two important themes that are worth registering. Geertz takes up the specific point that there is a crucial connection between relationship to the centres of social orders and the conferment of charisma. Being close to the centre and hence where momentous events occur, 'is a sign . . . of being near the heart of things' (Geertz, 1983). Geertz's approach is to take this theme and to align it with the study of what he refers to as the 'symbolics of power'. He takes three examples, of which one is Elizabeth Tudor and the symbolism that inhered in her procession on the day prior to her coronation and in her subsequent journeys to various towns. Geertz suggests that through these journeys and their associated pageantry, Elizabeth came to symbolize a cluster of virtues ordained by God (and most importantly a Protestant version), and that her charisma grew out of her fashioned association with these transcendent moral attributes.

This and the other examples employed by Geertz point to the importance to the charismatic political leader of establishing in the minds of others a direct connection between themselves and the central values of the society in question. This connection need not be a positive one: revolutionary leaders are equally concerned to associate themselves with the core values of a society, but of course will seek their inversion. Either way, what is critical is that charismatic leadership entails the connection between the leader and the cultural values that signify what it means to be 'at the heart of things'.

While Geertz's approach derives very directly from Shils's understanding, it carries a number of themes that are worthy of highlighting. One is that Geertz implicitly restores the Weberian notion that charisma is attributed to individuals. He does not seem to suggest that the values that are the source of charisma are themselves charismatic; instead, Geertz argues that charisma is conferred by virtue of association with such values. Weber did occasionally write about objects as possessing charisma (other than charisma of office), as when he wrote: 'Charisma is a gift that inheres *in an object* or person simply by virtue of natural endowment' (*ES* II: 400, emphasis added). However, by and large, Weber's analysis emphasized persons as bearers of charisma.

Second, Geertz seems to go much further than Shils in drawing attention to the strategies that leaders can pursue in order to enhance the likelihood of being regarded as charismatic. In particular, it is clear that the leader needs to develop a sensitivity to values which are central to the specific social order and must develop mechanisms for demonstrating that connection in the minds of others. The fact that Geertz sees political symbolism as a vital ingredient of this process draws attention to the fact that the prospective charismatic leader's connection to the centre and its values must be apparent to others. Moreover, Geertz suggests that it can be not just involvement, but also oppositional involvement, with the centre that may engender the attribution of charisma. This proposition suggests that a leader may be viewed as charismatic by seeking to break with existing central values, and must also be clearly recognized as doing so. But Geertz's ideas operate at the level of the nation-state and wider political leadership. Do they have relevance in the context of a focus on leadership in organizations? If we treat the organization as the focal point, we can view charismatic leadership in terms of the leader embodying a system of values which stand for the organization's core. Some leaders will seek deliberately to overturn cherished beliefs, possibly because of their perceived irrelevance to current circumstances. Geertz's elaboration of Shils's conception of charisma may be taken to imply that if the leader has overturned an organization's values, those which replace it will probably be best expressed in terms of the old and will probably need to be clearly signified to others as the new centre.

The psychoanalytic tradition

It is possible to distinguish within the study of charisma an approach which draws upon the works of Freud and psychoanalytic thinking. However, it is very difficult to do full justice to this tradition since it represents a number of contrasting strands. Freud himself never used the term 'charisma' but a number of commentators have noted that he seemed to draw attention to aspects of the charismatic leader–follower relationship without referring to it in these terms (for example, Freud, 1955). Later writers have taken Freudian concepts down a variety of avenues in seeking to explore the psychological dimensions of charisma. Downton, for example, has written:

> The charismatic tie is seen [in Freud's work] as an outgrowth of a psychological exchange arising from tensions within the follower's personality . . . Identification with a leader, diminished capacity to criticize, and complete submission are related directly to the ego's attempt to find a solution to conflicts that produce anxiety, guilt, inferiority, insecurity, and/or ambivalence. (1973: 222)

The general theme behind such ideas is that the follower undergoes regression to an infantile frame of mind when confronted with a leader who appears capable of resolving the intra-psychic problems that the follower experiences.

In understanding the process by which this occurs, Abse and Ulman (1977) propose that it is necessary to appreciate three elements drawn from psychoanalytic theory. First, they point to the unconscious, which represents a repository of individual experiences since and including childhood, which the individual carries around. Second, Abse and Ulman suggest that the processes of transference and counter-transference illuminate how elements stored in the unconscious may be projected on to others. Transference occurs when the individual displaces an old relationship with a person and its accompanying feelings (which are stored in the unconscious) on to a person in the present. Thus leaders, and charismatic ones in particular, often represent for followers a relationship with a parent. When this occurs, the follower replaces his or her own ego-ideal or superego with that of the leader. In this way, the leader is endowed with exceptional qualities associated with parents or other figures. Counter-transference occurs when the leader transfers to the followers 'the wishes and feelings from people in his own past life' (Abse and Ulman, 1977: 38). This process can arouse intense identification with followers and may engender an exalted view on the leader's part of him- or herself. The third element is the process of regression through which the follower 'loosens up'. 'Collective regression', as in the case of a charismatically led social movement, may provide a focus for coping with current problems. As a result, self-esteem is enhanced and past disappointments are salved.

By and large, the psychoanalytic approach appears to emphasize the position of the follower. The leader surfaces through the mechanism of counter-transference. Within the psychoanalytic tradition, one view of charismatic leaders is to perceive them as individuals who externalize their own problems to society as a whole. Their own problems become everyone's problems. The charismatic leader's vision encapsulates these projected problems which, if shared by others, are reinforced and become increasingly public concerns (Kets de Vries, 1990). It is not simply the receptivity to a parental figure that motivates the follower, but also the charismatic leader's specific message which awakens an awareness of the follower's own problems. The charismatic leader emerges when he or she can persuade others that there is an affinity between his or her message (which reflects the leader's problems) and their problems.

The role of such concepts can be discerned in Lindholm's account of Hitler's projection of personal loss. He notes that Hitler went temporarily blind on hearing of the armistice:

> The defeat of Germany had thrown Hitler into a condition of fragmentation and symbolic death, connected to the earlier deep trauma of the loss of his mother ... But Hitler did not disintegrate ... He received the call that reformulated his identity. Voices . . . told him to rescue the motherland from the Jews. His blindness miraculously vanished as Hitler suddenly knew himself to be the saviour of his adopted nation. Henceforth, he and Germany were, he felt, mystically merged, and he could act from his inner feelings with absolute certainty. (Lindholm, 1990: 109)

When he discovered the power of spellbinding oratory, Hitler discovered the means through which he could entice others to follow his perception:

In his speech, Hitler re-enacted for his audience his own violent drama of suffering, fragmentation, loss and eventual redemption through the assertion of a grandiose identity, and the projection of all evil outward. (1990: 109)

We can see in these passages the way in which the leader attempts to produce an affinity between his understanding of what is wrong with his society, a diagnosis that reflects unconscious traumas which he is seeking to relieve and which he projects into larger-scale universal predicaments.

The psychoanalytic approach has some possible use in the context of a Weberian approach to understanding charisma, because it attempts to deal with the vexing problem of the psychological mechanisms that prompt some individuals to develop a vision and to attract a following to bring that vision to fruition. On the other hand, as Willner (1984) has observed, there is a lack of clinical studies that relate directly to the phenomenon of charismatic leadership itself. Much of the thinking derives from Freud's writings on leaders and groups and from extrapolations from clinical research on patients. Whether either of these provides an adequate foundation for the understanding of charismatic leadership is questionable. There is psychohistorical research on charismatic leaders, but this tends to concentrate on highly prominent leaders, so that the universality of the concepts and approach is unclear. It is also not clear how people with the same impulses and problems as such leaders, but who do not become charismatic leaders, cope with these traumas. In other words, are there lots of unsuccessful but would-be charismatic leaders or do individuals have functionally alternative coping mechanisms? Finally, there is a slight tendency to associate charismatic leader–follower relationships with essentially pathological states, though this may not be overly surprising since psychoanalysis grew out of the examination and treatment of pathological phenomena. Thus, it is unnerving to find the three main cases in Lindholm's (1990) book, which is strongly influenced by psychoanalytical ideas, to be extremely destructive charismatic leaders: Hitler, Manson, and Jim Jones. Nonetheless, as suggested earlier, the approach may have a role to play in understanding some of the psychological mechanisms that lie behind the emergence of some charismatic leaders and their attraction to the people who follow them.

Conclusion

It is possible to glean from the foregoing discussion some of the controversial aspects of the concept of charisma. Weber's primary concerns seem to have been to locate it within an appreciation of the nature of legitimate authority, which in turn was linked to his concern with social change, and to provide a language for describing a certain type of leadership within the religious and political spheres. His discussion tantalizes the reader with a host of intimations of fascinating avenues of enquiry, but is flawed because of occasional inconsistencies. In contrast to the popular use of the term, Weber saw charisma largely as a social relationship; his insistence that it needs to be repeatedly validated is an indication of this point. On the other hand, he slips in the occasional comment that he perceives charismatic leaders as innately extraordinary and special.

Weber's use of the concept was a very bold one, in that he sought to divest charisma of its specifically religious denotation. He went even further in locating it in the modern world and not just treating it as a vestige of the past. There has been much controversy about these two aspects of his use of charisma. Perhaps there is a sense in which he used the terms 'charisma' and 'charismatic leadership' metaphorically when he was seeking to broaden out the range of contexts within which it may be applied, that is, beyond the religious and pre-modern environment. This interpretation would be moderately consistent with his insistence that the three modes of legitimate authority are ideal types. As with metaphors, the aim of the ideal type is to draw attention to certain striking features of the object in question. Nonetheless, the bulk of the research that will be discussed in the next two chapters leans heavily upon the insights and framework that Weber developed.

Note

1 Weber's best-known political essay (Weber, 1948) is an exception, in that it makes liberal use of the term 'charisma', although it also refers to Caesarism. However, as Baehr (1987) observes, the essay represents an exercise in both political commentary and broader sociological analysis, so that it is neither surprising nor inappropriate for charisma to appear in this context.

3
The Nature of Charisma

There can be little doubt that in the concept of charisma we find a seductive but irritatingly intangible way of discussing leadership. Nonetheless, the concept has appealed to many writers and has quite wide currency in certain circles. Definitions of charisma or the charismatic leader invariably and inevitably borrow heavily from Weber. Discussions of definitions are usually tedious and frequently degenerate into a quagmire of often minor differences among contending views of what should and should not be included. In this light, it is not proposed to begin a lengthy disquisition on the possible elements that might or might not be included.

On the other hand, it should be recognized that it is often very difficult to define charisma in such a way that some of its causes or consequences do not form part of the definition. We may depict the charismatic leader as someone who is viewed as extraordinary and special by followers. These followers allow the charismatic leader to have power over them and they submit willingly to his or her commands. The followers view the charismatic leader with a mixture of reverence, unflinching loyalty and awe. However, it could be argued that the nature of the followers' response to the leader is in fact a consequence of charisma, that is, they submit willingly to charismatic leaders and regard them reverentially because such leaders are regarded as extraordinary. However, if we take the view, which will in fact be adopted in this book, that the concept of charisma is about a particular kind of social relationship between leaders and their followers, then the inclusion of these elements is only to be expected. On the other hand, Willner (1984) has raised the question of how far the charismatic leader's sense of mission forms part of a definition, arguing that it is a cause of charisma and not a defining characteristic. However, since the charismatic leader's followers 'obey and follow him by virtue of his mission' (*ES* III: 1112) and since a charismatic leader who is bereft of a mission or vision is almost inconceivable, it is difficult to see how this element should be excluded from any conception of charisma which views the phenomenon as a social relationship. Accordingly, it seems appropriate to include the charismatic leader's sense of mission in our definition. In looking for instances of charismatic leadership, therefore, we will be concerned with relationships between leaders and their followers in which, by virtue of both the extraordinary qualities that followers attribute to the leader and the latter's mission, the charismatic leader is regarded by his or her followers with a mixture of reverence, unflinching dedication and awe. This devotion is due to the charismatic leader *qua* individual and not by occupancy of a status or position that is legitimated by traditional or legal-rational criteria.

This can be considered a working definition. It is sufficiently close to Weber's writings and definition that it cannot be accused of having lost its conceptual roots. Equally, it is sufficiently broad for a number of possible candidates on whom research has been conducted to be considered charismatic leaders. A large number of leaders have at some time or another been labelled charismatic and they constitute a very diverse collection indeed. In employing illustrations, I have been initially attracted to individuals who either have a reputation for being or having been charismatic leaders, or have been regarded as charismatic leaders by social scientists, historians and others who have carried out research on them. Occasionally, one comes across individuals who have been labelled charismatic, but in relation to whom there seems to be little evidence for such an attribution. Salaman (1977) has written a case study of 'Mr Brian', the company director of a British manufacturing company. While this is not the kind of milieu that will be considered in this chapter, it was a candidate for consideration in Chapter 5 onwards. Mr Brian did exhibit the personal influence that is often associated with charismatic leaders, since they do not exert authority by dint of their office, but his highly autocratic style seems to have alienated subordinates and substantially reduced their confidence. Charismatic leaders often do become autocratic, which can have deleterious effects upon their followers, but there is no evidence from Salaman's account of the kind of personal devotion implied by the definition. Cases like this are therefore omitted.

The definition is very broad and could be narrowed down by adding characteristics of charismatic leadership that would restrict the number of people that could be subsumed in this and the next chapter. In her discussion of charisma in the political sphere, Willner (1984) opted for an exclusive approach. She identified four characteristics of the charismatic leader–follower relationship: the charismatic leader is perceived as divine or semi-divine; he or she is deemed to possess extraordinary qualities, even super-human or supernatural ones; followers exhibit unconditional acceptance of the charismatic leader's personal authority; followers exhibit a high level of emotional commitment to the charismatic leader. However, because of this very rigorous approach, Willner was only able to find seven unambiguous cases of charismatic political leadership: Castro, Gandhi, Hitler, Khomeini, Mussolini, Roosevelt and Sukarno. A category of 'quasi-charismatics' is recognized but the analysis largely rests upon the magnificent seven. The approach adopted here is by comparison more cavalier, since a plethora of charismatic figures from a diversity of spheres, cultures and centuries will be examined, using the working definition as a guide as to who might be a legitimate target for inclusion. Another highly practical reason for preferring an inclusive approach is that when we come to examine charismatic leadership in the business sphere, even the most likely candidates for consideration, like Iacocca, would not even come close in the context of an exclusive definition.

In this and the next chapter, it is intended to examine information relating to the operation of charisma primarily in the religious and political spheres. Together, these two realms make up the *locus classicus* of the operation of charisma in view of the examples that Weber employed in his writings, so that they seem the most appropriate starting-points for its examination.

Charisma as a personal attribute

CHARISMATIC GENERAL MANAGER
For the most exciting retail challenge of 1987
Total Package c.£35,000 + car

The world's most famous toy store is about to make an even bigger name for itself.

We're revitalising and redeveloping one of London's leading shopping landmarks, adding an extra sales floor, increasing our vast product range and heading for a substantial increase in turnover.

But it won't be child's play. To achieve our targets will take the vision, style, flair and dynamism of a young and outstanding retail professional. Someone in their late 20's or early 30's with a meteoric record in a major department store or multiple group and the charisma to mould a high calibre management

team into a retail tour de force.

The challenge is exceptional but so are the rewards. A package of around £35,000 plus company car indicates the value of the role. Prospects will be precisely what you make them. Suffice it to say that the group has ambitious expansion plans – nationally and internationally – and will require talents such as yours to bring them to fruition.

If you believe your reputation is equal to ours, open further discussions by sending your career details in complete confidence to: Peter Hindley, Chairman, Hamleys of Regent Street Ltd., 188-196 Regent Street, London W1R 6BT.

Hamleys of Regent Street Ltd

THE FINEST TOY SHOP IN THE WORLD

Figure 3.1   *Charismatic leader wanted*

One of the commonest views of charisma is that it is something that people 'have' or do not have. The advertisement in Figure 3.1 shows that Hamleys were looking for a person 'with . . . the charisma to mould a high calibre management team into a retail tour de force'. Charisma would seem to be something that you either have or do not have, like brown hair, or an introverted personality, or an IQ of 142. Thus, it is sometimes suggested that there is a charismatic 'personality type'. Mike Brearley, the former Middlesex and England cricket captain, exhibits this view when he writes: 'Charisma is an effulgence of personal qualities, innate, or at any rate not capable of being acquired by study' (1985: 38). From the point of view of the more practical issues that will be addressed in Chapter 5 onwards, this approach would imply that securing charismatic leaders for firms would be a matter of selecting individuals with the right characteristics. There is a clear similarity here with the trait approach to leadership (see Chapter 1). Although the trait approach has not been quite as fruitless as is sometimes supposed, it has not been especially successful either. Consequently, some scepticism about the possibility of the charismatic leader being a particular personality type is inevitable.

A number of writers have denied that there is a charismatic personality type (for example Dow, 1969; Willner, 1984). For one thing, the sheer variety in the charismatic leaders who have been identified makes it unlikely that a single type can subsume such a diverse assortment of individuals, other than at a level that would probably be so general as to be virtually useless. The search for a distinctive charismatic profile is likely to be fruitless.

However, personal factors may come into play in relation to the question of who becomes a charismatic leader. Do charismatic leaders possess a distinctive collection of physical and/or psychological characteristics that determine who becomes such a leader? Again, the trait approach to leadership does not encourage optimism, but on the other hand, many commentators on particular charismatic leaders have drawn attention to their special characteristics. They are sometimes referred to as having 'a presence', a description used by Bromley and Shupe (1979) in connection with the Reverend Moon, leader of the Unification Church, and Schram (1967: 383) writing about Mao Tse-tung. However, such a notion is very difficult to tie down and probably masks a number of features that the writer has in mind.

Physical characteristics are sometimes cited by writers. Handsomeness has been cited as an important feature of Kwame Nkrumah, who led Ghana to become the first African country to achieve independence (Apter, 1968), Huynh Phu So (Tai, 1983), a Vietnamese Millenarian leader, and Sankara, who was President of Burkina Faso (Skinner, 1988), but such attributions are inevitably subjective and not mentioned with sufficient frequency to warrant a great deal of attention. The quality of the eyes of charismatic leaders is mentioned with striking frequency. Lindholm (1990) has noted the special quality of the eyes of Jim Jones who led his followers, who made up the People's Temple, to mass suicide after they decanted their activities to Guyana; while Charles Manson, who along with his followers was responsible for the killing of the actress Sharon Tate and a number of others, has been described as having 'hypnotic eyes' (Lindhlom, 1990). Huynh Phu So had a 'burning gaze' (Tai, 1983), due to a gaunt appearance deriving from a childhood illness. The eyes of Werner Erhard, the founder of the therapy and encounter cult, *est* (Erhard Seminars Training: the acronym is always in lower case), have been singled out by Stone (1982). When Jan Euden sat at the feet of Bhagwan Shree Rajneesh (see Box 3.1) in Poona, he too was struck by the man's eyes:

BOX 3.1   **Bhagwan Shree Rajneesh (1931–90)**

Formerly Rajneesh Chandra Mohan, Rajneesh was born in India and became a university lecturer. In the mid 1960s, he began to lecture widely in India and rapidly gained a reputation for his combination of powerful oratory and outrageous views on such topics as sex and religion. In 1970, he announced that he would be known as 'Bhagwan' (God) and a few years later founded an Ashram (religious community centred on a holy man) in Poona. In 1980, 5,000 followers lived in this community and there were around 15,000 disciples worldwide. The Ashram gained a reputation as a place where sex and drugs were readily available. There were also adverse reports about the effects of many programmes of instruction upon the minds of adherents. Numerous centres for expensive instruction in meditation grew up throughout the world. In 1981, Rajneesh disappeared and turned up in Oregon, where he had purchased a huge estate which became the new centre for the religion. He then entered a period of silence, which left the running of the estate to Sheela, who was the closest of the 'power ladies' (a group of women who ran his affairs) to him. He only spoke to her. During this period, the leadership became highly autocratic and venal, and many excesses were perpetrated. Bhagwan's accumulation of ninety Rolls-Royces, while followers were not allowed their own vehicles, was not the cause of much resentment, but numerous crimes were coming to light and were the subject of growing concern among insiders and outsiders. When he came out of his silence in 1984, Rajneesh sought to distance himself from the apparatus that Sheela had created and from her crimes. In 1985, he was arrested trying to leave the USA, but was later deported. In 1988, he re-established the Poona Ashram which soon became extremely popular. Recognizing the Oregon experiment as a mistake, he and his close disciples sought not to repeat the experience. More indicative of his influence than number of disciples is the immense capacity for work exhibited by disciples who, as in Oregon, often work twelve-hour days, seven days per week for tiny amounts of money. Why? According to Thompson and Heelas (1986: 92): 'They regard all that they do as acts of worship, to be performed with care, willingness, concentration; as opportunities to express their devotion.'

Sources: Barker, 1989: 201–5; Euden, 1990; Milne, 1990; Palmer, 1988; Thompson and Heelas, 1986

I listened to his discourse, trying to imagine how this almost comical character could possibly have inspired such deeds [building a huge business empire and a city in a desert, attracting a huge personal following, and possibly incitement to commit murder], until the ecstatic sobbing of the sannyasins drew my attention to his face. The eyes were as magnetic as they had seemed on film, and he had that ability of the true charismatic in seeming to lock into the gaze of each individual. (Euden, 1990: 19)

Willner (1984: 149–50) has also observed that the political leaders that she examined had been noted for the quality of their eyes, such as Castro's eyes being 'hypnotic in their intensity'. Quite how and why the eyes of charismatic leaders seem to be so significant can only be a matter of speculation, but will be returned to when the formation of charisma is examined.

BOX 3.2 **Kwame Nkrumah (1909–72)**

Nkrumah was the first African leader to engineer independence from colonial rule, when the British handed over sovereignty to Ghana. In 1947, after some years as a student in the UK and the USA, where he earned the reputation of a skilful organizer, Nkrumah was asked to return by increasingly affluent Gold Coast professionals and business men to help bring about independence. He helped to create the Convention People's Party (CPP) which gained political ground at elections and managed to bridge the gulfs between different regional and tribal groupings. At the time of the first election in which the CPP could compete, Nkrumah and other leaders were in prison for civil disobedience, which enabled him to be cast as a victim of oppression and as a martyr. His disciples organized his election campaign. The election was won by a landslide. On his release in 1951 he was appointed Leader of Government Business, and the following year was made Prime Minister. By 1957 independence had been achieved, but the road had not been an easy one, in that Nkrumah encountered sustained opposition from certain groups, such as the National Liberation Movement. Soon after independence, restrictions were imposed upon opposition groups. An inability to deliver economic prosperity, coupled with mismanagement of certain projects (in particular the disastrous Volta River Project) gave rise to considerable unpopularity. This unpopularity reached a peak when internment without trial in the interests of national security was adopted to curb opposition. The country seemed to limp towards chaos as imported food and pharmaceutical drugs disappeared, as did Nkrumah himself who became a virtual recluse. Following a number of assassination attempts and growing disquiet in the army, he was overthrown by the combined forces of the army and the police on 24 February 1966.

Not all commentators are agreed on Nkrumah's credentials as a charismatic leader. One of the main writers to favour Nkrumah with the attribution 'charismatic', Apter (1955), revised his view to suggest that it is not applicable after 1955 (Apter, 1968). Nkrumah's claim to status as a charismatic leader is based largely upon a number of distinctive features: his relentless pursuit of a vision, namely freedom and the development of a centralized nation-state; the adulation and loyalty that he received prior to independence; his capacity to move audiences through inspired oratory; and his success in bringing independence to fruition. However, the contrary views point to the difficulty of attributing charisma unambiguously to leaders. Moreover, Nkrumah's inability to manage the economy and his drift towards authoritarianism testify to the limitations of charismatic leaders.

Sources: Ake, 1966; Apter, 1955; 1968; Birmingham, 1990; Cohen, 1972; Runciman, 1963

The charismatic leader's voice has been singled out by several commentators. This is a difficult theme in certain respects, because it is well documented that charismatic leaders are powerful orators, which can also be seen as a personal characteristic that is determinative of charisma. It becomes very difficult to disentangle the voice, the words and the style of delivery. Nonetheless, the charismatic leader's voice has been noted as often having a special quality. Writing in *The Times*, Bernard Levin, normally a rather sceptical commentator, was moved by Rajneesh and noted that: 'His voice is low, smooth and exceptionally beautiful' (cited in Milne, 1990: 12). Apter (1968: 773) has described Nkrumah's (see Box 3.2) voice as follows: 'His voice, both deep and melodious, had a practiced resonance that audiences found attractive.' However, more commentators have pointed to the powerful and often spellbinding oratory of many charismatic leaders than to their voice as such. Very few charismatic leaders are poor speakers. Gandhi was not noted for his public speaking and even had something of a phobia about addressing the public (Lewy, 1979). Joanna Southcott (see Box 3.3) was not a strong speaker and is unusual in that she relied largely upon her fairly numerous publications for spreading her message (Harrison, 1979). The impact of the holy men, who in the fifth and sixth centuries attracted followings by virtue of acts of mortification (such as St Simon Stylites perched on a pole in the desert for many years) and their reputation for magic and miracles, was not based upon oratory (Brown, 1981). Thus, impressive oratorical skills are not a necessary feature of charismatic leadership, although it is certainly a notable aspect. However, it is questionable whether powerful oratory is entirely a matter of personal ability; in the section on the social formation of charisma, it will be argued that a powerful oratorical style may be developed to a very large degree.

BOX 3.3   **Joanna Southcott (1750–1814)**

Described by one source as 'the greatest prophetess of all' (Thompson, 1968: 420), Joanna Southcott received a vision in 1792: 'I was strangely visited, by day and night, concerning what was coming upon the whole earth. I was then ordered to set it down in writing' (quoted in Harrison, 1979: 88). Operating in a religious climate in which there was widespread anticipation of a second coming, which engendered a procession of would-be prophets, Southcott became a prodigious writer of pamphlets which allowed her apocalyptic message to be spread widely. Initially, she failed to secure adherents, but then gathered seven disciples who visited her in her home in Devon in 1801. The following year, she moved to London where her seven disciples became ever more active on her behalf in seeking to spread her word. One wealthy convert provided her with a home and acted as a patron. Converts received 'seals', which were pieces of paper with words which testified to new adherents' qualifications for the new millennium and then secured with a seal bearing the inscription 'I.C.' (for Jesus Christ). Southcott claimed that Christ had led her to find this seal while clearing out a house in Exeter. Demand for seals increased from 8,000 in 1804 to 14,000 in 1807. In 1814, there was much excitement when she announced that she had received a vision that at the age of sixty-five, she would give birth to Shiloh, the Son of God. Initially, she was able to point to signs of pregnancy, but these disappeared and she became increasingly ill and died at the end of 1814. Various individuals claimed to be her successor, but none gained a wide or consistent following, and so the movement gradually dissipated.

Sources: Harrison, 1979; Thompson, 1968: 420–8

Other personal characteristics often attributed to charismatic leaders include such things as energy, confidence and endurance. Stone (1982) mentions a catalogue of characteristics that Erhard's followers ascribe to him. He is seen as having immense powers of endurance, a feature which is evident in his activities at *est* training weekends when he would lecture each day for more than ten hours, return to his office to take care of administration, sleep for three hours, and then return refreshed for further training. Stone also wrote in his research notes that Erhard 'radiates energy and confidence' (Stone, 1982: 146). House et al. (1988: 116) compared charismatic and non-charismatic US presidents and found the former to be 'extremely active, assertive, and energetic'. Tales of many other charismatic leaders attest to their energy and endurance, though the two do not always go hand in hand;

the holy men of late antiquity impressed by virtue of their endurance rather than their energy (Brown, 1981). Stone (1982) also refers to Erhard's confidence, as does Schweitzer (1984) of Hitler, while House (1977) also suggests that this is an important characteristic of charismatic leaders, along with a tendency to dominate, strong conviction for beliefs and a need to influence others. In an examination of US presidents, House et al. (1990) have confirmed the importance of such traits as need for power in distinguishing charismatic from non-charismatic presidents. Simonton (1988) also finds charismatic US presidents to have a high need for power. His data also suggest that a tendency towards interpersonal dominance, an outgoing nature and an absence of shyness are features of charismatic presidents.

There is also a suggestion that many charismatic leaders exhibit a special ability to feel intuitively what people want. Lindholm (1990: 105) has suggested that Hitler had a capacity to woo prospective converts by making them feel that he was responding to their dormant wishes. Schweitzer (1984: 248–9) attributes a capacity for empathy to F.D. Roosevelt. However, whether this phenomenon can validly be called a personal characteristic is questionable. It may be that the leader who successfully lays claims to being regarded as charismatic has developed an understanding of what potential followers want, moulds his or her mission to what is felt will appeal to them, and focuses their attention on certain issues that are connected with what their followers want to hear. In other words, the charismatic leader makes people think that he or she knows what they want, when in fact he or she is bolting some of their desires and hopes on to the mission. Ralston, for example, writes of the charismatically inspired leaders of Ashram-based movements: 'They were able to focus and shape ideas already present in an obscure manner in the consciousness of their followers' (1989: 57). In many cases, then, the apparent capacity for empathy may have more to do with impressing on potential followers how the mission will meet their needs, which the leader gives a focus to.

There is certainly evidence for a number of personal characteristics to be associated with the propensity to become a charismatic leader. However, the evidence makes it difficult to say that any one characteristic is a feature of all or even a majority of charismatic leaders. Writers on particular leaders tend to emphasize certain qualities that their subjects exhibit, or are seen by followers as exhibiting, and this creates an impression that such features are important in generating charismatic leaders. However, the evidence is invariably sketchy and impressionistic, with few common features being in evidence across the full range of leaders. Further, many personal attributes are probably exaggerated by leaders themselves or in the hagiography that succeeds them. It also has to be remembered that although prospective charismatic leaders may have special qualities, these have to be recognized and acknowledged as extraordinary by putative followers, and that the leader's mission will be just as influential in creating the charismatic leader–follower relationship. When we look at the stories of charismatic leaders of the past, it may appear inevitable that individuals with certain characteristics achieved their positions by dint of those characteristics, but there may have been many candidates for charismatic leadership status with the same features in equal profusion who never achieved the same status. The problem here is that we know relatively little about unsuccessful claims to charismatic leadership. Another problematic feature of an excessive reliance upon personal attributes in the understanding of charisma is that it probably fails to give sufficient attention to the role of contextual factors in the genesis of charisma. Carson has noted that the perception of Martin Luther King almost certainly exaggerates his personal attributes at the expense of 'the impersonal, large-scale social factors that made it possible for King to display his singular abilities on a national stage' (1987: 448–9), such as the wider influence of the black movement. Moreover, before accepting as determinative the role of personal attributes we would have to explain the case of William Wadé Harris (1865–1929), a self-styled prophet who engaged in a brief but highly successful preaching mission in 1913 and 1914 in the Ivory Coast and the Gold Coast during which he had a considerable impact on many thousands (Wilson, 1975). His unsettling influence led to his deportation at the end of 1914. He attempted to preach in a number of regions afterwards, but aside from some success in Sierra Leone, he never achieved the impact and status as a charismatic leader that he had attained previously. Undoubtedly, the impact of cultural and other contextual factors played a major role in his lack of success elsewhere, implying that the special features of the charismatic leader are unlikely to be a sufficient explanation.

Charisma as a social relationship

Rather than to treat charismatic leadership as something that resides in the individual leader, the point of view preferred here is to depict it as inhering in a particular kind of social relationship between leaders and their followers. This notion can be found in the works of a number of other writers on charisma, such as Dow (1969), Theobald (1978) and Wallis and Bruce (1986a), and is an explicit feature of the working definition articulated on p. 41. But what does it actually mean to say that charismatic leadership is a social relationship?

For one thing, as Weber recognized, a leader cannot be said to be charismatic unless his or her claim to charisma has been validated by others. Thus, the followers form an integral element in charisma. Their importance continues since the leader's charismatic claims are in constant need of reaffirmation. If charismatic leaders do not bring benefits to their followers, or if their special abilities (for example, magical, prophetic, healing) appear to desert them, their claim to charisma may be diminished and even disappear. Once the leader's charisma has gone, he or she no longer has power over the followers and is no longer their leader. A possibly extreme example can be seen in the case of a Sufi 'saint', Muhammad al-Wali (1786–1806). Sufism is a mystical form of Islam in which the saint (*wali*) occupies a special position in relation to Allah. According to Last (1988: 184), this saint lost his *baraka* (an

Islamic concept denoting numinous power which has affinities with charisma) when he inadvertently caused an old talismanic Qur'ān, which had been wrapped in goats' skins and then hides, to be opened. He was ejected from his office and killed.

The charismatic leader and his or her followers are therefore locked together in a relationship of interdependence. The leader must have the followers' support, their preparedness to submit to his or her will. Charismatic leaders may even depend upon their followers for economic support. In Hasidism, the mystical Jewish tradition begun by Rabbi Israel Ba'al Shem Tov in the eighteenth century, the *zaddikim*, spiritual leaders around whom Hasidic communities clustered and who were regarded as having special powers, relied upon their followers for financial support (Berger, 1986). For their part, followers willingly acknowledge their own dependency and even submission, but in return they expect that advantages will accrue to them as a consequence of their submission (such as salvation, spiritual enlightenment, a way out of political oppression or poverty), although Bendix (1986) has suggested that followers may seek to withhold complete surrender of self-determination in case effective leadership in exchange for their subservience is not forthcoming.

Charismatic leaders may engage in strategies to enhance their followers' dependence upon them, especially since the need for charisma to be continually reaffirmed renders it a very precarious element. Jim Jones secured converts to the People's Temple in the early days by offering free food and help in securing jobs (Johnson, 1979). Their dependency was often then enhanced by requiring that they contribute a large proportion of their economic resources to the group and that they sever outside ties. Indeed, the programming and 'brainwashing' associated with certain religious cults, which have occasioned considerable controversy (Beckford, 1985), can be seen as strategies to create or enhance dependency on charismatic leaders. David 'Moses' Berg, the leader of the Children of God, has shown an unusual tendency to change his exhortations to his members about their beliefs and practices (see Box 3.4). Wallis (1982) suggests that one reason for this predilection is that he wants to be seen as the ultimate source of his followers' beliefs and lifestyles so that their dependency upon him is not diminished.

In viewing charismatic leadership in terms of a relationship of reciprocal interdependence we are close to conceptualizing it as an exchange relationship. The followers agree to submit to the charismatic leader in exchange for his or her preparedness to meet their needs for salvation etc. They also acknowledge their preparedness for unflinching loyalty. The charismatic leader agrees to bring them benefits provided that they are prepared to submit to his or her will. Each becomes reliant on the other but the exchange is an asymmetric one in the end, for it is the charismatic leader who holds the reins of power. Inevitably, a further element in the relationship is trust, since the followers and leader must trust that each will keep their end of the bargain. From the followers' point of view, the charismatic leader may need to have failed them on a number of occasions before he or she is regarded as having broken that

BOX 3.4   **David 'Moses' Berg (1919–)**

Formerly a minister in a conservative denomination in the USA, Berg became increasingly involved in the Jesus movements that formed part of the 1960s counterculture. The religious movement that he formed has been known by a number of names, but has been most frequently referred to as the Children of God. It is now often called the Family of Love. Berg claims to have received a number of revelations which are primarily concerned with the end of the world. His vision entails gathering converts who can be saved and can become participants in the new millennium. Members view the world as essentially evil. They are expected to give up worldly possessions when they join. Berg's methods have been controversial since at one time they included 'flirty fishing' – offering sex for successful conversion. In fact, an obsession with sex is one of the hallmarks of Berg's writings and remarks. However, Berg has been unusual in his propensity to alter the movement's focus in matters of belief and practice. A number of examples have been documented by Wallis (1982). Initially, followers were enjoined not to take conventional jobs, but at a later stage, a more lenient approach could be discerned. There were corresponding changes in tolerance towards followers mixing with members of Christian churches. In matters of internal organization, he has been shown to promote individuals into positions of leadership and then to humble them. The movement has spread into many regions of the world, though worldwide membership is not large (perhaps between 5,000 and 10,000).

Sources: Barker, 1989: 171–3; Beckford, 1985; Wallis, 1982; Wallis and Bruce, 1986a

trust. Jacobs's (1987) research on individuals who have become disaffected with religious movements led by charismatic leaders shows that they often do not attribute their disillusionment to the leader *per se*. But what does the exchange comprise?

Power

Power is a critical element in the conception of charisma in terms of an exchange, because in the charismatic leader–follower relationship it is a central resource in the exchange. There is the obvious sense that has just been explored, namely, that the charismatic leader is allowed by his or her followers to have power over them, by virtue of what he or she can promise them in the context of the proclaimed mission. But there is a sense in which, because of their association with the leader and his or her mission, the followers are empowered in return. The power that they receive is not necessarily power over others but a sense of having come into contact with special forces or of being part of a movement for change. The power that we are talking about here is the association with forces and agencies that can make things happen.

Not only is the charismatic leader a person who enjoys power over followers; he or she is also regarded as a person 'with' power. Through the charismatic leader, followers can participate in some of that power, that awesome capacity to make even the impossible happen. They can benefit through and by their association with this source of power. In Sufism, the saint is a man of power which is believed to emanate from Allah (Cruise O'Brien, 1988; Brenner, 1988; Last, 1988). In order to attain sainthood the saint will have used his power for the benefit of his followers. In essence, the followers are empowered by their association wtih this source of power. In late antiquity, holy men were men of power and 'to visit a holy man was to go where the power was' (Brown, 1981: 121). The holy man would engage in what Brown calls 'stylized gestures' which demonstrated the capacity for power. By visiting a holy man one became empowered oneself. Bromley and Shupe report in relation to the Reverend Moon and the Unification Church:

> The extraordinary qualities embodied by the movement leader give members a sense that the movement is linked to powerful forces that will assure them ultimate victory. (1979: 144)

Schweitzer (1984: 9) cites a follower of the Romanian charismatic leader, Codreano, as saying: 'He is our hope and the hope of Romania tomorrow. We get strong through him. We are feared through him. We shall win through him.' McClelland reports a study in which, shortly after the assassination of John F. Kennedy, business students were shown a film of his inaugural address, which is described as 'a highly moving presentation of a charismatic leader' (1975: 259). Compared with a control group, those who watched the Kennedy film 'were apparently strengthened and uplifted by the experience; they felt more powerful' (1975: 259). Lindholm (1990: 110, 120) reports that Hitler's audiences frequently felt 'energized' by him and that a convert to Manson's Family felt 'energy' from joining the group. While energy may not quite be the same as the empowerment that we have been referring to, it conveys a sense of being associated with someone with a capacity to make things happen and for the individual to be a part of that movement.

A distinction offered by Howell (1988) seems relevant to the issue of charisma and empowerment. Howell distinguishes between socialized and personalized forms of charismatic leadership. The latter is based on followers' needs and their right to develop as individuals. The follower is empowered and capable of pursuing the charismatic mission independently of the leader. With personalized charismatic leadership, the mission is a reflection of the leader's personal motives, from which he or she believes that followers will benefit. This form of charismatic leadership engenders follower obedience and submission, as well as dependence upon the leader. This distinction appears relevant because it suggests that only socialized charismatic leaders produce the empowerment that has been the focus of this section. However, the distinction is not easy to apply because charismatic leaders seem to be complex mixtures of both types. Howell acknowledges that a leader can exhibit both tendencies. She views Jim Jones as a clear instance of the personalized type, and there is much to confirm this description, though Lindholm (1990: 149) asserts that Jones's followers 'felt energized by his presence'. On the other hand, many other leaders seem to reflect both tendencies. Hitler's mission, for example, was a reflection of his personal motives, but there is little doubt that many Germans felt empowered by his vision of a powerful Germany. In fact, most charismatic leader–follower relationships probably entail mixtures of dependency and empowerment for followers, so that although it is useful to draw attention to the two types of charismatic leadership, the possibility that they simply reflect differences in the balance between the two elements limits the distinction's usefulness.

The evidence to support the notion that power is a key element in the relationship between charismatic leaders and followers is inevitably sketchy, but if further research were to lend it further credence it would add to our understanding of followers' reasons for supporting charismatic leaders in such a selfless way and might enhance our understanding of the differences between charismatic and non-charismatic leaders.

The role of crisis in the emergence of charisma

Weber recognized that eruptions of charisma are frequently associated with periods of social crisis. Indeed, a central focus of attention in the missions of charismatic leaders is their programme for relieving their current and prospective followers of the circumstances associated with crisis. A number of overviews of charismatic leaders, which have sought to quantify aspects of the emergence of charisma, have confirmed the important role that crisis plays in establishing charismatic leaders (for example, Barnes, 1978; Cell, 1974; Toth, 1981).

The notion of crisis can take a number of different forms, but the most prevalent is that of profound social dislocation and the discontent that accompanies it. Fourteen of the fifteen charismatic founders of religions examined by Barnes (1978) made their impact during periods of social upheaval. Brown (1981) relates the rise of the holy man in late antiquity to the erosion of classical institutions. Gilsenan (1973) ties the founding of the very successful Sufi brotherhood, the Hamidiya Shadhiliya, by Salama ibn Hassan Salama (1867–1939) to a period of considerable crisis in Egypt. Stewart has described the situation confronting Henry Alline, a religious leader in Nova Scotia in the 1770s and early 1780s, and the northern Yankees who were receptive to his message as 'one of fear, uncertainty and confusion' (1974: 141). This uncertainty arose as a result of the ambiguous position in relation to the American Revolutionary War of Yankees living in Nova Scotia. Alline's interpretation of the war as sinful and as producing chaos delivered a message appropriate to the Yankee predicament during the war. Ignored or threatened by the Americans, suspect or harassed by the British, subjected to privateer raids, fearful of an American invasion or of British conscription to fight against friends and relatives, the people of the out-settlements lived in an atmosphere of instability and confusion. (1974: 144)

Sometimes, the sense of crisis and distress is tied more exclusively to economic problems. In reality, it can be difficult to distinguish a sense of economic crisis, but in some cases the rise of charisma seems to be associated with economic distress. The followers of the millenarian movements of the nineteenth century, like the Southcottians, seem to have been motivated by the prospect of spiritual deliverance from economic hardships. In India, the Bhoodan Gramdan, which under the charismatic leadership of Vinoba Bhave aimed to redistribute land, was in many respects a response to a sense of crisis and discontent spurred on by an awareness of the need for land reform (Oomen, 1967).

Frequently, of course, the sense of crisis and dissatisfaction is due to a combination of economic and social factors. This seems to have been the case in Germany, where the ravages of depression and hyper-inflation coupled with the trauma of defeat in the First World War and a loss of social cohesion provided a fertile context for Hitler's message. Equally, supporters of Perón saw him as someone who could deliver them from economic distress and the effects of social disorganization (Madsen and Snow, 1983).

The charismatic leader may also project a message that is relevant to the psychic needs of certain targeted groups. Galanter (1982) has observed that many of the people who join religious cults are not economically deprived individuals, but young people from middle- and upper-middle-class backgrounds in relatively stable societies. They sometimes come from troubled family backgrounds and have a history of psychological distress. They often have few social ties prior to joining. There is evidence to suggest that on joining, such individuals improve psychologically as a result of the feelings of belonging to a group that are fostered (Galanter, 1981).

The usual interpretation of the connection between charisma and crisis and discontent is that charismatic leaders gain a following by fitting their message or mission to the situation at hand. Alternatively, through their mission they may draw attention to critical situations of which subsequent followers were only dimly aware at the outset (Oomen, 1967; Willner, 1984). Oomen believes that Gandhi fits this second category better than the other, as perhaps do many other charismatic leaders who headed independence movements. Likewise, Cruise O'Brien (1988: 7–8) has observed that in Islamic societies in Africa, charismatic leaders often achieved significance by virtue of their interpretation of the society around them as in a state of crisis. Thus, while there is a good deal of evidence to associate the rise of charismatic leaders with a sense of crisis and distress, aspects of this impression may sometimes be the creation of the leaders themselves. When this is the case, the leaders are contributing to the social formation of charisma, which is the focus of the next section.

The social formation of charisma

Having established doubts about the virtue of viewing charisma in terms of personal characteristics and a preference for treating it as a form of social relationship, we cannot escape the question of how charisma arises. To say that it emerges from the interaction of leaders and followers is true and entirely consistent with the view of charisma as a social relationship, but it is not very illuminating. In this section, it is proposed to present some ideas about the activities of leaders and their followers in generating charismatic leadership – the social formation of charisma.

The starting-point for the understanding of charisma that is proposed here is what might be called 'a cultural model of charismatic leadership'. This is a set of prescriptions about the sorts of things that a prospective charismatic leader should do or exhibit in seeking to make a successful claim to charisma. It is these actions that will help to convey the sense of extraordinariness that is constitutive of charisma. This is not to say that anyone who does the right things will automatically become a charismatic leader; the mission may be unacceptable, the situation may not be propitious to the prospective leader's message, he or she may not exhibit the right personal characteristics for attracting a following, and so on. Moreover, in talking about a cultural model, all that is being suggested is that prescriptions will vary from culture to culture; there is no suggestion that cultural prescriptions do not change, or that there can be no subcultural models. Attention is simply being drawn to the possibility that what will pass as a legitimate set of actions in one time period or place may not work in another.

Writers on Sufism have successfully delineated a cluster of activities in which the putative charismatic leader (possibly seeking to become a sheikh or even a saint) should engage. These activities help to project a sense of an exceptional individual. A period of retreat and possibly seclusion in one's early years seems to be important, since it represents a special capacity for piety (Cruise O'Brien, 1988). Salama ibn Hassan Salama devoted himself to a variety of ascetic practices, many of which caused him profound physical discomfort (Gilsenan, 1973). Second, the prospective man of *baraka* usually needed to demonstrate a capacity for intensive study and literacy. Literacy alone can convey a sense of mysterious power when the population is largely illiterate. Knowledge of Arabic is especially efficacious in creating a sense of numinous power because it was the language in which the Qur'ān was revealed to Muhammad. However, as literacy spread, knowledge of Arabic had to be accompanied by other signs, and Cruise O'Brien suggests that this development generated greater emphasis being laid upon religious retreat. Third, the prospective sheikh or saint must have visions and demonstrate a capacity for miracles. The miracles may be subject to a variety of interpretations: they may be manufactured (Constantin, 1988), or seemingly ordinary events may be deemed miracles (see some of the examples in Gilsenan, 1973: 20–35). A vision legitimates the holy man's right to be considered a leader; the vision may be rejected but is nonetheless a *sine qua non* in the production of a figure who will become a sheikh (Gilsenan, 1973). In Salama's case, his vision instructed him 'to follow the path of the Saints and to form an Order' (1973: 36). Fourth, a capacity for medicine seems to have been a useful asset to develop. Fifth, saints seem often to have been good mediators in disputes (Constantin, 1988: 89). There is an interesting connection here with the holy men of late antiquity who have been described by Brown (1981) as ombudsmen in social life. It seems likely that those who have developed a capacity for intercession in human affairs will be seen as having special abilities to intercede on behalf of others with respect to divine agencies.

In the case of the charismatic leader in Sufism, we see a pattern of activities that are necessary to the later attribution of charismatic status. Personal qualities may help: as a child Salama was an impressive student and had the advantage of being able to trace his descent from the Prophet (Gilsenan, 1973), but these would hardly be sufficient to become a charismatic leader in the environment of Sufism. In addition, he needed to conform to a number of features associated with the cultural model of the charismatic leader in the Sufi tradition. The notion of the charismatic leader seeking to become a vessel of holiness in the manner of the Sufi leaders is not peculiar to that tradition. While representing a quite different tradition and route, Gandhi dressed in the garb of a Hindu holy man in order to legitimate his political message with Hindus, although in the process he alienated Muslims (Perinbanayagam, 1971).

A critical stage in the career of many prospective charismatic leaders is the emergence of a coterie of supporters. It is not just that these individuals support the putative leader; they reinforce his or her sense of mission and are prepared to act on his or her behalf. In the case of Salama, Gilsenan (1973) reports that early recruits were carefully selected according to strict criteria. These early disciples acted as his emissaries, spreading his mission and recruiting others. In these early days of support for a charismatic leader one discerns the charismatic community (*Gemeinde*) about whch Weber wrote, but equally the germs of routinization of charisma are present since the leader's retinue is soon allocated tasks and responsibilities and their roles are given some stability. However, the specific issue of the routinization of charisma is reserved for the next chapter. The significance of the prospective charismatic leader's early coterie of followers at this juncture is that they act as the bridge between the leader him- or herself and a wider following or mass movement. If they fail to recruit others and to spread the message, the chances are that they will lose interest if their belief in the prospective leader fails to be reinforced by the emergence of further supporters. As such, the 'charismatic leader' is likely to be a footnote in history, assuming that he or she even gets that far. The followers, therefore, have a vested interest in the successful promotion of their leader, who will be well aware of the necessity of having their support in order to make a wider impact.

Numerous illustrations can be found of the charismatic leader's early reliance upon an initial band of followers. Apter (1968: 766) notes that Nkrumah had a small group of supporters who were able to create the movement that led to independence and to collect supporters. Joanna Southcott was especially in need of a band of supporters since she was a poor speaker and, although she made good use of publications as media for spreading her message, her influence was bound to be restricted at a time when illiteracy was not uncommon. Hitler relied heavily upon a small group of dedicated followers and consistently surrounded himself with acolytes who reinforced his ambitions and delusions. Ellen White, who effectively started Seventh Day Adventism, was initially accepted as a prophet by a small band of followers who were prepared to do her bidding (Theobald, 1980).

The sequence of events depicted in Figure 3.2 can be employed to represent the process that has just been described. It demonstrates the crucial role of the initial devotees upon the subsequent attraction of a wider following and how the failure to attract a wider following may have an adverse effect upon the devotees. The model probably works especially well with the genesis of charismatic leadership in relation to religious movements and to some political leaders as well. However, the role of enthusiastic disciples pervades a number of aspects of the social formation of charisma and does not rest simply in terms of spreading the word and recruiting followers.

The importance of oratory

For many people, the charismatic leader is a person who is a spellbinding, or at least highly effective, orator. The ability to hold an audience in one's thrall through powerful oratory is not an especially important feature of Sufi saints and sheikhs, nor was it of Brown's holy men of late antiquity. Oratory cannot be absolutely definitive, because we would be hard put to explain the continued support of imprisoned or exiled charismatic leaders, such as Mandela, Khomeini and Gandhi. Nonetheless, the association in many people's minds of charisma with impressive oratorical skill is apparent. In the West, there is often a tendency to associate charisma with powerful oratory. Thus, there are instances where a person's lack of evident skill at speaking is treated as evidence of an absence of charisma. The verbal blunders of Dan Quayle, who at the time of writing is Vice-President of the USA, seem to be a prominent factor in the suggestion by one of Quayle's aides that he 'does not have a lot of charisma' (Lichfield, 1989: 9). One instance may suffice from a newspaper report:

> In the course of a speech to the Young Republicans National Federation in Nashville . . . the Vice-President said America was about to celebrate 'the twentieth anniversary of Neil Armstrong and Buz Luken walking on the moon'. As every American school child knows, it was Buzz Aldrin who made the second biggest step for mankind on 20 July 1969 . . . Donald E. 'Buz' Lukens is a Republican congressman from Ohio who was recently tried and convicted of sexual misconduct with a 16-year-old girl. (1989: 9)

John McGregor, when UK Secretary of State for Education, was described as 'a really boring minister, devoid of charisma, short on vision, so bad on television that producers never want him on their programmes' (Wilby, 1989:

FIGURE 3.2 *Model of the Social Formation of Charisma*

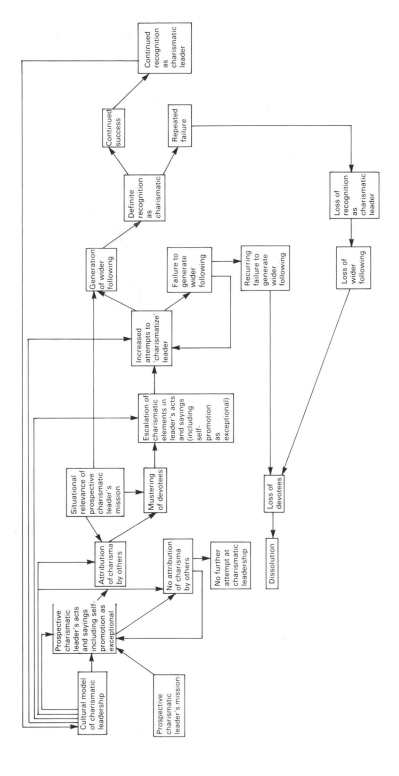

19). To take one final example, in a discussion of Don José María Arizmendiarrieta, who masterminded the immensely successful and admired Mondragón cooperative in Spain, Whyte and Whyte (1988: 250–1) dismiss the possibility that he is a charismatic leader largely because of his poor public speaking. Certainly, many charismatic leaders appear to have been very competent orators. While one thinks most obviously of leaders like Hitler and Mussolini in this regard, many other figures like Nkrumah, John L. Lewis (see

---

BOX 3.5   Huynh Phu So (1919–47)

In 1939, Huynh Phu So founded a millenarian religious sect which operated in the Mekong delta area of Vietnam. His message was one of an impending apocalypse in relation to which he offered salvation for the movement's adherents. He projected himself as the reincarnation of a previous charismatic religious figure in the area, the Buddha Master of World Peace (1807–56), whose message initially gave So's sect its name. Later, the movement became known as the Hoa Hao sect. At an early age, Huynh Phu So received a revelation and was soon accepted as a holy man. He built upon his reputation both by exhibiting an unswerving belief in his mission and by gaining converts through healing sessions. With the help of devotees he quickly built up a following, and by 1939 the sect numbered 10,000. A year later, the followers of a rival sect joined the Hoa Hao. In this same year, the sect's success prompted the increasingly concerned authorities to purge it. Huynh Phu So was incarcerated in a hospital, where he was diagnosed as insane, and he took the opportunity to convert some of the staff. Ten months later, he was transferred and put under house arrest, but the area then attracted followers in droves. He was later rescued with the help of the Japanese who gave him protection. The sect continued to gain followers, even though for some time So was unable to leave Saigon. His devotees recruited in his absence, but were not averse to threats to achieve their aim. So increasingly became concerned that the movement lacked a clear ideology, and he seems simultaneously to have decided to compete with the communists. The sect became more political and developed a structure. In fact, So oscillated between confrontation and cooperation with the communists. He was assassinated by the Viet Minh. His body was dissected into many pieces and buried in different places so that Hoa Hao followers would be less likely to anticipate his reincarnation. By late 1944, there had been nearly one million followers.

Source: Tai, 1983

Chapter 4) and Huynh Phu So (see Box 3.5) have exhibited great oratorical skill.

It may be that many of these leaders were 'naturally' great speakers, but we should be wary of seeing oratorical ability too readily in these terms. For one thing, it is apparent that many charismatic leaders who are also stirring speakers make abundant use of carefully constructed rhetoric to get their message across. Hitler imbued his nationalistic speeches with a religious rhetoric in order to convey the impression that there was a God-given basis for his ideology (Schweitzer, 1984: 69). The use of religious imagery is quite a common device among political leaders which Willner (1984) has also discerned in relation to F.D. Roosevelt. Mao Tse-tung's message was more effectively put across by virtue of earthy humour and metaphors from Chinese folklore (Schram, 1967). Indeed, the deployment of metaphor seems to be a striking feature of the oratory of many charismatic leaders, and this almost certainly contributes to their effectiveness as speakers, since there is clear evidence that metaphors contribute greatly to the capacity of the leader to persuade others (for example, Bosman, 1987). There is a very strong possibility that the use of metaphor is a deliberate tactic on the part of many leaders, thereby adding weight to the notion that powerful oratory is in large part stage managed and an important ingredient of the social formation of charisma.

In addition, speakers who are regarded as charismatic seem to employ a number of oratorical devices in greater profusion than others. Atkinson (1984) has shown that stirring speakers make greater use than others of techniques such as three-part lists. Tony Benn, the Labour Party Member of Parliament, makes particular use of a technique that Atkinson calls 'refusing invited applause', which is where his supporters are given every indication as to when they should applaud (note the role of followers here) but he carries on speaking during their acclamation. This conveys an impression of the speaker having to fight to make himself heard because he has had such an immense impact upon the audience. The latter find that they must become active participants in the proceedings, since they must anticipate the appropriate moment in order to be able to give the speaker the acclamation that is deserved. Atkinson demonstrates that two other charismatic leaders made use of this particular technique – J.F. Kennedy and Martin Luther King. Fairclough has noted that the latter learned many oratorical artifices from black clergy and 'became a past master at manipulating audiences' (1990: 48).

Moreover, the stirring speaker frequently uses gestures and eye contact to make an impression. Hitler not only prepared his speeches carefully, he also studied his gestures in a mirror and acted out particular points of his speeches (Schweitzer, 1984: 66). Bull (1986) has demonstrated how hand gestures can add substantially to the impact of the rhetorical techniques described by Atkinson. In addition, Atkinson (1984) has shown that eye contact can be extremely important in the creation of charismatic speaking. He notes that Tony Benn rarely uses a script. While this gives the impression of greater spontaneity, it also means that greater eye contact gives the audience the impression that he is speaking directly at them and at the same time he is able to monitor their reaction. Also, Atkinson notes that few great orators wear spectacles when making speeches, since this makes their eyes difficult to see and hence affects communication. This observation could be taken to imply that even the importance of the charismatic leader's eyes (see p. 44) is at least an impression that they create. It may also help us to understand the afore-mentioned capacity to read others' minds that is sometimes attributed to charismatic leaders, since it may be that the effect of eye contact is to form an impression of being able to see into the individuals in the audience.

Audience reaction is an important part of the way in which a speaker is perceived. This can also be stage managed. Hitler certainly strategically arranged followers in the audience to maximize the opportunity for copy-cat clapping to take the audience over. He also used halls that were too small to create the impression of people clamouring to hear his words. Standing ovations, such as those enjoyed by Tito (Drachkovitch, 1964), can be created to convey a sense of a stirring speaker.

The association of charisma with powerful speaking is a strong one. It is certainly true that many charismatic leaders have been potent speakers and it is not surprising therefore that in the popular mind there is a tendency to connect charisma with a style of speaking. It is easy to view oratory as an innate ability, but we should recognize that even if some people are naturally better public speakers than others, the charismatic leader and his or her followers often conspire through a variety of techniques to enhance that ability. In other words, even striking oratory can be at least in part formed.

Creating myth and legend

A further aspect of the social formation of charisma can be the creation of myths and legends about the charismatic leader. These myths and legends can be vital ingredients of the process by which the charismatic leader comes to be seen as special or extraordinary. Sometimes, the leaders fashion the circumstances out of which myth and legend may arise on their own, but in many cases their closest followers are wittingly or otherwise active participants in the process. Miracles may be fixed, for example. Constantin (1988) has suggested that many miracles performed by Sufi saints are constructions. Sometimes, the fabrication may appear pitifully obvious, such as Jim Jones's use of rotting chicken livers to create an impression of having extracted cancers (Johnson, 1979); Joanna Southcott's discovery of seals with the words of Christ, which were later distributed to believers, can be seen in a similar light. Charles Manson enhanced perceptions of his potency by developing the legend that during a particularly passionate act of fellatio, his partner bit off his penis, which miraculously grew again (Fine, 1982). Alternatively, apparently ordinary events may be subsequently construed as miracles.

The leader's initial vision or revelation may become the subject of considerable interest to followers who invest it with special significance. Werner Erhard's 'catalytic freeway experience' is one such example. While driving on a freeway in California, Erhard had an 'enlightenment experience' (Stone, 1982: 149) that made him feel that he had acquired a special understanding of himself and his purpose, a revelation that led to the founding of *est*. Initially, Erhard gave little prominence to this experience in his teachings, but it was very important to his staff, who, as they themselves became successful practitioners of *est* methods, were able still to believe in his specialness because it was he who had had the experience. Here again we see the important role that the charismatic leader's immediate disciples play in the creation and maintenance of charisma. Their role can become even more decisive when, as has occurred in a handful of cases, charismatic leaders wittingly or unwittingly enhance the mythology that surrounds them by becoming remote from the bulk of their followers. Rajneesh's prolonged silence would be one such example, as would David Berg's disappearance in 1970 which generated a sense of mystery about him among his followers (Wallis and Bruce, 1986a).

A further aspect of the mythologizing of the charismatic leader can involve the enhancement of his or her unique qualities or past. In the case of the Reverend Moon, aside from the stories about his communication with Jesus at the age of sixteen, he is reputed by his followers to have had a profound sense of justice and morality since a very young age and only to need three to four hours' sleep each night (Bromley and Shupe, 1979). John Noyes, the leader of the Oneida Community, a nineteenth century sect of Christian perfectionists, was described by his mother as having always possessed a special ability to command respect and loyalty (Olin, 1980). Kimmel and Tavakol (1986) report that when Khomeini's potential as a charismatic leader was recognized, his biography was rewritten to imply the inevitability of his ascendancy to power. Such developments of myth and legend can greatly enhance the sense of the leader and his/her mission as extraordinary.

Creating innovation and success

A clear theme in Weber's writings on charisma is the notion that the charismatic leader is a revolutionary, someone who possesses an innovative solution to the predicaments of his or her followers. This aspect of charisma is likely to be intrinsic to the leader's vision and mission. The leader may prophesy that the last days are nigh, as do millenarian leaders like Southcott, Berg and Moon, and promise a better future for their followers; or charismatic leaders may promise a new social and political order which will release followers from the injustices and inequalities of the present, as with Nkrumah, Mandela, King and Hitler; or charismatic leaders may inveigh against the moral bankruptcy of the present and offer the prospect of a new set of values, as with Khomeini. The mission may take other forms and even involve combinations of the foregoing and other types. What appears common to most illustrations is that the charismatic leader is innovative, promising profound change and often offering novel ways of going about effecting change.

An interesting conceptual difficulty about this aspect of charisma has been raised in the context of the Northern Ireland Protestant loyalist politician, the Reverend Ian Paisley, by Wallis and Bruce (1986b). They observe that Paisley appears to have modelled himself upon the Old Testament prophets, who for Weber were the archetypal charismatic leaders. Paisley has a loyal following, possesses a clear mission, and is noted as a fiery orator. He would seem to have a great many of the attributes that one would associate with a charismatic figure. But Wallis and Bruce are uneasy about viewing him in these terms because his 'identity, style and message rely so heavily upon reference to the traditional past of Ulster Protestant society' (1986b: 88). Because of this apparent reliance upon an appeal to tradition, Wallis and Bruce argue that Paisley's authority is better described as based upon tradition. They summarize their position thus:

> *Charismatic authority* . . . can only be accorded to leaders who are not only seen to possess charismatic endowments, but whose legitimacy to command, rebuke, praise or prescribe for others, arising from these endowments, is relatively unconstrained by instrumental, ideological, rational-legal or traditional considerations. The greater the constraint, the further the departure from charismatic authority . . . Ian Paisley is constrained by tradition to such an extent that it makes no sense to regard him as a charismatic leader. (1986b: 107)

This is an interesting argument. However, it is difficult in the absence of precise indicators to know how to interpret 'relatively unconstrained' or to describe apparently mixed types. As regards the latter point, it is clear that the Old Testament prophets are difficult to classify in these terms. Wallis and Bruce quote Southwell (1982: 61) as saying that the teachings of these prophets were innovative. However, Southwell also notes that Old Testament prophets drew on older traditions and notes the 'puzzling coition of radical and conservative, revolutionary innovator and protagonist of ancient inherited traditions that is so marked a feature of prophetic teaching' (1982: 63). Indeed, many purportedly charismatic leaders display the admixture to which Southwell refers. Khomeini's radical mission against the West was grounded in a commitment to the reassertion of fundamental Muslim virtues (Kimmel and Tavakol, 1986; Kimmel, 1989). The aim of Vinoba Bhave who, as leader of the Bhoodan Gramdan movement in India which sought to redistribute land to the landless, is regarded as a saint and as superhuman (Oomen, 1967: 89), was to re-establish a traditional order. The possibility exists, therefore, that the charismatic leader may indeed be an innovator or revolutionary, but a major component of the change that he or she wants to induce may entail a resurgence of traditional ways and virtues. As such, what distinguishes charismatic and traditional authority is the nature of the relationship between leaders and their followers and of the characteristics that the latter ascribe to the former.

However, this discussion is in some respects something of an aside and was introduced in order to draw attention to a problematic aspect of the concept of charisma. The point that is to be raised specifically here is that innovation may be a feature that prospective and actual charismatic leaders seek to cultivate.

Writing generally about political leadership (rather than charismatic leadership in particular), Edelman (1988) has argued that leaders invariably have to give the impression of innovation in order to mark themselves off as distinctive and to conform to an expectation that such persons will be innovative. He argues that leaders use a variety of linguistic devices and dramatic gestures to imply innovation, while simultaneously barely departing in their actions from the maintenance of the status quo. This view suggests that in so far as charisma is associated with innovation, many charismatic leaders may cloak their actions and intentions with a rhetoric and dramaturgy that is aimed to disrupt the status quo as little as possible. It may be that one of the reasons why some charismatic leaders (or aspirants) appear innovative, while appealing to traditional virtues and ways, is that they cover their intentions with a revolutionary and innovative gloss.

A similar kind of point can be made about the role of success in charismatic leadership. Weber took the view that charisma needs recurrent validation in order for the aura of extraordinariness to be maintained. It becomes important to exhibit a continued capacity for the kind of ability that got the leader noticed as a bearer of charisma in the first place. Success in performing miracles, defeating opponents, prophesying and so on must be redemonstrated, although some commentators (especially, Theobald, 1975; Wallis and Bruce, 1986b) have suggested that truly charismatic leaders will have secured the devotion of their followers to such a degree that they will not lose their followers in spite of failure. Even Nelson Mandela, the African National Congress leader who was imprisoned for twenty-seven years and is regarded as a charismatic figure by the media (for example, Carlin, 1990) and social scientists (for example, Rosenbach and Hayman, 1989) alike, lost some of the sense of his extraordinariness soon after being released from jail. Just six months after his release, it was being suggested that as a consequence of his failure to achieve a resolution to the bitter fighting between ANC and rival Inkatha members, the image of him 'as a demigod, capable of achieving results no mere mortal could contemplate' (Dunn, 1990: 17) was fading.

Failure need not necessarily engender a loss of charisma. For one thing, as Edelman (1988) notes, political leaders often seek to construe apparent failures in terms that will be favourable to them. Military failures can be depicted by leaders as indicative of their own courage; disastrous economic policies may be glossed over and treated as signifying the leader's firmness and commitment to a mission. Alternatively, they may divert attention from problems. Nasser, who is often viewed as a charismatic figure, has been interpreted as seeking the Six Day War in order to divert attention from economic problems in Egypt and to restore his waning charisma (Entelis, 1975). Second, leaders can treat a continued capacity to win new followers as pointing to success, in which case they are to a certain extent specifying the criteria of success. Dow (1968) notes how the charismatic leaders of pre-independence movements in Africa retained the faith of their followers in spite of many years of failure. He attributes this continued support in particular to the role of mass rallies in validating their charisma. Third, they can accept the view that all success relating to the movement or whatever can be attributed to them. Bromley and Shupe (1979) suggest that the Reverend Moon is credited with having organized many successful events even though it was his followers who were largely responsible. He in turn appears quite willing to accept this view of his role in success. Fourth, they may be adept at deflecting blame from themselves for failures and mistakes. Ronald Reagan, who is referred to as a charismatic leader by a number of writers, earned the sobriquet 'the Teflon President' as a result of his capacity to ensure that no charge for errors or misdemeanours ever stuck to him (Foley, 1990). Thus, 'objective' failure does not necessarily result in the dissipation of charisma.

Overview of the social formation of charisma

The discussion thus far suggests that components of charismatic leadership that are frequently cited by commentators as important features of charisma can be viewed as part of its social formation. This conception of charisma has implications for the distinction between true and manufactured charisma (see Chapter 2), which has been a concern for a number of authors (for example, Bensman and Givant, 1975; Ling, 1987). The perspective that has been enunciated here suggests that there is a strong manufactured element in all instances of charismatic leadership. To cling to some kind of notion of 'true' charisma is to imply that some individuals are so overwhelmingly special that they deserve to be separated apart from those whose charisma has to be consciously fabricated. Weber showed a tendency to slip into this style of reasoning, when he wrote of two types of charisma: that which 'is a gift that inheres in an object or person simply by virtue of natural endowment' and that which 'may be produced artificially in an object or person through some extraordinary means' (*ES* II: 400). This kind of contrast is flawed because the 'special qualities of natural endowment' are, as we have seen, difficult to pin down in any systematic fashion. On the other hand, there is ample evidence that even among leaders whose status as charismatic leaders is relatively undisputed, the manufacture and reproduction of charisma by the leader and his or her followers is a recurring theme. Luke (1986) has examined the role of television in the creation of charisma in American political life and essentially argues that the media, campaign aides, party officials and the leaders themselves have come to appreciate the capacity of charisma to be socially formed. Indeed, the creation of the aura of charisma has become a central ingredient of the persona that the candidate for political office (and supporters) seeks to engender in order to present him- or herself as a legitimate candidate for public office. However, to view this form of charisma as bogus, as implied by the notion of 'manufactured' charisma, is to miss the point, because these are simply modern (perhaps even post-modern) forms of the kind of process depicted here as the social formation of charisma.

The leader's status as charismatic may even be created or enhanced after his or her death. Schwartz (1990) has shown how Abraham Lincoln was not a very popular leader while alive, but the Lincoln Centennial celebrations in

1909 created a view of him as special and accorded him greater warmth than he enjoyed from his contemporaries. Schwartz does not describe Lincoln as a charismatic leader, but his characterization of the twentieth century view of Lincoln is highly consonant with the attributes that such leaders are supposed to exhibit:

> In the twentieth century . . . Americans . . . saw the Saviour of the Union who takes upon himself the pain of the people. They saw the great moralist, the prophet of democracy, the Great Emancipator, the giant who changes the course of history. They saw the man that can never be reached: a man, for sure, but too good, and too big, to be treated as a man. (Schwartz 1990: 98)

But these features were not identified by Lincoln's contemporaries, so that what we see here is a kind of *post mortem* charismatization, which suggests that the depiction of him as a charismatic leader is almost exclusively a matter of social formation. Equally, there may be a need to protect the charismatic leader from *post mortem de*charismatization. A musical based on the life of Martin Luther King received a hostile reception in certain quarters because it portrayed him as 'a womanizer', 'cunning rather than great', and 'despite his reputation for oratory, often less than eloquent' (Chittenden and Roy, 1990: 28).

Another especially interesting case in the political sphere in the light of viewing charisma as socially formed is that of Gladstone (1809–98), who in his later years was the subject of what amounts to a personality cult. Gladstone was also one of the only political figures of modern times who was identified by Weber as charismatic. Hamer (1978) has shown how a number of biographies of Gladstone appeared in the last twenty-five years of the nineteenth century, which copied much from each other and collectively created a body of mythology about him:

> In the biographies, Gladstone often appears in strongly dramatic terms. He is shown as almost superhuman, not an ordinary politician at all but able to bend circumstances to his will . . . the great episodes [were] described again and again in such a way as to make Gladstone appear the chief protagonist, not subject to any of the normal restraints on the ability of a politician to control circumstances . . . The illustrated biographies convey this dramatic quality particularly vividly. Gladstone is often depicted in heroic or dramatic poses or against romantic backgrounds . . . His features become more hawklike and fierce, and in the later part of his life he looked – or could be made to look by the artists – like some Old Testament prophet or patriarch. (Hamer, 1978: 34)

For his part, Gladstone, with the politician's ability to recognize an opportunity, lived up to the part that the biographers and others were creating for him. His love of tree-felling was well known and almost always covered by his biographers. Gladstone in turn was quick to ensure that he was seen engaging in this highly symbolic activity. Other politicians were sometimes inclined to ridicule this tendency towards self-glorification. In 1884, Lord Randolph Churchill described him as 'the greatest living master of the art of political advertisement' (1978: 39). In the end, Hamer suggests, it was not Gladstone the person who was so revered, but the Gladstone who had been created by the biographers and other contributors to the hagiography that surrounded him. Gladstone himself then became the embodiment of the myths.

Conclusion

The main aim of this chapter has been to examine a number of ways in which charisma, and charismatic leadership in particular, can be conceptualized. This examination has not been favourable to the popular view that charisma is something that resides in the person. There is a tendency in general speech to perceive charisma as an attribute that a person possesses. This chapter has taken the view that this does not represent an especially helpful framework for the analysis of charismatic leadership. Drawing upon a number of theoretical ideas in the relevant literature and the abundant research on charismatic leadership in the religious and political spheres, two themes have received special attention in this chapter.

First, the working definition supplied on p. 41 and the subsequent presentation of evidence have been concerned to suggest that charismatic leadership is essentially to do with a particular kind of relationship between leaders and followers which can be regarded as a form of exchange. This view is not especially novel; nor is it entirely inconsistent with an emphasis upon the special qualities of charismatic leaders, since these can be viewed as an aspect of an exchange relationship (for example, Lindholm, 1990). However, since some scepticism has been levelled in this book at the view that charisma reflects innate abilities and characteristics, the depiction of charisma as an exchange has tended to emphasize resources – and power in particular – as the key ingredient of the exchange. The notion of charismatic leadership as a type of social relationship means that followers are heavily implicated, since it is not simply a matter of the special qualities of the leader. In suggesting that the relationship is one of exchange, and in proposing power as an important constituent of the exchange, an attempt is being made to address the issue of why followers enter into the relationship and what they seek to extract from it. If there was no examination of this issue, the depiction of charisma as a social relationship would not take us very far. We would be forced to regard the charismatic leader's followers as mesmerized puppets. Such a description may be apt some of the time, but the devotion of followers almost certainly involves a greater degree of instrumentality and sentience than it implies. It should be appreciated that this injection of a rational element into the present elucidation of the nature of charisma is to a large degree in contrast to Weber's conceptualization. As a number of authors have observed (for example, Albrow, 1990; Baehr, 1990), for Weber charisma belonged to the realm of the irrational, because the followers' support for their leader is largely emotional and not amenable to rational explanation. However, the adoption here of an approach to charisma that is not posited upon a notion of irrationality is consistent with the suggestion that Weber probably underestimated the complexity and purposiveness of followers' motives (Baehr, 1990).

Second, it has been argued that charisma can be characterized as something that is socially formed by the leader and others to produce the kinds of effect with which the phenomenon of charisma is associated. Perhaps such a perspective on the genesis of charisma, like the presentation of charisma in terms of an exchange relationship, implies too much rationality and purposefulness in human affairs; however, it is hoped that it provides something of a corrective to the excessive tendency to seek to separate out certain individuals as special and extraordinary by dint exclusively of personal characteristics, a notion which pervades much popular commentary of charisma and to which Weber was occasionally prone. Equally, the notion of the social formation of charisma is highly consistent with the idea of charismatic leadership as a social relationship in at least three ways: both sets of ideas point to the importance of followers in the affirmation of charisma; they both imply a greater degree of purposefulness in charisma than is typically the case (perhaps even by Weber); and they are both antithetical to the notion that charisma is purely a personal attribute. It is hoped that together they will provide a helpful backcloth to the material that follows in later chapters.

4
Charisma, Organization and Routinization

Like the previous chapter, this one will deal with a number of interrelated issues. The linking theme in this chapter is the question of the relationship between charisma and organization. It is evident from Weber's writings that he saw the two as antithetical. Charisma was seen as something that arises in opposition to conventional arrangements, usually authority structures based upon traditional or legal-rational criteria, and the organizational structures with which they are associated. Moreover, as noted in Chapter 2, he viewed the inevitable process of routinization as involving the development of organizational structures which were often in opposition to the pristine and highly original charisma. In the present chapter, a prominent theme will be the degree to which routinization and its associated organizational forms result in the stultification of charisma. Initially, the idea of routinization will be explored. While this term represents a number of issues, both in Weber's work and that of later researchers, it is possible to distil much of the literature so that it reveals two main areas of concern – the problem of succession and the development of structure. The notion of 'the development of structure' is meant to act as a short-hand for the emergence of organizational structures and the codification of beliefs following the initial burst of charisma. The two issues – succession and structure – are by no means unrelated, but they are meant to serve as simple organizing themes for an examination of theory and research. This discussion is followed by an examination of the question of whether charismatic leadership can emerge in the context of formal organizational structures, since Weber regarded such structures as inimical to the emergence of charisma. This examination will entail an exploration of the operation of charismatic leadership in formal organizational contexts outside the religious and political spheres that have tended to dominate the discussion of charisma so far, and is meant to act as a bridge with the material to be covered in the later chapters.

Routinization: the problem of succession

Precisely because charismatic leadership is a personal form of leadership, followers are often concerned about what will happen once the leader dies. Charismatic leaders may recognize this concern and seek to take steps to initiate a successor. Weber wrote about six methods of solving the problem of succession. First, there may be a search for a person with the right qualifications for the position of successor. The chief example of this type is the search for the Dalai Lama. Second, the new leader may be revealed through the examination of oracles, divine judgements and the like. Third, the charismatic leader may designate a successor, which is a common method, as Weber noted. John Noyes, the leader of the Oneida Community, nominated his son as successor, while Gandhi had clearly primed Nehru to succeed him. Fourth, the successor may be designated by 'the charismatically qualified administrative staff' (*ES* I: 247). Fifth, the successor may be decided by heredity, whereby succession is associated with a kinship line and is acknowledged as such. Within Hasidism, the position of *zaddik* is decided by such a criterion. Whitaker (1990) has provided a graphic description of the process with reference to a sixteen-year-old boy named Umar, who, following the murder of his father by gunmen eleven days earlier, was preparing himself to become the spiritual leader of Kashmir's six million Muslims. Meanwhile, 'more than 50,000 Muslims are waiting for him in the huge Jama Masjid mosque . . . to see the turban of office being wound on to his head' (1990: 18). Finally, there is charisma of office, whereby charisma becomes associated with incumbency of a position with which charisma is associated. At this point, the succession issue becomes intertwined with the development of a structure, since it often provides the framework within which charisma of office occurs. Weber cited the anointing of priests and the coronation of monarchs as illustrations of the process whereby charisma of office may come about.

Of course, as Weber recognized, the charismatic leader and his or her followers may do nothing to initiate a foundation for dealing with the succession. It may be, as with Rajneesh's view of himself, that the leader feels that he or she cannot be succeeded. David 'Moses' Berg has also done little to initiate the process of securing a successor. It seems unlikely that the Reverend Moon will be succeeded, partly because the view is taken that he cannot be and also because there is a sense in which he is believed to have fulfilled his role (Barker, 1987: 143). Does it matter if no successor is secured at the time of the charismatic leader's departure?

If the leader and his or her followers fail to provide for a successor, there is a fair amount of evidence that the movement or group will either dissipate or continue but with a strong tendency to disintegrate. When Joanna Southcott died fairly suddenly there was no obvious successor, as a result of which various factions arose which disputed the future path of the movement. Many of the factions were led by prophets who claimed to follow in her footsteps but none appears to have secured a consistent or large following (Harrison, 1979). Huynh Phu So's early demise at the hands of the Viet Minh meant that no successor had been secured. His father was made leader but he does not seem to have been able to make the same impact as So, perhaps because his right to leadership was not apparent. The movement did not disintegrate, because So had routinized his charisma through the development of a structure (see below), but the absence of a recognized charismatic leader made it harder for the movement to gain new followers (Tai, 1983). When the Prophet

Muhammad died in 632, he had failed to name a successor or a means of election. Nor was there an obvious successor from his marriages. His successor, Abu Bakr, was related (his daughter was Muhammad's main wife) and was responsible for public worship when Muhammad was ill. But the association of leadership with kinship to Muhammad was broken at a later stage by Abu Bakr's successor, 'Umar I, who insisted that his successor should be selected by a group of men and that his own son should not be elected. This development lies at the heart of some of the current divisions within Islam, with the Shi'a claiming that only members of Muhammad's clan can truly succeed him (Turner, 1974). It is not only the death of the charismatic leader that can lead to the kind of fission that has been described. The deportation of Simon Kimbangu, a charismatic leader who attracted many followers within a six-month period in 1921 in the Congo through a mission which combined Christianity and anti-colonialism, created what Wilson (1975) has called a 'charismatic demand', which led to the emergence of a number of local prophets who claimed to be following directly in his footsteps, though none seems to have come very close to achieving the same extent of a following. A final example is the case of the successor to the charismatic founder of the National Council on Alcoholism (NCA) in the USA. Following the latter's retirement (although she remained on the premises with secretarial support), the organization's board of directors appointed an executive director to succeed her. The successor is described by Trice and Beyer (1986) as a professional administrator with little knowledge of alcoholism problems. The founder's supporters were divided in their support, but many were concerned about the new director's apparent shift of the organization's perspective on the nature of alcoholism towards viewing it as a disease. Moreover, the founder and the successor were soon locked in a bitter conflict, with the latter insisting that the former withdraw more and more from having an interest in the NCA's affairs. Four years after his appointment the successor left.

These illustrations would seem to suggest that if either a successor or a framework for securing one is not suggested by the charismatic leader, the group's continuation is threatened. One other possibility for the charismatic leader is to put the leadership in the hands of a number of individuals following his or her death. However, this approach can lead to an organization racked with conflict, as suggested by Rochford's (1985) description of the International Society for Krishna Consciousness (ISKCON) in the years after the death of its charismatic founder Srila Prabhupanda in 1977. In 1970, Prabhupanda had set up a governing body commission to oversee the movement's affairs and it was assumed that this body would take over government after his death. However, some months before his death, Prabhupanda appointed eleven close disciples to act as initiating gurus (who would be responsible for initiating new disciples) for the movement. The idea was that these gurus would be viewed by their disciples as spiritual masters, much as Prabhupanda's disciples viewed him as their spiritual master. The gurus and the fourteen commission members were to be jointly responsible for ISKCON's administrative affairs. Although matters were not helped by economic decline following Prabhupanda's death, there then followed a period of intense conflict and rivalry within the movement. For example, there was much concern and resentment over one of the initiating gurus who demanded the same treatment and consideration as Prabhupanda himself. This prompted concern about the role and position of the gurus both in terms of the nature of their succession to the movement's founder and relative to the commission.

Had Prabhupanda not sought to introduce the guru system, thereby leaving the commission to get on with the administrative affairs of ISKCON, it is possible that the movement would have been riddled with conflict to a much lesser degree. But the commission was a predominantly bureaucratic entity, relying for its authority on legal-rational considerations, and it seems likely that Prabhupanda wanted to continue a charismatic line through the appointment of the gurus. Certainly, the initiation by Mary Baker Eddy, the founder of Christian Science, of a board of directors which governed the movement prior to her death and continued to do so afterwards has meant that the splintering effect that is observed in ISKCON has not occurred to anything like the same degree (Wilson, 1961: 146). In part this can be attributed to the fact that there is an absence of the countervailing authority system that is seen at ISKCON, but also there is a tendency among guru authority systems towards fission (Robbins, 1988: 120).

It might appear that the problem of succession will be dealt with more effectively if the charismatic leader either names a successor or initiates a framework within which one can be generated. However, there are numerous instances of failure in such cases too. John Noyes's decision to nominate his son as his successor as leader of the Oneida Community led to an outcry. This event appears to have been the first stage of the loss of Noyes's charisma in the eyes of many members of the Community, some of whom began to question his authority over other matters as well (Olin, 1980). In the late nineteenth century, Sri Ramakrishna gathered a diverse group of disciples who were attracted to his apparent spiritual abilities. He designated as his successor one of his most promising disciples, Narendranath Datta, who became Swami Vivekānanda. However, Ramakrishna's followers refused to accept Vivekānanda's succession because they disliked his commitment to social reform and to direct dealings with the world and his criticism of excessive piety. Vivekānanda became an itinerant missionary (in India, North America and Great Britain) in which capacity he gained a personal following and achieved the status of a charismatic leader in his own right. He founded the influential Ramakrishna Order on his return to India (Ralston, 1989).

Sometimes, the success of the charismatic leader's nominated successor is more partial than these two cases suggest. The Mahdi of Sudan, who died shortly after the fall of Khartoum, had designated as his successor the Khalifa Abdallahi, who had been his assistant. The Mahdi asserted that Abdallahi's role had been revealed to him through the Prophet Muhammed, thereby legitimating the latter's position. Abdallahi did a great deal to continue the work of the Mahdi in creating an Islamic state. He reaffirmed his legitimacy as successor by claiming visionary experiences in the manner of the Mahdi. However, Abdallahi failed to gain the unequivocal support of the Mahdi's kin. He also 'had to rely on conventional power tactics to perpetuate his authority over the disparate tribal structure of the Sudan' (Dekmejian and Wyszomirski, 1972: 209). His tendency to suppress opposition and his inability to command unambiguous support played a part in the eventual diminution of loyalty to the Mahdi's mission.

Dekmejian and Wyszomirski (1972) liken the 'transference of charisma' between the Mahdi and Abdallahi to the case of Gandhi and Nehru. However, Bendix (1986) has suggested that the transfer between these two was fairly smooth because Nehru was seen as the embodiment of Gandhi's charisma. During his campaigns to make contact with Indians, Nehru was able to view at first hand the degree to which he possessed Gandhi's charisma. Here would seem to be a fairly successful designation by a charismatic leader of a successor, but although other instances exist of a relatively smooth transfer, they are few and far between.

It is tempting for any successor to a charismatic leader, no matter how he or she comes to this position, to seek to follow directly in the style and conduct of the predecessor. However, this impulse can lead to a loss of support, rather than an increase. While Nehru was well aware of his dependence for his own charisma upon Gandhi, as Bendix (1986) observes, he parted company with his mentor over certain issues and practices which meant that he did not become a carbon copy of Gandhi. Nehru was more westernized than Gandhi and this had an impact upon his approach to the relationship between prophecy and teaching, giving greater weight to the second of these than Gandhi. Bendix perceives this as a potential difficulty for Nehru, arguing that Indians sought a greater emphasis upon prophecy. On the other hand, it may be that in not seeking to be a replica of his great predecessor, Nehru gained more support than otherwise.

Two examples will be used to illustrate this general point. Salama, the founder of the Egyptian Sufi order Hamidiya Shadhiliya, was a highly revered figure whose death represented a considerable problem for the brotherhood. He was succeeded by his son Ibrahim, which is believed to have been Salama's preference. However, Gilsenan (1973) argues that Ibrahim's succession derived not from a descent principle but because, as a first-generation relative of the founder, he participated directly in his predecessor's *baraka*, which is seen as transferable. Nonetheless, some members of the order doubted Ibrahim's ability to perform miracles. This doubt was reinforced by the fact that he was after all one step removed from the founder's *baraka* and was a boy of thirteen when he acceded to the position. Gilsenan suggests that Ibrahim responded to the ambiguity of his role by recognizing that he was not regarded as having the same capacity for miracles and with the awe that his father attracted. He responded by increasing the social space between himself and his followers compared with the approach of his father. Whereas Salama made himself available to members of the order, so that they could share in his *baraka*, Ibrahim restricted contact so that access to his *baraka* became more difficult to attain and therefore more sought after. The order's officials restricted access to him, so that any irritation over his remoteness devolved to them. In this way, Ibrahim created a sense of mystery for himself and enhanced his position by making his *baraka* a scarce and valued commodity to be dispensed only on rare occasions. In this illustration, we see not only another clear instance of the social formation of charisma, but also a strategy for the successor in dealing with the questionable legitimacy of his status as a charismatic leader. The latter is achieved at least in part by not adopting the same style as that of the original charismatic figure.

The Jehovah's Witnesses furnish another interesting case. The founder of the movement, Charles Taze Russell, enjoyed two sources of authority: charismatic authority as a preacher and as pastor to the movement's network of ecclesias, and legal-rational authority as the editor of the movement's successful publishing house (Beckford, 1972). His death in 1916 provoked a crisis for the movement, especially since it followed a failure of prophecy two years earlier. A bitter power struggle ensued out of which Joseph Rutherford emerged victorious in 1917. There was considerable resentment in some quarters at Rutherford's rise, but he seems to have been very astute at carving out a niche for himself within the movement that quelled some of the disquiet about his assumption of Russell's position. He appears to have recognized that he could not follow directly in Russell's charisma, such was the attachment in the movement to its founder. Instead, he sought to take over Russell's largely bureaucratic functions. Rutherford instilled a rational framework within which the proselytizing and business of the movement could take place, though at the same time he sought to weaken the importance of Russell's charisma in the movement.

This case is especially interesting since the routinization of charisma often means that the charismatic leader is forced to occupy bureaucratic roles in the resulting structure. The degree to which charismatic leaders involve themselves in the day-to-day running of the organization varies a great deal from case to case (see next section). While we do not usually find the sharp bifurcation of sources of legitimate authority that are discerned in the case of Russell, the example of the Jehovah's Witnesses suggests that it may be futile for a successor to claim to share in the founder's charisma. Instead, he or she may do better to absorb the leader's functions as an official. Ibrahim chose a different strategy, perhaps in part because routinization had not been accompanied by a legal-rational ethos to the same degree. Together these two illustrations point to the possible importance of the successor resisting the temptation of presenting him- or herself as a duplicate of the original charismatic leader.

There can be little doubt that succession to the charismatic leader is rarely unaccompanied by at least a modicum of discomfort for followers and successors alike, regardless of the timing of the succession itself. In this section, an attempt has been made to stipulate some factors that may accompany relatively effective successions. Succession is only one aspect of routinization, but as will be seen, it rears its head again in the context of a discussion of the emergence of a structure that accompanies routinization.

Routinization: the development of structure

Weber recognized that a certain degree of routinization is bound to occur almost as soon as the initial charisma of the leader is acknowledged by others and a following develops. In particular, a structure of tasks, obligations, rules and so on is likely to develop and is often accompanied by a codification of the movement's beliefs. Disciples come to rely on the emerging structure for their status and may receive rewards for their activities. The wider movement wants some kind of structure to emerge in order for a sense of continuity to be infused. These issues were explored in Chapter 2. As Weber indicated, the emergence of a structure is to varying degrees likely to quell the originality and fervour of the initial charismatic impulse. Zald and Ash (1966) have suggested that the officialdom that takes over the everyday running of what they call 'social movement organizations' tends to adopt a more accommodating position in relation to society at large. This tendency can be seen in the John Birch Society, an extreme right-wing political movement in the US, in which the initial fervour and radicalism of the movement's founder, Robert Welch, a self-styled charismatic leader, was gradually suppressed by 'organization men' (Broyles, 1964). Because of their commitment to a career within the movement, these officials sought to enhance their job security by making the ideology less extreme and so more attractive to a wider range of people.

From the charismatic leader's perspective a number of issues arise. How far should the process of routinization be encouraged and welcomed? If it is encouraged at least to a degree, should it be introduced early or later in the movement's development? How far should the charismatic leader be involved in the structure that arises? These broad themes will be addressed in this section, along with a consideration of the question of whether the routinization of charisma *necessarily* engenders the stultification with which it is often associated.

The encouragement of routinization

One significant feature of the John Birch Society is that the emergence of a structure may result in a loss of control on the part of the charismatic leader. This tendency is especially evident in the Elim Foursquare Gospel Church which came into being as a result of the activities of a charismatic evangelist, named George Jeffreys. Early on, Jeffreys initiated a formal system of overseers, within which he was the principal overseer along with three others. One of these others was E.J. Phillips, the secretary-general. There was also a council, of which both Jeffreys and Phillips were members, which held property in trust. It is apparent that Jeffreys came to rely more and more on Phillips's expertise in administrative matters. Wilson asserts that Phillips's role became the most important in the Elim administrative structure, which grew at a rapid rate in the late 1920s and 1930s. He argues that Jeffreys became a figurehead, but 'his power was curtailed by the new organisational structure' (1961: 47). Jeffreys seems to have been largely unaware of the implications of these developments, and possibly would have remained so, had not Phillips become ill in 1937 and had not Jeffreys decided to deputize for him. Jeffreys rapidly became aware of the growing concentration of authority in the administrative bureaucracy and in Phillips's hands in particular. A power struggle ensued, but that is not of special concern here, since the chief point to be made is that charismatic leaders may have much to lose from the structure that they participate in creating but which could subsequently engulf them. Wallis (1984) suggests that this kind of example represents a form of routinization in which the charismatic leader encourages the process, but fails fully to appreciate its ramifications.

An interesting comparison can be drawn with the case of Rajneesh, who approved of the activities of his 'power ladies' in seeking to create an efficient Ashram (Palmer, 1988). When Rajneesh entered his period of silence, he effectively allowed the power ladies untrammelled power to set up an institutional framework, which they duly did. They appointed officials and created a business infrastructure to help pay for the movement's growth. When he realized the excesses to which the ladies had subjected members of the movement and others, Rajneesh attempted to reassert control over the process of routinization. There are similarities with the Elim case, but it might be suggested that Rajneesh encouraged routinization to a greater extent than Jeffreys, partly because he believed that through such strategies as ensuring that his photograph was omnipresent and by prompting rivalries among the power ladies (so that they would not develop into undisputed charismatic figures in their own right), his charisma would be retained. But again, the Rajneesh case illustrates the potential for a loss of control.

Some leaders may seek to resist the process of routinization of their charisma altogether. John Noyes disliked constitutions and a legalistic approach to religious affairs and sought to minimize their introduction into the Oneida Community (Olin, 1980). Ironically, it was precisely because of his failure to routinize the running of the sect that his charismatic authority was later challenged. Another case is David 'Moses' Berg who has engaged in a number of conscious strategies to resist the incursions of routinization. He has expressed his dislike of the tendency towards elaborate structures in many sects and denominations and has criticized some of his leaders for wanting to create structures from which they could create their own power bases. Berg shows a tendency to change direction in his thinking so that his message does not ossify into a creed. He has also put many of his followers to the test in order to weed out those whose commitment to the Children of God had become tenuous. Wallis (1982; 1984) suggests that these strategies can be viewed as a deliberate attempt to resist routinization of both structure and doctrine, so that Berg can remain at the core of the group. Bromley and Shupe (1979) suggest that the Reverend Moon has also sought to minimize the growth of bureaucracy in the Unification Church, because he wanted to restrict the extent to which members developed entrenched interests in positions within the movement. However, the Unification Church is much larger than the Children of God, so that the ability to resist the emergence of structures has been more difficult in the former. Growth, coupled with the followers' and possibly the leader's desire for stability and continuity, constitute forces for the growth of structures that are difficult to resist in the longer term.

Developing societies have provided a laboratory for examining the consequences of the failure to routinize charisma. Many of the individuals who have risen to power within these societies have presented themselves as saviours who could deliver the people either from the tyrannies of colonialism or from economic hardships or sometimes from both. Not unreasonably, many of these leaders have been regarded as charismatic because of their sense of mission and the adulation that accompanies them, especially if they are successful or close to being so. However, there is also a fair amount of evidence to suggest that many of these leaders were poor at creating structures to routinize their charisma and that this accounts for their frequent failure to build stable social systems.

Dow (1968) has pointed to a number of difficulties that confront the charismatic leader who delivers the country from colonial rule: they no longer have a clear mission which suffuses all their aims and actions; they must concern themselves with routine affairs of state; and they must begin to concern themselves with the running of the economy. These activities are largely inconsistent with the lofty aims that were associated with the pre-independence mission upon which their charisma was based. Failure in any of the areas can begin to contribute to a loss of charisma. Nkrumah is a case in point. He struggled largely unsuccessfully to create economic prosperity and a social revolution after independence, but because he took personal responsibility for these developments he came to be seen increasingly as the source of the problems facing Ghana. As a result, he was subjected to riots, coups, assassination attempts and mutinies, to which he responded by becoming increasingly repressive.

In the view of a number of commentators, the failure to routinize his charisma contributed to the problems, a deficiency which Nkrumah shares with a number of other post-independence leaders. Horowitz (1972) has suggested that such leaders need to create *party charisma*. This is the party 'which embodies the charismatic leadership responsible for making the national *revolution of development*' (1972: 317; emphasis in original). The creation of party charisma permits charismatic leaders to dissociate themselves from the problems that are consequent on independence and so to retain their charismatic authority. Nkrumah had created the Convention People's Party, but he never succeeded in routinizing his charisma through it because of his direct involvement with the party. Equally, the creation of party charisma means that the party can dissociate itself from the loss of the leader's charismatic authority, whilst simultaneously injecting an element of stability into the new regime to compensate for the instability of charisma. As a number of commentators have observed (such as Horowitz, 1972; Runciman, 1963; Dow, 1968), this process of routinizing the leader's charisma in an institutional framework did not occur in Ghana.

The foregoing suggestions imply that the routinization of charisma may be an essential prerequisite for countries undergoing rapid social development through the leadership of a charismatic figure. On the one hand, the leader's charisma may be protected; on the other hand, stability for the structures he or she creates may stand a better chance of survival. Following Robinson (1988), we would probably do better to refer to institutionalization here, since the charismatic leader will probably fare better if the party and other structures are associated with the fervour of the original charismatic leader–follower relationship. Juan Perón represents an interesting special case, because the routinization of his charisma was essential to the maintenance of his influence during his exile between 1955 and 1973. The process of routinization was intensified after his exile and his personal influence necessarily declined in these years. Data collected in Argentina in 1965 reveal an interesting pattern, suggesting that some of those surveyed were committed to Perón as a person but were not very enthusiastic about Peronism, while others were committed to Peronism as a movement (the routinized form of Perón's charisma) but were unenthusiastic about him as a person (Madsen and Snow, 1983; 1987). The former were enthusiastic about the man because he had been seen as a solution to the social and economic crises that had impinged upon them and from which Perón promised deliverance; Peronists were either younger or better off or both and had therefore not experienced the same crises as the supporters of the man. The routinization of Perón's charisma probably played a part in his continued influence in exile, but the case also demonstrates how the political movement can become uncoupled from the charismatic leader as such.

The chief purpose of this section has been to draw attention to the difficulty of retaining charisma in the absence of adequate routinization. This message has been implicit on a number of occasions in this book, but the aim here has been to reinforce some of the earlier observations.

The timing of routinization

The case of the Children of God suggests that routinization may be resisted without the demise of the movement with which the original charismatic impulse is associated, although it is hard to see how the movement could survive Berg's death for very long. On the other hand, it is often suggested, for example by Weber, that charisma disappears without routinization. In this section, the focus will be on the timing of routinization: that is, are there any general lessons to be learned regarding the question of how soon the charismatic leader should develop structures to routinize his or her charisma? The early routinization of Salama's charisma, which was undertaken through the fixing of structures of the Hamidiya Shadhiliya, was highly instrumental in its success and continuation (Gilsenan, 1973). A 'quasi-bureaucratic charter' was created, which, like the fact of very early routinization itself, is very unusual in Sufi orders. Gilsenan suggests that Salama exhibited a fervent desire to establish continuity for the order and to restrain the tendency toward fission to which it might have been subjected. As Gilsenan observes:

> The setting up in full detail of the means of control, administration, and regulation within the brotherhood, often a long process of development in religious groups, was closely integrated here in its inception. (1973: 39)

By contrast, Huynh Phu So was much slower to routinize his charisma, as a result of which the Hoa Hao sect had little sense of purpose because the followers, although numerous, were poorly integrated (Tai, 1983). So recognized that in order to make a wider impact, he would need to routinize his charisma. He moved in this direction when he became more interested in secular ideologies and developed political ambitions that could not be met without a stable organizational base. He codified cultic practices, developed rules of admission, and built an organizational machine that could outlive him. In spite of the disastrous choice of So's father as a successor, the Hoa Hao sect continued after So's death largely because of the routinization that he had set in motion. However, in the end the communists triumphed over the sect because of their clearer vision (Tai, 1983: 172). While this may be due in part to So's early death, it may also be because he was slow and perhaps even slightly reluctant to set routinization in motion. Another possible example of the hazards of delaying routinization can be detected in Nasser, who, as President of Egypt, was widely regarded as a charismatic figure. Entelis (1975) has argued that Nasser relied on his *baraka* for his personal appeal and was very slow to develop structures to routinize his charisma. In the 1950s his prominence on the world stage and a number of apparent diplomatic victories confirmed Nasser's charisma. But in not creating structures which routinized his charisma at an early stage, his *baraka* was seen as personal in that it derived from a transcendental source. This in turn meant that when in the 1960s his charisma began to wane as a result of a number of problems, his attempts to create late in the day an organizational framework which reflected his charisma were doomed to failure. Instead, he was forced to revive his charisma through other tactics, such as war. Moreover, precisely because state agencies were independent of his charisma they never received the legitimacy that he enjoyed.

It is clearly hazardous to draw general implications from case studies like these, which are so divergent in character, but it would seem that routinization will be more successful, in the sense of providing for the continuation of the movement or group that is brought into being by the charismatic leader, if it is begun earlier rather than later. To some extent, this principle arises because the leader and his or her followers cannot predict when he or she will die; an early demise like So's may mean that routinization will not have gone very far or may even not have begun. Also, early routinization may send signals to followers and others regarding the leader's commitment to the movement's perpetuation.

Assuming that a structure of offices and regulations is brought into being, should the charismatic leader remain aloof from the day-to-day running of the organizational apparatus that has been created? Trice and Beyer (1986) tend to the view that routinization of charisma may be hampered by too much involvement on the part of the charismatic leader in the ensuing structure. They compare the routinization inaugurated by the leader of the NCA with that associated with the charismatic leader of Alcoholics Anonymous. Neither leader is named by Trice and Beyer in deference to the AA's norm of anonymity. Trice and Beyer regard routinization as a good deal more successful in the latter case because of a number of differences between the two movements. One of these differences is that in the AA the charismatic leader was much less involved in the workaday administration of the organization than his NCA counterpart. The authors argue that the more entrenched the leader becomes in the running of the movement, the less he or she comes to be seen as exceptional and special. In a sense, the charisma begins to dissipate. Another reason for suggesting that the charismatic leader should be aloof from the products of routinization is that, to the extent that followers occasionally criticize aspects of the structures that are produced, he or she can deflect such disapproval on to others. Lindholm (1990) notes that Hitler distanced himself from the Nazi Party so that he could dissociate himself from the corruption and inefficiency with which it was seen as riddled. Here may lie one reason why former members of religious movements led by charismatic leaders often express disaffection not with the leaders but with the officials who are responsible for 'carrying out the directives and laws established by the spiritual figurehead' (Jacobs, 1987: 298).

The case of Ellen White, the founder of the Seventh Day Adventists (a religious movement which began in the USA in the 1840s), provides further general confirmation of the suggestion that the charismatic leader should be minimally involved in the products of routinization. As the movement grew, the pressures for routinization became great in the 1850s. Doctrinal uniformity was established, an economic basis for the ministry was introduced, and a bureaucratic structure emerged to organize rapid growth of membership. However, according to Theobald (1980), White remained outside the legal-rational framework which she and others had been instrumental in creating. In 1888, she and two others had become concerned about the legalism that pervaded the movement and sought to restore 'a position in which the person of Christ and the notion of righteousness by faith became central' (1980: 93). Many members of the central administration had much to lose by such proposed changes and successfully resisted them. Thirteen years later, White reintroduced the same issues and on this occasion was successful in achieving her aim. Theobald argues that White never occupied a formal position within the complex bureaucracy that accompanied routinization and therefore had to rely upon personal influence through her charisma to achieve change. However, since the organization had moved in a legal-rational direction, her ability to employ charisma to instigate change had dwindled. By 1901, things had changed: influential opponents who had earlier resisted change had come to accept the need for a Christ-centred reorientation; other opponents had disappeared from the scene; and there was a widespread belief that change was necessary. In other words, by 1901 the climate within the movement (in part because of her continued appeals) had shifted in a direction which was broadly more receptive to her initiatives. This illustration points to the risks that non-involvement in the routine administration of the movement may present to the charismatic leader. In Ellen White's case, she had lost control to a degree which almost recalls the example of Jeffreys and the Elim Foursquare Church. Had the climate not shifted and she not been persistent she might not have been able to make an impact. On the other hand, had she occupied a formal position in the bureaucracy, she might well have found it difficult even to be listened to. As a charismatic leader she at least commanded an audience, but as has been seen, complete non-involvement can be a high-risk strategy.

Although Gilsenan (1973) does not address this issue directly, Salama does seem to have been actively involved in the mundane affairs of the Hamidiya Shadhiliya, but this apparent divergence may have something to do with the perceived role of Sufi brotherhoods and the manner in which the charismatic founder is perceived. Cruise O'Brien (1988) has suggested that active involvement of brotherhoods in political and economic affairs had become an established pattern by the mid nineteenth century, so that the charismatic leader's participation in the routine administration of a brotherhood's affairs would have considerable legitimacy and would even be an expectation.

This example apart, the general message would seem to be that charismatic leaders should minimize their involvement in the products of the routinization process that they inaugurate. A useful tactic would seem to be to separate the leader's charismatic basis of authority from the legal-rational (or possibly traditional) grounds on which he or she functions when participating in routine management and administration. This seems to have been Russell's approach in relation to the Jehovah's Witnesses, where he combined charismatic with rational-legal authority. According to Bromley and Shupe (1979: 46), this has also been the approach of the Reverend Moon in the context of the Unification Church both in Korea and in the USA. Political leaders who have been identified as charismatic almost always have to separate their charismatic appeal from their incumbency of a position as head of state or leader of a political party. The experience of leaders like Castro and Nkrumah suggests that this can be a very difficult balancing trick.

Routinization clearly imposes on charismatic leaders a series of decisions such as whether and when to routinize and how involved the leader should be in the structures that emerge. The experiences that have been cited in this section suggest few general principles. However, it is difficult to see how charisma and the associated following can be retained in the absence of routinization. Routinization may lead to a transformation of the leader's original message. Also, the leader in most instances is probably advised to embrace routinization as soon as possible and to be only slightly involved in routine administration. Some contact with the structures that he or she creates is likely to be necessary so that vestiges of control are not lost.

Routinization and the maintenance of charisma

It is clear from Weber's writings that he saw routinization as both necessary and inevitable for charisma to persist. However, it is also apparent that he regarded routinization as antithetical to charisma in as much as it tends to extinguish its innovativeness and the passion associated with the reverence accorded to the charismatic leader. The sense of wonder and excitement induced by charismatic leaders gives way to dull routine and mundane operations. Is this process inevitable?

A number of writers in various ways and in a variety of contexts have questioned Weber's views about the loss of excitement that follows routinization. To some extent, it is possible to see this suggestion in Shils's writings (see Chapter 2) when he argues that Weber was referring in much of his work to a particular type of charisma, that is, an especially intense and concentrated form. In this section, some indications that it may be wrong to treat routinization and charisma as contradictory forces will be examined.

First, there is a suggestion that in some religions charisma is not quelled by the onset of routinization. Nelson (1969) has observed that unlike many religious movements, Spiritualism was not founded by a charismatic leader and so the routinization of the founding charismatic leader's charisma has not posed any problems for the movement. There has been a succession of prominent figures in the movement who could reasonably be described as charismatic leaders, but there has rarely been an impulse to routinize their charisma. Moreover, at the local level charismatic leadership has played a prominent part: 'The local, group, society or church has always been founded and based on the charisma of a medium' (1969: 242). A formal structure often grew up around these mediums, but it does not seem appropriate to regard this as indicative of a routinization of their charisma; rather it seems to have had more to do with providing a framework for the efficient administration of their special skills.

Second, there may be periodic resurgence of charisma within organizations that are the outcomes of routinization. Stark has observed that the Roman Catholic Church, which can be viewed as a product of the routinization of Christ's charisma, has enjoyed a 'periodical re-awakening of charisma' (1965: 206). He argues that charismatic figures have always coexisted within the Church with solidly bureaucratic ones. He refers to St Carlo Borromeo as a functionary within the Church who reversed the tendency to ossification, and to the immense personal following attaching to Jean-Marie-Baptiste Vianney, a parish priest whose reputation as a confessor was legendary. Although aspects of Stark's article smack of Catholic apologetics, there is some virtue in not losing sight of his basic premise that charisma is not necessarily snuffed out by the onset of routinization.

Third, charismatic leaders may be able to limit the effects of routinization by keeping themselves at the hub of operations. It is inconceivable that a charismatic leader like Hitler could have made a great impact without a substantial degree of routinization of his charisma. However, it is evident that he adopted a number of strategies to limit the impact of the structures of government with which he was surrounded. Lindholm (1990: 111) notes that Hitler kept himself at the core of decision-making. He also did not enunciate specific policies and therefore kept people guessing about what he wanted, so that he could not be taken for granted. As a result, as Nyomarkay (1967: 4) has suggested, 'the Nazi Party was based on charismatic legitimacy.' Nyomarkay also points out that Hitler employed a variety of organizational devices (such as promoting competition among subleaders in the movement so that they were not inclined to cooperate, and by limiting their authority) to ensure that 'all lines converged on Hitler' (1967: 32). Factions existed but not in opposition to him; instead their aim was to gain his patronage.

Fourth, an attempt may be made to institutionalize the leader's charisma. It is common to find the terms 'routinization' and 'institutionalization' being employed interchangeably in the literature on charisma. Robinson (1988) has sought to distinguish the two in an attempt to reformulate Weber's ideas on this issue. She suggests that institutionalization is a process through which charismatic leaders and/or their successors try to retain the original vitality of charisma. Robinson argues that the Dengist regime in China has sought to clothe itself with a sense of Mao's original charisma in order to legitimate its own authority. She shows that Deng Xiaoping has sought systematically to publish his writings and to formulate policies in such a way as to link directly in a line back to Mao. Moreover, in their quest for a vision that 'will energize the population spiritually' (1988: 366), the regime has again sought to employ Mao's thought and tactics, with a specific emphasis upon their revolutionary character, although it has also been critical of Mao's Cultural Revolution. Also, since Mao saw a strong party as an essential ingredient of the revolutionary ethos, the Chinese Communist Party's position is enhanced. Robinson is less than sanguine about the capacity of the Chinese leaders to bring off institutionalization, and the events in Tiananmen Square in 1989 suggest that their strategy has been unsuccessful. However, Robinson's notion of institutionalization refers to the *effort* to retain the vitality of the charisma of the original leader and does not carry any connotation of success. More recently, the Dengist regime has sought to renew its association with Mao in order to regain legitimacy following the suppression of the pro-democracy movement (Swain, 1991).

Fifth, Kanter (1968; 1972) has suggested that organizations can be suffused with charisma through the creation of 'institutionalized awe' which permeates a social entity with 'power and meaning' (1968: 514). She examined historical data relating to thirty utopian communities in the USA and was able to distinguish nine successful ones from the remaining unsuccessful ones. A successful community was deemed to be one which had survived twenty-five years or more. It is not clear from Kanter's work whether she believes all of the communities to have been founded by charismatic leaders, but she regards an important factor in determining success to be a community's capacity to induce members to surrender themselves to that community. This is the kind of posture that charismatic leaders seek to create among their followers, but, in order for surrender to persist independently of the presence of the leader, charisma must be diffused throughout the group. It is in this context that the creation of institutionalized awe comes into play because it

> consists of ideological systems and structural arrangements which order and give meaning to the individual's life and attach order and meaning to the social system . . . Such arrangements . . . elevate the group to the level of the sacred, setting it apart as something wonderful, remarkable and awful, and, at the same time, indicate the system's mastery of or control over human existence. (1968: 514)

Kanter delineated a number of mechanisms that were used by both successful and unsuccessful communities to induce surrender in their members. Of special interest to the student of charisma and its routinization is that successful communities were much more likely to: invest power in individuals believed to have special abilities; employ higher-order principles as a means of legitimating demands on members; relate group ideology to historically important figures; have leaders who had been groomed by their predecessors; sanction special prerogatives and immunities for leaders; and reserve separate residence for leaders, who also receive special forms of address and are able to make decisions on an irrational basis (such as on the basis of intuition). Kanter's study is of interest because it suggests that routinized structures can become imbued with a sense of charisma, but its precise relevance to the present discussion is slightly ambiguous because it is not specifically concerned with the routinization of charismatic leadership.

A similar instance is reported by Trice and Beyer (1986) in the context of the routinization of the charisma of the founder of Alcoholics Anonymous. Unlike his NCA counterpart, the AA founder created a strong organizational culture, particularly through rituals and ceremonies and a strong oral tradition which perpetuated his charisma and dispersed it throughout the organization. Trice and Beyer note that the AA never mounted a serious attempt to find a successor; instead, a number of administrative mechanisms which the founder had set in motion in the twenty years before his death created a structure of offices from which his personal charisma emanated. It may be that the strong culture that had been created played a part in suffusing these structures with a legitimacy that derived directly from his charisma.

The similarity between Kanter's research and the case of the routinization of the AA founder's charisma is striking. In each case, structures seem to have emerged which reinforce the original charismatic impulse. It would be misleading to suggest that what is being witnessed here is the same form of charisma that was responsible for bringing these movements into being in the first place. They are clearly forms of what Weber would have called transformed charisma, but they are not strictly speaking instances of routinized charisma. Following Robinson's (1988) distinction they are probably better viewed as illustrations of institutionalization wherein an attempt has been made to retain the original vigour of charisma, albeit in a transformed state.

In each of the five instances delineated in this section can be seen indications that charisma and routinization are not quite the contradictory tendencies that Weber and others have portrayed them. On the other hand, it is essential to recognize that at no time is it suggested that charisma is unaffected by routinization (or even institutionalization). Rather, it is necessary to appreciate that routinization is not just a necessary evil and that vestiges of original charisma can be retained and stored.

Charisma and organization

If it is accepted that charisma and the organizational structures consequent on routinization are not necessarily entirely antithetical, the possibility of charismatic leadership arising within formal organizations is raised. It is easy to view organizations as stifling the opportunity for eruptions of charisma, but this view can be misleading. In the previous section instances of charisma occurring within heavily routinized organizations were mentioned, such as Stark's (1965) view of the periodic resurgence of charisma in the Roman Catholic Church and Theobald's (1980) discussion of Ellen White's restoration of the impact of her charismatic authority among the Seventh Day Adventist movement. Similarly, in an examination of fifteen charismatic leaders who had founded religions, Barnes (1978) shows that four operated within an organizational framework. This is a larger figure than might have been expected in the light of Weber's depiction of charismatic leaders as emerging from outside conventional organizational arrangements, and has points of affinity with Berger's (1963) assessment of Weber's misunderstanding of the institutional position of Old Testament prophets. The issue of the possible inconsistency between charisma and organization is of considerable importance in relation to the question of charismatic leadership in business organizations which will constitute the focus for the remaining chapters of this book.

John L. Lewis (1880–1969) was a trade union leader who both worked through and created organizational structures and is widely regarded as a charismatic leader. However, his significance appears to run even deeper than this for our understanding of the nature of charisma:

> The word *charisma* was introduced into American journalism for the first time . . . in *Fortune* magazine in 1949, when a writer used it to describe the qualities of John L. Lewis. The managing editor, scanning the first draft of the article, questioned the use of a clumsy foreign term that would be unintelligible to the reader, and struck it out. On the page proof, however, an eleven-character word was needed for the caption under Lewis's picture to justify the line, and over the loud objections of the editor, the word *charismatic* was inserted, because no comparable word with the same number of letters could be found. (Bell, 1966: 704)

Since then, as Bell notes, the term has endured a wide and often loose currency among journalists. But it is of considerable interest to the present discussion that it was used for the first time by a journalist in relation to someone who operated within conventional organizational structures. What was it about Lewis that prompted others to see him as a charismatic leader?

It is impossible to do proper justice to the complex figure that emerges from the pages of Dubofsky and Van Tine's (1977) biography of Lewis. Two factors appear to stand out. One is that he was a man with a mission. Almost to the point of obsession, he was concerned to improve the lot of the American working class. His first major appointment in the labour movement was in 1917 as a statistician for the United Mineworkers (UMW), though he had held a number of other, less important positions between 1908 and 1916 both in the UMW and in the American Federation of Labor (AFL). Within the UMW his rise was meteoric, and by 1918 he was acting president of the UMW. He pursued his mission of improving the position of the mineworkers with zeal, though Dubofsky and Van Tine believe that his power in the union had peaked by 1924. His mission to enhance the position of the working class changed course somewhat after his return from a visit to Europe in 1934 following a meeting in Geneva with trade union leaders at the International Labour Organization. As a result of this encounter, Lewis became convinced of the need to organize American mass production workers and to build a broad-based labour movement. Out of this conviction the Committee for Industrial Organization (CIO) was created, with the first office opening in November 1935. Lewis's mission was pursued at some cost, and it is possible to see in him the tendency to personal sacrifice to which many charismatic leaders are prone in pursuit of their calling. In particular, Lewis's family life suffered greatly owing to his frequent absence from home. Also, in spite of his considerable size and appearance of robust health, he was prone to a number of illnesses, which he sought to conceal from the media in case he was viewed as having weaknesses.

The second factor is that he was an immensely effective speaker. Time and time again, Dubofsky and Van Tine refer to rousing speeches which were attended by thousands of unionists and which received a fervent response. When he needed to arouse emotions, he had a stock of biblical and Shakespearean phrases that he had previously tried out on private audiences. Dubofsky and Van Tine write:

> Lewis's voice alternately bellowed and modulated, crooned and cursed. He charmed and cajoled his audiences, entertained and taught them, agitated and pacified them. So fine was his voice modulation, so smoothly could Lewis change moods, that listeners became hypnotized by him and cheered platitudes, inappropriate classical allusions, and outright solecisms. For Lewis, speech was an instrument to sway audiences, not to enlighten them. (1977: 66)

Such powerful oratory, with its capacity to attract and enthral large audiences, both provides a vehicle for the transmission of the mission and conveys a sense of the speaker as exceptional. For his part, Lewis sought to enhance his charismatic appeal by dressing smartly so that he could appear on a par with the bosses with whom he negotiated, by making himself inaccessible, and by emphasizing his impressive appearance. As regards the last of these, an acquaintance of Lewis was rebuffed for a year because he had been photographed towering over him at a lunch. The acquaintance was told by one of Lewis's associates: 'John resents anyone towering over him. You should have been sitting' (1977: 283). Moreover, like many charismatic leaders, Lewis demonstrated a tendency towards autocracy. Dubofsky and Van Tine (1977: 287) describe his behaviour as exhibiting a 'combination of secrecy, brutality, and egotism'.

In John L. Lewis we find someone who can reasonably be described as a 'charismatic labor leader' or as a 'charismatic leader of the masses' (1977: 315, 389), thereby following in the footsteps of the *Fortune* writer. But Lewis both worked through and created organizational structures. He represents a case in which charisma arises within the context of organizational arrangements. Nor do we find it too difficult to find other illustrations, albeit less dramatic ones.

One such example is a school superintendent in a school district near a Midwestern US city who has been described as a charismatic leader (Roberts, 1985; Roberts and Bradley, 1988). Six months into the superintendent's new job, her district suffered a major budgetary crisis, mainly due to the curtailment of public funding. Instead of submitting to the crisis and allowing morale to collapse, she not only helped the district to survive but also revitalized and energized it. Central to her leadership was a strategic vision which was supplemented by a clear succinct statement of her mission. The simple mission statement involved a recognition of the child as a unique individual with unique potential. She continually reiterated this mission and its implications in every context that presented itself, no matter how informal. Her strategic vision entailed infusing an awareness of societal trends and their implications for schools, and developing by consensus a programme to meet their challenge. The central ideas were disseminated through meetings and workshops with teachers, administrators and others. Part of her aim in these sessions was to create dissatisfaction with the status quo, because once people shared her dissatisfaction, change would be easier to bring about.

She also created a structure for change. She replaced people in key positions with new, more receptive personnel. Temporary task forces were created to participate in decisions about budget cuts. These groups comprised teachers, administrators and support staff. Suggestions about possible areas for pruning were submitted to the task forces from a wide constituency of people, including 13,000 students who met in quality circles. The combination of a clear sense of direction and the calculated involvement of a variety of stakeholders allowed the budget to be achieved without acrimony, in spite of the loss of both jobs and funding for many programmes. In addition, district personnel felt more involved, understood the system better, and are reported as feeling energized and excited by their work. A major component of being able simultaneously to push through cuts and to empower others was the climate of trust that she had created. Moreover, it is apparent that she received the special kind of personal adulation that is associated with charismatic leaders.

Here again, we see an individual who has many of the hallmarks of the charismatic leader but who has established her position within an organizational context and who, like Lewis, works through and creates organizational structures. In the case of the school superintendent, there is an interesting postscript to the story. After her success, she moved to a new job at state level as head of the Department of Education. It is apparent that none of those with whom she was associated in her new position perceived her in terms that could remotely be treated as indicative of charisma. This case illustrates the unreliability of treating charisma exclusively as a personal phenomenon, because it was clearly not something that could be transferred to the second situation.

There are other illustrations of the basic theme that charismatic leadership can and does arise in solidly organizational contexts which could have been employed. Day (1980) has provided an interesting account of the emergence of charismatic leadership within a small maternity home in the USA. Clark (1972: 180) has provided a fascinating account of Arthur E. Morgan who in 1919 took the reins of Antioch College, a small liberal arts college which had begun life sixty years earlier, and who is described as 'a charismatic utopian reformer'. Clark writes:

> He began in the early 1920s an institutional renovation that overturned everything. As president he found it easy to push aside old, weak organizational structures and usages. He elaborated a plan of general education involving an unusual combination of work, study, and community participation; and he set about to devise the implementing tool. Crisis and charisma made possible a radical transformation out of which came a second Antioch, a college soon characterized by a sense of exciting history, unique practice, and exceptional performance. (1972: 180)

Swidler (1979) has explored the emergence of charisma among teachers in 'free schools' in the USA, that is, schools which sought to abolish formal authority. In both of the schools she studied, many teachers developed relationships with their students that she describes as indicative of charisma, so that they could gain a personal following in the absence of a formal position of authority. Two tactics for creating charisma stood out. One was to engage in self-dramatization: the teachers 'exaggerated personal eccentricities, and worked to appear unpredictable and mysterious while adhering to the school's ethic of intimacy and openness' (1979: 76). The other tactic was to embody group values, which meant reinforcing one's commitment to the values of a free school.

These illustrations of the appearance of charisma in organizational settings imply that it is not as inconsistent with formal organizational arrangements as is sometimes suggested by writers like Weber. It may be more difficult for charismatic leaders to emerge in such settings, but even that view is debatable. However, the evidence examined in this section has provided a backcloth to the examination of charismatic leadership in business organizations. On the basis of this examination, the prospect for investigating charisma in the world of business is at least promising.

Conclusion

There can be little doubt that routinization is an inevitable consequence of the emergence of charisma, in that without it the original charismatic impulse appears doomed to failure. There are a number of factors which influence the likely success of routinization and these have been discussed in this chapter, which has highlighted two aspects: the problem of succession and the emergence of a structure for the perpetuation of charisma. In addition, there has been an attempt, drawing on a variety of sources, to suggest that charisma and organizational arrangements are not necessarily incompatible. On the one hand, charismatic leadership can arise within formal organizational settings without being in opposition to them; on the other hand, the emergence of an organizational apparatus does not necessarily stifle the charismatic stimulus that was responsible for its inception. This issue is of great importance to the subsequent chapters. If it had been shown in this chapter that formal organizations inhibited charismatic leadership, it would have been necessary to be suspicious from the outset of those New Leadership writers concerned predominantly with business organizations who have emphasized charisma. It would have been unlikely that we would have found genuine illustrations of charismatic leadership in such milieux, if there was little or no evidence of it in educational and union organizations. In fact, as we shall see, there are a number of leaders in the business world who fit the working definition presented in Chapter 3 fairly well. People like Iacocca of Chrysler, Steve Jobs the founder of Apple and Mary Kay Ash of Mary Kay Cosmetics have many of the attributes that we have seen in political and religious charismatic leaders. They are invariably visionary, are viewed as exceptional by others, and are regarded with considerable devotion and awe. Thus, the issues covered in this and the previous two chapters should be treated as providing the background for an understanding of charismatic leadership in business organizations, as well as related forms of New Leadership writing.

5

The New Leadership and Charisma

Up to now, the chief focus of attention has been upon the operation of charismatic leadership in the context of religious and political movements and organizations. Some instances of charisma in educational and trade union organizations also appeared towards the end of the previous chapter. However, until the second half of the 1980s, charismatic leadership in the context of business and commercial organizations (as well as large public sector organizations) was given scant attention, in spite of the voluminous literature on leadership in organizations. In this chapter, the early attempts to include charisma within the purview of leadership theory and research will be examined. More recent attempts to study charisma will be explored in the context of the emergence of a number of other approaches with which charismatic leadership shares common elements. Collectively, these approaches to leadership are referred to as 'the New Leadership'.[1] It is important to realize that the approaches within the New Leadership tradition that do not take charisma as an explicit focus exhibit certain similar themes to discussions of charismatic leadership in business organizations, but this should not be taken to imply that they are somehow indirectly concerned with charismatic leadership. Indeed, as will be seen, in some cases New Leadership writers explicitly reject the use of charisma.

In this chapter, some early contributions to theory and research about charisma in formal organizational settings, especially business organizations, will be discussed. There then follows an examination of a number of recent theoretical contributions from the New Leadership literature that either are explicitly concerned with charismatic leadership or address highly adjacent themes. Prominent among these is the notion of transformational leadership, with which charismatic leadership is sometimes equated or on other occasions depicted as a component. Other important distinctions within the New Leadership are then introduced and some potential problems of terminological confusion are examined. Research relating to many of these ideas is then examined in the next chapter.

Early explorations of charisma in leadership and organization theory

Aside from instances in which charisma was examined as a largely residual category, one of the earliest attempts to include it can be found in Etzioni's work, although even here it was not a major concern (Etzioni, 1975; first published 1961). Etzioni provided a very general definition of charisma which facilitated its exploration in the context of 'complex organizations'. He defined charisma as

> the ability of an actor to exercise diffuse and intense influence over the normative orientations of other actors. This suggests that charisma is a form of normative power which ultimately depends on the power of a person. (1975: 305; emphases removed)

By normative power Etzioni (1975: 5) meant power 'which rests on the allocation and manipulation of symbolic rewards and deprivations'. The chief problem with this approach is that, in redefining charisma so that it has a broad application across a wide span of organizations, the resulting definition is so inclusive that it lacks a specific referent. It is therefore not surprising that Etzioni's definition, while frequently cited, has not had the impact of the book in which it was enunciated.

On the other hand, Etzioni makes an important distinction which transcends the specific definition that he provided. He distinguishes between charisma of office, a term that has been encountered in Chapters 2 and 4, and personal charisma that arises during the incumbency of an office. Extending this distinction somewhat implies that there may be three manifestations of charisma in an organizational milieu: charisma of office; personal charisma that arises during the incumbency of an ordinary office; and personal charisma that arises during the incumbency of charisma of office. A bishop illustrates the first of these; John L. Lewis and the school superintendent cited in the previous chapter are illustrations of the second; and Geertz's (1983) depiction of Queen Elizabeth I (see Chapter 2) is an illustration of the third.

Berlew (1974) provided a treatment of charisma in the context of expressing some disillusionment with traditional leadership research. He argued that leadership research tells us little about what excites people in organizations and that it is largely to charismatic leadership that one must look for an appreciation of the factors that generate excitement. Berlew saw charismatic leadership as exhibiting three forms of leader behaviour which are likely to produce excitement. First, the leader develops a common vision for the organization. The vision expresses a set of goals that are valued by the organization's members. Second, there is the creation of 'value-related opportunities and activities' within the vision's frame of reference. Examples of such possibilities are offering the opportunity to be tested, or the opportunity to engage in activities that will benefit the community, or the chance to perform a task especially well. Third, the leader makes members of an organization feel stronger and less powerless. The first of these three aspects of leader behaviour, the emphasis on vision, can be discerned in the material covered in Chapter 3 in the form of the charismatic leader's sense of mission. It is also a central motif of much of the New Leadership. The third aspect betokens the notion of empowerment that was addressed in Chapter 3. The second aspect of charismatic leadership cited by Berlew is slightly idiosyncratic and connects only loosely with a number of themes concerning charisma that have been previously encountered.

Oberg (1972) was concerned to show how the concept of charisma could be applied to a 'secular, profit-seeking organization', thereby divesting it of its religious overtones. He suggested that the capacity to affirm individuals as charismatic is declining and that this tendency is to the detriment of all organizations, because leaders who can produce the same kind of loyalty enjoyed by charismatic leaders would produce considerable advantages for their organizations. Oberg argued that charismatic leaders would be especially important in crisis situations and that they have a particularly important role in the promotion of institutional values. He then examined the factors that can lead to the attribution of charisma, which were seen as comprising five main types. First, Oberg specified a number of personal qualities, including: the ability to demonstrate significant past achievements; the ability to empathize with followers; a presence; and appropriate personality traits. The second set of factors relates to the followers and included: the employees' fears and troubled feelings; age and length of service (younger people being more likely to attribute charisma); and the nature of the employees' psychological contract (individuals with a narrow view of their obligations to the organization will be less receptive to charisma). Third, charismatic leadership is most likely to emerge when decisions involve unclear means and goals. Since these characteristics of decisions are most likely to occur at the apex of an organization, charismatic leadership is most likely to occur at the top. Fourth, there are 'deliberate myth-making or charisma-building efforts' (1972: 28). This set includes: the employment of symbols denoting prestige (such as large desks, special privileges); the use of rituals; and 'executive dramaturgy'. Finally, a corporate creed or ideology can contribute to charisma, such as a mission statement which fulfils the role of something like Mao's Red Book.

In Oberg's analysis we end up with an interesting array of factors which contribute to charisma, but they are a mixture of personal traits, follower beliefs, situational characteristics and the kinds of element that were referred to in Chapter 3 as part of the social formation of charisma. There is no indication of the relative importance of different factors. It is also difficult to see what role the leader has in some of these elements; for example, are organizational creeds or symbols of prestige created by the charismatic leader or are they simply enabling factors which facilitate his or her emergence as a charismatic figure? There is a sense in which we are left with a catalogue of factors which are relevant to charisma, but which await systematic analysis. Nonetheless, although it borrowed heavily from Thompson (1963), Oberg's (1972) article represents an important elaboration of charisma in an organizational setting.

House's theory of charismatic leadership

Probably the major application of charisma to the study of formal organizations can be found in House (1977). In this work, House developed a number of testable hypotheses about the characteristics and behaviour of charismatic leaders, situational factors, and other issues. He also specified a number of effects of charismatic leadership: trust of followers in the veracity of the leader's beliefs; creation of similarity of belief between followers and the leader; unquestioning acceptance of the leader by followers; affection for and obedience willingly given to the leader; emotional involvement of followers in the leader's mission; enhanced follower performance in relation to task; and a belief among followers that they will contribute to the mission's consummation. This list is regarded as being both a set of dependent variables *and* the criteria which distinguish charismatic leaders. It might be argued that to define a concept in terms of its posited effects is less than ideal, since it detracts from the content of the concept as such, and has been specifically rejected in the context of charisma by Willner (1984).

According to House, the personal characteristics that contribute to charismatic leadership are: a high level of self-confidence, a tendency to dominate and a need to influence others, and a strong conviction in the integrity of one's own beliefs. A number of aspects of the behaviour of charismatic leaders are specified by House's theory. First, charismatic leaders, through role modelling, represent the values and beliefs to which they want followers to subscribe. If the potential follower regards the charismatic leader favourably, this role modelling will result in followers accepting his or her value system regarding the benefits of effective performance. Second, two types of leader behaviour are seen as important to the creation of a favourable perception on the part of followers: charismatic leaders engage in image building to create an impression of competence and success, and express ideological goals which represent a set of ideals for the organization's direction. Third, the charismatic leader communicates high expectations of followers and exhibits confidence in their ability to accomplish the lofty goals that they have been set. As a result, followers are more likely to accept the leader's goals and to seek to strive to meet his or her exacting expectations. Finally, the charismatic leader is more likely than the non-charismatic leader to arouse motives that are relevant to the execution of the mission. Such motives may include a need for affiliation or achievement, a felt need to overcome an enemy or competitor, and a need for the achievement of excellence in one's work.

House follows a number of writers in seeing charismatic leadership as most likely to arise in stressful situations. Such a sense of crisis operates in conjunction with the afore-mentioned characteristics and behaviour of the charismatic leader to enhance the probability that he or she will be deemed to be charismatic.

House's (1977) article undoubtedly provides the most comprehensive approach to the analysis of charismatic leadership in formal organizations prior to the 1980s. Its explicit combination of personal traits, leader behaviour and situational factors renders it highly reminiscent of the approaches that were encountered in Chapter 1. There is an ambiguity in the approach in that it is not always clear how far the types of behaviour which are specified by the theory are determinants of the probability that charisma will be attributed or how far they are exemplified by the established charismatic leader. To be fair, a similar accusation could be levelled at much of the research on charisma that has been encountered in previous chapters, but in House's case the problem is exacerbated by the fact that processes like image building and the articulation of ideological goals seem to belong to an early stage in the genesis of charisma, while the enhancement of followers' performance expectations seems to refer to a later stage in which the charismatic leader is established.[2]

The emergence of transformational leadership

In spite of the suggestiveness of the contributions to the understanding of charisma in organizations that have been examined, there is a fair chance that charisma would have remained a fairly marginal category in leadership research had it not been for the growing interest shown in the notion of 'transforming leadership'. However, in order to reach the connection between transforming leadership and charisma, a number of prior paths will need to be trodden.

Burns on transforming leadership

The term 'transforming leadership' was coined by a political scientist, James McGregor Burns (1978), in the context of a contrast with another approach to leadership which he dubbed 'transactional leadership'. This second form of leadership entails an exchange between leader and follower, such as the follower receiving wages or prestige for compliance with the leader's wishes. There is a kind of implicit contract beyond which the followers are not prepared to venture in meeting their formal obligations. Leadership takes place but it does not bind 'leader and follower together in a mutual and continuing pursuit of a higher purpose' (1978: 20).

By contrast, transforming leadership entails both leaders and followers raising each other's motivation and sense of higher purpose. This higher purpose is one in which the aims and aspirations of leaders and followers congeal into one. The transforming leader seeks to engage the follower as a whole person, and not simply as an individual with a restricted range of basic needs. Transforming leadership addresses the higher-order needs of followers and looks to the full range of motives that move them. Both leaders and followers are changed in pursuit of goals which express aspirations in which they can identify themselves.

This contrast seemed to raise the possibility of a quite different under-standing of the nature of leadership from the normal focus of leadership research. The bulk of the research that has been carried out in terms of the approaches examined in Chapter 1 can be construed as elucidations of transactional leadership. Burns's ideas seemed to suggest that such leadership is almost bound to have a limited impact because of its failure to raise the aspirations of leaders and led. Herein may lie one reason for the disappointing results of so much leadership research, since it is possible that most of it was not concerned with leadership that would make a substantial difference to subordinates in organizations.

Peters on leadership

In view of such possibilities, it is not surprising that writers on organizational issues should alight on Burns's distinction. It was used to especially good effect by Peters and Waterman, who extolled the virtues of transforming leadership because it 'builds on man's need for meaning [and] creates institutional purpose' (1982: 82). They noted that the 'excellent' companies that they studied all had strong, coherent corporate cultures, that is, systems of belief and values underpinned by legends, myths and rituals. Behind these cultures, which Peters and Waterman see as important because of their capacity to instil purpose and direction, can be detected the activities of at least one transforming leader at some stage in the organization's development:

> While the cultures of these companies seem today to be so robust that the need for transforming leadership is not a continuing one, we doubt such cultures would ever have developed as they did without that kind of leadership somewhere in the past, most often when they were relatively small. (1982: 82)

Such a view accords a very important role to transforming leadership in a modern organization.

The emphasis upon transforming leadership can be discerned in Peters's later books (Peters and Austin, 1985; Peters, 1987), but in these works the focus is upon leadership as such. Following on from the leads of writers like Bennis (1976) and Zaleznik (1977), Peters and Austin refer to leadership as distinct from management. They write that from the highly effective leaders who form the basis for their reflections, they have learned of 'passion, care, intensity, consistency, attention, drama, of the implicit and explicit use of symbols – in short, of leadership' (Peters and Austin, 1985: 265). The kind of leadership that they claim to be talking about is in fact what Peters and Waterman, following Burns, had earlier called transforming leadership (Peters and Austin, 1985: 420), but now it is referred to simply as leadership. This terminological shift implies that transforming leadership was increasingly coming to be seen as 'true' leadership. By implication, transactional leadership comes to be associated with management, with each being regarded as a somewhat mundane set of activities involving short-term problem-solving and decision-making. In other words, transforming leadership equals leadership; transactional leadership equals management.

These equations echo the view of Zaleznik (1977) that, unlike the manager, the leader

> is active instead of reactive, shaping ideas instead of responding to them. Leaders adopt a personal and active attitude toward goals. The influence a leader exerts in altering moods, evoking images and expectations, and in establishing specific desires and objectives determines the direction a business takes. The net result is to change the way people think about what is desirable, possible, and necessary. (Zaleznik, 1977: 71)

This conception of leadership is redolent of Burns's notion of transforming leadership. Together, these assessments suggest that it is true leadership (that is, transforming leadership) that entices individuals to transcend everyday routine and to have their horizons stretched beyond the here-and-now. It is this kind of leadership that breeds commitment and loyalty and which allows organizations to be propelled to new levels of activity.

These reflections invite a consideration of whether the type of research which was assessed in Chapter 1 was actually about leadership at all. By equating transactional leadership with management and by viewing both as humdrum activities with limited horizons, we might suggest that consideration and initiating structure are really *management* styles rather than leadership styles. Indeed, in view of the frequency with which the two terms are employed interchangeably (Bryman, 1986), it could be argued either that generations of leadership researchers have not been studying leadership at all or that at best they have been studying an extremely limited aspect of it.

An important theme in Peters and Austin's (1985) book, which was followed up in Peters (1987), is that of *vision*. This theme was implicit in Peters and Waterman (1982), but was very prominent in his later works. As Peters and Austin put it:

> You have got to know where you are going, to be able to state it clearly and concisely – and you have to care about it passionately. That all adds up to vision, the concise statement/picture of where the company and its people are heading, and why they should be proud of it . . . The issue here, in our discussion of leadership, is not . . . the substance of the vision, but the importance of having one, *per se*, and the importance of communicating it consistently and with fervor. (1985: 284)

The emphasis upon vision has become a central motif of much recent writing on leadership and will figure a great deal in this and the next chapter. The significance of Peters's writings is not just that he was an early advocate of the significance of vision for leadership, but that he played an important role in the dissemination of the notion of transforming leadership. The other major publicist of the term is the focus of the next section, and it is here that we begin to return to charisma.

Bernard Bass and transformational leadership

Bass (1985; 1990b) has written about and conducted a great deal of research into transforming leadership, taking Burns as his starting-point. Along with Tichy and Devanna (1990), he seems to have been responsible in large part for the tendency to write about transformation*al* rather than transform*ing* leadership. In this section, the chief concern will be to outline some of the main themes in Bass's writings; the research findings deriving from his conceptual scheme will be examined in the next chapter.

Like Bass, Burns draws a distinction between transactional and transformational leadership, but goes further at the conceptual level in at least three major respects. First, whereas Burns conceived of the two types of leadership as opposite ends of a continuum, Bass views them as separate dimensions. The difference between the two conceptions is important because there is the implication for Bass that a leader can be *both* transactional and tranformational. Second, Bass seeks to outline the components of the two types of leadership, and as such is concerned to specify their content more precisely than in Burns's somewhat broad-brush account. Third, they differ over the ascription of transformational leadership. For example, for Burns (1978: 48), Hitler after 1933 was not a transformational leader, because he relied on tyranny and was therefore not responding to the wants and needs of his followers. Bass (1985: 20) disagrees, arguing that nonetheless 'Germany was still transformed.' This is a potentially risky argument in that it implies that transformational leadership may be identified by its effects. The chief problem with such an argument is that one cannot be indifferent to the question of the causes and mechanisms of transformation, since it may be produced by a number of types of leader behaviour which have little or nothing to do with transformational leadership. In any event, it is difficult to argue that Hitler's vision of a stronger Germany was not at least partly a product of his perception of the needs and wants of the population even after 1933.

Bass sees transactional leadership as an exchange in which the leader rewards subordinates for compliance with his or her expectations. The problem with this way of leading is that it usually fails to raise subordinates' performance beyond the leader's and their own expectations. They are unlikely to inject those extra increments of effort that make the difference between mundane and extraordinary performance. By contrast, transformational leaders motivate subordinates to commit themselves to performance that exceeds expectations. Bass suggests that transformational leaders raise followers' propensity to expend greater effort in at least three ways: they raise awareness about the importance of certain goals and the means for their attainment; they induce followers to transcend their self-interest for the good of the whole (such as an organization); and they stimulate and satisfy followers' higher-order needs (such as for self-esteem and self-actualization; cf. Maslow, 1943). Together these three elements boost the value that followers ascribe to outcomes, such as greater effort and commitment to the organization.

In tandem, transformational leaders enhance followers' confidence and hence their expectation that they can attain greater performance. These effects on followers operate in conjunction with the tendency of transformational leaders to seek to change the organizational culture, which alters the ways in which followers think about themselves and the organization, and their position within it. Together these factors enhance followers' preparedness to attain outcomes, and hence they produce the greater effort which leads to performance beyond expectations. Transactional leadership is a component of all of this since it both defines expected performance and establishes the ground-rules for rewards.

Both transactional and transformational leadership comprise separate dimensions which vary slightly in Bass's writings, but the following are mentioned consistently. Transformational leadership comprises:

Charisma Here at last, we begin to see the connection between transformational leadership and the chief subject matter of this book. Bass's (1985) treatment of charisma elaborates upon House (1977). In addition to the effects that charismatic leaders may have upon followers (see above), Bass argues that they reduce resistance to change and by dint of the emotional arousal initiated by the charismatic leader, a sense of excitement is generated. In his more recent work, Bass defines charisma as: 'Provides vision and sense of mission, instills pride, gains respect and trust' (Bass, 1990b: 22).

Inspiration Bass sees inspiration as 'a subfactor within charismatic leadership' (1985: 62). He suggests that charismatic leadership clearly inspires, in that it arouses and incites, but that inspiration can occur without charismatic leadership. In the bulk of the early research emanating from Bass's framework, inspiration is treated as a component of charisma, but in the more recent writings it is treated as a separate dimension in its own right. The early conception of inspirational leadership seems to have revolved around the notion of the capacity to act as a model for subordinates. In Bass (1990b: 22) it is described as: 'Communicates high expectations, uses symbols to focus efforts, expresses important purposes in simple ways.' In Bass and Avolio (1990b), inspirational leadership seems to be more specifically concerned with the communication of a vision.

Individualized consideration This component of transformational leadership is very similar to the Ohio State notion of consideration (see Chapter 1). Individualized consideration entails the leader giving personal attention to followers and their needs, trusting and respecting them, and helping them to learn by encouraging responsibility.

Intellectual stimulation The leader provides a flow of new ideas which challenge followers and which are supposed to stimulate a rethinking of old ways of doing things.

Transactional leadership comprises the following dimensions:

Contingent reward The leader rewards followers for attaining performance levels which he or she has specified. Like consideration, there is a sizeable literature on this dimension which shows that performance-contingent leader reward behaviour is associated with both subordinate performance and satisfaction with different aspects of jobs (for example, Podsakoff et al., 1984; see Bryman, 1986: 108–12 for a summary of such research). In more recent research, a distinction has been introduced between providing contingent *rewards* and *promises*. The idea of contingent promises is that the leader promises rewards in return for conformity with expected levels of performance. This distinction seems to involve a splitting of contingent reward into two separate aspects of leader behaviour.

Management-by-exception   This component denotes an approach to leadership in which the leader takes action when there is evidence of something not going to plan. In later writings (for example, Bass, 1990b), this dimension of transactional leadership has been split into two modes: *active* and *passive*. The former suggests a leader who looks out for deviations from established procedure and takes action when irregularities come to light. The passive form signifies a tendency to intervene only if established procedures are not being followed. The dividing line between these two forms is rather fine, but in the former the leader actively searches out deviations, whereas in the passive mode they must materialize.

In addition to transformational and transactional leadership, Bass has more recently introduced the notion of 'non-leadership' which is synonymous with one component:

Laissez-faire   This component refers to a tendency to abdicate responsibility towards one's subordinates, who are left to their own devices. In a sense, *laissez-faire* leadership indicates an absence of leadership.

In Bass's conceptual framework, charisma is an aspect of transformational leadership, albeit a prominent one (see the research findings presented in Chapter 6). An important implication of Bass's writings is that charisma alone is not sufficient for generating both system-wide change and the alteration of followers' moods and propensity to expend effort. The actual effects of transformational and transactional leadership (and their constituent components) are explored in Chapter 6.

An issue which is bound to be of concern in the context of the study of leadership in organizations is that of how far transformational leadership is the product of personal predisposition or whether it can be developed in leaders. This issue echoes the tendency which was depicted in Chapter 1 to think of effective leadership as a reflection of personal traits or as a matter of appropriate behaviour in which leaders can be instructed. Since charisma is a component of transformational leadership, this issue is of special interest because, as has been noted on a number of occasions in this book, charisma is often depicted purely as a personal trait. In fact, Bass treats transformational leadership both as exhibiting elements of a cluster of personal traits and as pointing to transferable skills. In the next chapter, Bass's general approach to the development of transformational leadership will be presented.

Lewis and Kuhnert (1987) place greater emphasis than Bass upon the personal characteristics of leaders in attempting to distinguish between transactional and transformational leaders. The authors argue that leaders may proceed through personality stages. At the first stage, which they call 'lower-order transactional', leaders are oriented to immediate concerns and issues and lack the ability to reflect on future possibilities. They do not have a notion of future lines of action that they want to take. The here-and-now dominates their thinking and action and they are much more preoccupied with their own concerns and needs than those of others. At the second stage, 'higher-order transactional', leaders are much more reflective about their own and others' needs and begin to formulate 'personal goals and agendas' (1987: 652). Therefore, second-stage leaders are more responsive to and concerned about their subordinates and show a capacity to look beyond the immediacy of present events. The authors suggest that we see in these leaders the germs of transformational leadership, but they have not acquired the capacity to alter the values and horizons of their followers. At the third stage, that of transformational leadership, the leader formulates end values which serve to inject their environment with meaning. They have acquired an understanding of their strengths, goals and mission which together provide a lens through which the world is interpreted. Having come to this understanding, they seek to convert others to their world-view. Their enthusiasm conveys itself to their followers who are more easily persuaded of the merits of the leader's world-view than if it was presented as a bland policy statement.

The capacity of leaders to progress to the second or third stages is circumscribed to a very large extent, according to Lewis and Kuhnert, by personal differences among leaders. However, they also note that the capacity of stage three leaders to get their world-view across is affected by the leaders' ability to communicate values to others. As some of the material covered in Chapter 3 implies, however, this process may have much more to do with the conscious development of oratorical skills and symbols than an innate capacity of the kind that the authors seem to be implying.

Avolio and Gibbons (1988) summarize the results of research by the second of the authors that has some bearing on Lewis and Kuhnert's approach. Based on their answers to the Multifactor Leadership Questionnaire (see Box 6.2), sixteen senior executives were classified in terms of their tendency to be transactional, transformational, a mixture of both, or *laissez-faire*. Detailed retrospective clinical interviews were then carried out to determine some of the personal antecedents to transformational leadership. It was found that transformational leaders were more likely to have had: parents who set high expectations and offered a great deal of encouragement; family circumstances that were neither excessively lavish nor overly trying; a learned capacity to deal with emotions such as conflict; and previous experience of leadership roles. They also have: a strong desire to engage in personal development; a tendency to respond very positively to learning experiences; and a propensity for reflectiveness. Such findings are consistent with Lewis and Kuhnert's model in that they go some of the way towards identifying the kinds of personal factor that contribute to a leader's capacity to move to a higher stage. On the other hand, as Avolio and Gibbons recognize, retrospective data are far from ideal for the examination of such issues.

It is clear that while there is some disagreement about the extent to which transformational leadership is a matter of individual predisposition or something which can be developed, the role of personal factors is generally acknowledged. Equally, while Avolio and Gibbons emphasize individual

differences they seem not to discount the possible development of transformational leadership, although it is not clear whether some kind of 'propensity'
for such leadership needs to be ascertained in advance. For example, they
suggest that precisely the same development experiences that Gibbons
identified as contributing to transformational leadership can be used to
change leaders to adopt a more transformational approach, such as enhancing
confidence and encouraging self-development.

Conger and Kanungo's behavioural theory of charismatic leadership
in organizations

Conger and Kanungo (1987; 1988) have provided a framework for the study of
charismatic leadership which is specifically concerned with its emergence in
business and other complex organizations. The behavioural theory that is
enunciated is well versed in the literature on charisma and has been broadly
tested in research reported in Conger (1989), which will be examined in the
next chapter.

Conger and Kanungo conceive of charismatic leadership as primarily an
attributional phenomenon, that is, as an attribution made by individuals who
work in organizations in respect of certain leaders. In view of this emphasis,
the key issue becomes that of revealing the types of behaviour that are most
likely to lead to the attribution of charismatic leadership. In other words, in
what kinds of behaviour do leaders engage that result in their being viewed as
charismatic by others? The starting-point is a vision – an 'idealized goal that
the leader wants the organization to achieve in the future' (1987: 640) – which
breaks with the status quo. Charismatic leaders engage in activities that
represent considerable personal risk in order to achieve the vision. Because of
this preparedness to take personal risks, the leader is more likely to be seen as
trustworthy. They often use unconventional methods to move towards
achieving the vision. They are sensitive to the organization's environment and
the threats and opportunities that it offers, so that they will seek to implement
their vision when the time is ripe. They portray the status quo as insufferable
and their vision as leading to a viable alternative. They express confidence in
their capacity to lead and a concern for the needs of their followers. They use
personal power, for example based on their acknowledged expertise, in order
to influence others, rather than their position. They often engage in
entrepreneurial or exemplary behaviour to exert power. If they act as
administrators or managers, their charisma fades. This implies that if a
charismatic leader's charisma is routinized, there may be some dissipation of
the awe with which he or she is regarded. A particular context, like crisis, may
engender dissatisfaction with the status quo and 'triggers the emergence of a
charismatic leader' (1987: 644–5). This last point is somewhat ambiguous in
that it could be interpreted to mean either that crises facilitate the attribution
of charisma or that crises somehow entice leaders to engage in behaviour that
will be deemed charismatic. The authors' discussion of this issue implies that it
is the latter possibility to which they are drawing attention. Lee Iacocca (see
Box 5.1) and John DeLorean are taken to be charismatic leaders in terms of
their framework.

BOX 5.1   Lee Iacocca: Chrysler Corporation

Iacocca became president of Chrysler in 1979 after he had been
fired at Ford. On the day that it was announced that he was to take
over at Chrysler, the company reported a third-quarter loss of
almost $160 million. In 1983, an operating profit of $925 million was
made. When Iacocca joined Chrysler, he found a chaotic organization with no direction or coherence. In order to stave off
bankruptcy, he took the following steps: halved the work force to
80,000; reduced fixed costs; inaugurated a major initiative to
improve product quality; and brought in executives who would be
committed to bringing order to the chaos. It is tempting to see these
changes as manifestations of Iacocca's vision for a revitalized
Chrysler, as Tichy and Devanna (1990) do, but in fact it is not easy to
see what his vision actually was. Westley and Mintzberg (1988)
suggest that one must look to the way in which Iacocca justified, to
Congress, bankers and others, Chrysler's right to survive when it
was clear that the company would need to be bailed out. They
suggest that Iacocca did this by conveying the notion through
metaphors that 'Chrysler *was* America: Chrysler was a loyal, hard-
working family, of which Iacocca was the father, struggling to
survive in the face of war and famine' (1988: 194). As Westley and
Mintzberg acknowledge, this notion of vision constitutes a very
different idea from the normal one of a desirable way forward.
Kotter (1988: 18), by contrast, suggests that Iacocca instilled 'a bold
new vision . . . of a competitive and profitable firm that produced
much higher quality products, provided better employment
opportunities, and was strong enough to survive in the increasingly
competitive automobile industry'. Thus, there is some dispute
about the nature of his status as a visionary. Nonetheless, Iacocca
became a hero as a result of his turnaround of Chrysler and is the
individual who seems most frequently to be cited as an illustration
of a charismatic leader in business. In fact, this lack of forward
thinking may account partly for the fact that by the late 1980s
Chrysler was slipping into trouble again. Another factor may have
been that the demands on Iacocca's time deriving from his celebrity
status, following his success and the publication of his autobiography, may have diverted his attention. In any event, there is a view
that a lack of focus to his thinking played a part in Chrysler's
problems. As a result he has been accused of spending money and
energy on acquisitions which were marginal to improving Chrysler's
competitive position, while not investing in new cars in the mid- to
large-car range that could have been a substantial source of
revenue. At the point that this book was close to completion, it was

reported that in the last three months of 1990, Chrysler sold 7.2 per cent fewer cars than in the corresponding period of 1989. Iacocca's response has been to engage in an austerity drive, slashing costs in a variety of areas (Taylor, 1991). The cynic might see very little that is visionary in his response.[3]

Sources: Iacocca, 1984; Judis, 1990; Kotter, 1988; Taylor, 1991; Tichy and Devanna, 1990; Westley and Mintzberg, 1988

Conger and Kanungo's theory is of considerable significance since it represents an attempt to apply ideas from the substantial literature on charisma to business and similar organizational settings. Unlike Bass's work, they concentrate on charisma as such. In emphasizing the behavioural precursors to the attribution of charisma, Conger and Kanungo appear to imply that charisma is not a mystical quality that only very special individuals exhibit. While leaders may differ in terms of their capacity to transmit their vision, by and large Conger and Kanungo seem to imply that they are dealing with a fairly mundane pattern of behaviour that enhances the likelihood of being deemed charismatic and which is potentially learnable by many leaders.

Confusing transformational and charismatic leadership

In spite of Bass's insistence that charisma is just a component of trans-formational leadership, there is a discernible tendency to treat the two as synonymous. There is an irony here, because Burns (1978) expressed his dislike of the term 'charisma'. He argued that the variety of meanings that the word is capable of assuming has meant that it has lost its utility as a tool of analysis. Burns proposed the term 'heroic leadership' instead and saw it as a manifestation of transforming leadership.

The tendency for charismatic and transformational leadership to be confused or at least indistinguishable from each other manifests itself in a number of ways. Some writers use the formulation 'charismatic/trans-formational leadership' (for example, Avolio and Gibbons, 1988), implying that they are barely distinguishable. The subject index to the *Academy of Management Review*, volume 14, 1989 has the entry: 'Leadership, trans-formational. *See* leadership, charismatic.' The tendency towards possible confusion of the two is revealed in the study of a school superintendent which was referred to in Chapter 4. In an initial presentation of the case study (Roberts, 1985), the superintendent is referred to in relation to 'transforming leadership'; in a later publication which updated the superintendent's experiences, the research was referred to in relation to 'charismatic leadership' (Roberts and Bradley, 1988).

It might be tempting to deride these cases as instances of sloppy conceptualization. On the other hand, and somewhat to anticipate themes relevant to the next chapter, there is some excuse for the treatment of the two as at least difficult to distinguish. In Bass's research on transformational leadership, charisma is by far the major component of transformational leadership (see the next chapter). Second, in some of the most widely known research which is directly or indirectly concerned with transformational leadership, there is a tendency to treat it as implying an approach in which the articulation of a vision which animates followers and creates intense loyalty and trust are central ingredients (for example, Bennis and Nanus, 1985; Tichy and Devanna, 1990). These themes are very similar to those which are associated with charismatic leadership in both the popular imagination and the research that has been examined in earlier chapters of this book. Thus, although there is an implicit agreement with Bass's view that there is more to transformational leadership than charisma, in reality there is little to distinguish them in many people's eyes.

Trice and Beyer (1990) have tried to draw a distinction between charismatic and transformational leadership by suggesting that while both forms of leadership are essentially innovative in approach, and as such inaugurate new organizational cultures, charismatic leaders typically create new organizations (and hence new cultures) whereas transformational leaders are concerned to change existing organizations and their cultures. The former operate like the leaders of social movements in attracting followers and uniting them in pursuit of a common cause; the latter are concerned to change an old culture and to replace it with a new one. There is something to recommend this suggestion. Steve Jobs (see Box 5.2) is widely seen as a charismatic leader (Rose, 1989) who was extremely effective in securing the loyalty of co-workers. He has demonstrated this ability at both Apple and NeXT (Conger, 1989), but he was far less successful at operating within the framework of an existing organization. This inability led to his eventual dismissal from Apple by John Sculley (see Box 5.2).

BOX 5.2   Steve Jobs and John Sculley: Apple Computer Inc.

Steve Jobs was the co-founder of Apple, a personal computer company which he helped to build up from a small outfit that operated out of a garage and which marketed its first major product in 1977 (when Jobs was only 21) to a company which in 1982 had sales of over $580 million. Jobs is often referred to as charismatic and as a visionary who saw the computer as a route to changing the world. He created an organization in which people were totally committed to Jobs's vision, but Jobs felt that the company was in need of greater organizational solidity. In 1982, moves began to hire John Sculley, executive vice-president of Pepsi-Cola, as chief executive to meet this need. Sculley is often seen as a more staid organization man than the flamboyant Jobs. Eventually, Sculley was enticed away by Jobs, who at one point asked him: 'Do you want to spend the rest of your life selling sugared water or do you want a chance to change the world?' (Jobs, quoted in Sculley, 1987: 135). However, after a honeymoon period, the relationship between Jobs and Sculley deteriorated, as Apple lurched into a crisis which had a number of manifestations: the company's first loss in 1985; rivalry between the divisions; Jobs's favouritism over the Macintosh computer; and technical problems in getting new technologies to the market. In September 1985, Jobs resigned as chairman and started a computer company, NeXT, which aimed to build a revolutionary new computer which simulates learning experiences. It was left to Sculley to infuse Apple with a new vision; he presented it as the same as Jobs's ('one person – one computer'), but added to it the notion that the company should be more sensitive to what people want to do with computers and that Apple computers must be able to connect to other computers (a principle that was fiercely resisted by Jobs). His vision entailed a commitment to keep the excitement of the company but to enhance its accountability to customers. However, at the beginning of 1990, Sculley was facing a revolt from 150 Apple staff pressing for his removal. Not only was the company's market share declining and its new laptop faring poorly, but also there was concern that Apple's uniqueness was being compromised. In June 1991, Sculley came in for considerable criticism from within the company for his plans to lay off a large number of workers.

Sources: Guilliat, 1991; Morrison, 1984; Rose, 1989; Sculley, 1987; Uttal, 1985

Trice and Beyer's conception of charismatic and transformational leadership implies either that charismatic leaders are unlikely to arise within organizations or that it is inappropriate to designate as charismatic leaders the chief executives who transform existing organizations and their cultures. According to this view, a figure like Lee Iacocca, who turned Chrysler around from huge losses to profitability and is widely regarded as an archetypal charismatic leader in business, would not be regarded as charismatic. It would seem premature to close off the question of whether individuals like Iacocca can genuinely be called charismatic leaders in the manner implied by Trice and Beyer, since charisma is in large part a matter of the nature of the relationship between leaders and followers. It has been shown in Chapter 4 that leaders in existing organizations can produce the kinds of loyalty and commitment in followers that are typically associated with charismatic leadership. John L. Lewis and the school superintendent studied by Roberts (1985) were among those for whom the category 'charismatic' would not be inappropriate or involve a debasement of the word. Thus, while the tendency to confound charismatic and transformational leadership in some areas of the literature may be undesirable, Trice and Beyer's proposal for a solution does not necessarily help to move the issue forward a great deal.

Other conceptions of leadership

The problem of conceptual confusion has not been helped by the emergence of a number of cognate terms to describe notions of leadership which appear similar to charismatic and transformational leadership. It becomes very difficult to know where one starts and the other finishes and where areas of overlap are supposed to be. Together the terms employed stand for ideas about what leadership should entail. They are referred to here as 'the New Leadership'. The main terms are presented in Table 5.1.

Table 5.1 *Major distinctions in recent leadership theory and research*

Old leadership	New Leadership	Sample contributors
Non-charismatic leadership[1]	Charismatic leadership	Conger, 1989; Conger and Kanungo, 1987, 1988; House, 1977; Nadler and Tushman, 1990
Transactional leadership	Transformational leadership	Bass, 1985; Bennis and Nanus, 1985; Peters and Waterman, 1982; Tichy and Devanna, 1990
Management/managers	Leadership/leaders	Bennis and Nanus, 1985; Bennis, 1989; Hickman, 1990; Kotter, 1990; Peters and Austin, 1985; Zaleznik, 1977, 1990
Non-visionary leadership[1]	Visionary leadership	Sashkin, 1988; Westley and Mintzberg, 1989
Non-magical leadership[1]	Magic leadership	Nadler and Tushman, 1989

[1] These terms are not always employed by the authors concerned, but are implied by the present author from the terms used in the New Leadership column.

Sashkin (1986; 1988) writes about the *visionary leader* whose primary concern is the transformation of an organizational culture in line with the vision that he or she articulates of where the organization should be heading. Individuals like Iacocca, John F. Welch (see Box 5.3) and Jan Carlzon (see Box 5.4) are regarded as classic visionary leaders. Sashkin sees the personal capacities and abilities of certain individuals as crucial to their potential as visionary leaders (especially need for power), though he also refers to ways in which such leadership can be developed. There are clear affinities between Sashkin's approach and many of the ideas that are central to both charismatic and transformational leadership. However, in an extension of these ideas, Sashkin and Burke (1990) have sought to distinguish their approach from

---

BOX 5.3   John F. Welch: General Electric (GE)

In 1981, Welch was promoted to become the youngest ever chairman of GE. At the time, GE was regarded as a financially healthy if unexciting company. His vision was of a highly competitive company and to this end he constantly told people that he wanted GE to become first or second in each of the business sectors in which it operated. He saw foreign competition in the 1980s as likely to engender an intensely difficult market environment. A central plank of the implementation of his vision was waging war on GE's cumbersome bureaucracy which he believed stifled innovation and was unresponsive. He also aimed to instil a greater preparedness to take risk and to be more entrepreneurial by reducing GE's cultural emphasis on the company being a safe place in which to work. He created reward systems to support the changes and sought to educate managers in the new ways of doing things at the company's management development institute. To get GE employees behind his vision and to foster their empowerment, Welch has been a champion of Work-Out, a series of intensive meetings in which employees are encouraged to reflect on what they like and do not like about the company and their work and to offer proposals for change. By 1989, earnings per share had risen by 7.6 per cent per annum during his tenure, compared with 4.9 per cent under his predecessor, while 350 product lines or business units had been changed into 13 businesses, each first or second in its field. Welch is known as an aggressive and tough boss with a tendency towards a quick temper. He has also sloughed off uncompetitive business lines at a cost of 100,000 jobs.

Sources: Morrison, 1982; Potts, 1984; Sherman, 1989; Stewart, 1991; Tichy and Charan, 1989; Tichy and Devanna, 1990

Bass's in particular. They argue that their emphasis on visionary leadership differs in its combination of three central features exhibited by visionary leaders: distinctive personal characteristics (such as need for power); decisive impacts on organizational functioning (such as changing the organization's culture to express the vision); and distinctive behavioural patterns. The Leader Behavior Questionnaire (to be distinguished from the Ohio State LBDQ) has been developed to tap these ideas. It is difficult to agree with the authors that their approach is quite as distinctive as they claim, since Bass (1985) examines a host of personal and behavioural criteria which distinguish transformational from transactional leaders. Also, he views transformational leaders as seeking to change the organizational culture in line with their vision as a route to generating extra effort (Bass, 1985: 22–3). What is somewhat different is that Sashkin and Burke are adamant that they are concerned with

---

BOX 5.4   Jan Carlzon: Scandinavian Airlines (SAS)

Following successful turnarounds at the SAS subsidiary Vingressor (a package tour company) and the SAS affiliate Linjeflyg (a domestic airline), Carlzon took the helm at SAS itself. It was his job to return SAS to profitability in spite of unfavourable market conditions. He developed as his strategy (which he also refers to as a vision) the aim of becoming 'the best airline in the world for the frequent business traveler'. Cost cutting and expenditure were oriented to this concern. The vision was systematically conveyed to employees and the culture became increasingly geared to the need to provide a service. Responsibility for implementing the vision was devolved to the employees who were thereby empowered. An appropriate structure emerged which was flatter and did not stifle individual initiative. Carlzon believes that the employees became substantially more motivated. However, by 1984 the momentum seems to have slowed down. Carlzon realized that what was required was a new set of goals, now that the original ones of the return to profits and the implementation of the broad vision had been achieved. Carlzon hit on the need to prepare for freer competition in the skies as the new strategy, though it is not clear whether he regards this as a vision or a component of his original vision. However, in January 1991, Carlzon announced that 3,500 people were to be dismissed in response to a decline in the level of traffic.

Sources: Betts et al., 1991; Carlzon, 1987

---

executives (that is, senior managers) rather than middle managers, supervisors or foremen. Bass, by contrast, has tended to the view that transformational leadership should not be thought of as something that can only be exhibited at the apex of an organizational hierarchy.

Nadler and Tushman (1989) write about *magic leadership* which shares many of the themes that have been mentioned in this and the previous section. This term is supposed to be applicable to Iacocca, Sculley and Welch. Vision and driving leadership from the top are again prominent themes, but these authors are also concerned to assess why magic leadership does not always have a positive impact.

Elsewhere, these same authors write about charismatic leadership (Nadler and Tushman, 1990). They see charismatic leadership as having an important role in regard to organizational change which involves 're-orientation', that is, change which is both anticipatory and strategic (as against reactive and incremental respectively). For Nadler and Tushman, the label 'charismatic leader' denotes 'a special quality that enables the leader to mobilize and sustain activity within an organization through specific personal actions combined with perceived personal characteristics' (1990: 82). This notion has certain affinities with Weber's conception, but pays little attention to the personal devotion and loyalty that the charismatic leader is supposed to engender. Nadler and Tushman view charismatic leaders as engaging in three categories of behaviour that distinguish them from other types of leader. The first category is *envisioning*, which entails creating a vision, communicating it through the expectations of others, and acting as a model for the vision through one's own behaviour. Second, *energizing* involves generating the motivation to act, through such activities as exhibiting personal excitement and confidence in one's own capacity to succeed. It also entails proclaiming and celebrating successes which lead to the vision. Finally, *enabling* involves helping people to accomplish the tasks which lead to the vision being achieved and includes such activities as giving people emotional support, demonstrating empathy, and expressing confidence in their ability to achieve the vision. While this work provides a further illustration of the use of the term charisma in a business organization setting, the nature of charismatic leadership is very similar to the same authors' notion of magical leadership.

Still other writers, taking their lead from Zaleznik (1977) have concentrated on distinctions between managers and leaders and between management and leadership. This tendency can be found in some research-based studies which will be considered in the next chapter (such as Bennis and Nanus, 1985). According to Kotter (1990: 4–5), the fundamental difference between management and leadership is that the former is concerned with activities which are designed to produce 'consistency and order', whereas the latter is concerned with 'constructive or adaptive change'. These differences can be discerned in three core contrasts:

1   Planning and budgeting versus establishing direction: management entails setting short- to medium-term targets and resourcing the plans accordingly; leadership entails the creation of a vision and developing strategies for its implementation.
2   Organizing and staffing versus aligning people: management comprises the allocation of tasks in line with plans and staffing them appropriately; leadership comprises communicating the vision so that others understand and become committed to the vision.
3   Controlling and problem-solving versus motivating and inspiring: management involves monitoring results of a plan and identifying and resolving any problems with the plan; leadership involves ensuring that people are moving in line with the vision despite obstacles 'by appealing to very basic, but often untapped, human needs, values, and emotions' (1990: 5).

Individuals who are regarded as exhibiting predominantly leadership include Mary Kay Ash of Mary Kay Cosmetics, Carlzon and Iacocca.

Kotter also makes a few remarks about charisma. He notes that charisma is often viewed as genetically determined, but observes that in fact the aura of charisma can often be created. He cites the case of Mary Kay Ash, who is often regarded as charismatic because of her impressive oratorical displays and their effect on audiences. However, she herself takes a different view:

> People are often amazed at how I can talk about the firm so naturally and spontaneously, without any notes. What they don't realize is that it has taken me years to get to the point where I can do this as well as I do. Oh, I'm sure I have some natural ability, but that's only one part of it. (Mary Kay Ash, quoted in Kotter, 1990)

This kind of view has a clear affinity with the notion of the social formation of charisma that was presented in Chapter 3. However, Kotter also states that Mary Kay Ash is the only one of the leaders whom he discusses in his book who is regarded as a charismatic leader by colleagues and others. This leads him to conclude that charisma must be of little importance to leaders. Zaleznik makes a similar point when he suggests that charisma 'is not a necessary ingredient of management and . . . inclines towards elitist and mystical conceptions [of leadership]' (1983: 38). However, there is a close correspondence between the characteristics of leaders and leadership, as portrayed by writers like Kotter and Zaleznik, and charismatic leadership in organizations, as in the work of Conger and Kanungo, House, Bass and others. The emphases on vision, on the dramatic effects of leaders on the motivation and effort of subordinates, and on the leader as an instrument of change are central themes in both sets of writings, as they are in most discussions of transformational leadership. Table 5.2 represents an attempt to single out themes which are common to the recent approaches to the study of leadership, which are referred to as the New Leadership. Not all of the themes can be found in each of the distinctions presented in Table 5.1. However, Table 5.2 provides a representation of core ideas which are common to a

Table 5.2 *Themes in New Leadership literature, inferred from the old/New distinctions in Table 5.1*

Less emphasis needed on	Greater emphasis needed on
Planning	Vision/mission
Allocating responsibility	Infusing vision
Controlling and problem-solving	Motivating and inspiring
Creating routine and equilibrium	Creating change and innovation
Power retention	Empowerment of others
Creating compliance	Creating commitment
Emphasizing contractual obligations	Stimulating extra effort
Detachment and rationality on the part of the leader	Interest in others and intuition on the part of the leader
Reactive approach to the environment	Proactive approach to the environment

number of the pairs of labels which figure in Table 5.1. Equally, Table 5.2 does not include ingredients of the New Leadership (and by implication of the 'old' leadership) which are not common to a number of authors. Thus, House's (1977) suggestion that charismatic leaders exhibit high performance expectations is not evident among other writers on the New Leadership and is therefore omitted from the table. In fact, it is difficult to find much evidence from the cases examined in Chapters 3 and 4 that the demonstration of high performance expectations is a notable feature of charismatic leaders, but that is a separate issue.

Hickman (1990) has also emphasized the manager/leader distinction, which he presents in terms of over forty ways in which the two types of individual differ from each other. The essence of these differences is that 'managers tend to be more practical, reasonable, and decisive, while leaders tend to be more visionary, empathetic, and flexible' (1990: 2). As with many of the writers discussed in this chapter, Hickman views the leader as someone who creates a vision of a future state for the organization. Indeed, all of the writers cited in Table 5.1 emphasize the importance of vision. Managers, however, are concerned with implementing the vision by providing 'versions' of the visions created by leaders. Like Kotter, Hickman believes that organizations require both managers and leaders. He argues that it is essential to appreciate the tensions between leaders and managers, since a successful integration of their respective talents and abilities can provide the basis for sound organization.

Should any significance be attached to the use by some writers of a distinction between lead*ers* and manag*ers*, but by others between leader*ship* and manage*ment*? Bennis has been especially prone to drawing on different distinctions. In an early article he writes about lead*ing* and manag*ing* (Bennis, 1976); then later about leadership and management, even though the book was entitled *Leaders* (Bennis and Nanus, 1985); and more recently about managers and leaders (Bennis, 1989). The leader/manager pairing seems to imply a focus upon the personal capacities and dispositions of individuals. Zaleznik (1990) in particular appears to take this view when he summarizes his stance as follows:

> Managers and leaders . . . differ in what they attend to and in how they think, work, and interact. Above all, [they] have different personalities and experience different developmental paths from childhood to adulthood . . . Managers perceive life as a steady progression of positive events, resulting in security at home, in school, and at work. Leaders are 'twice-born' individuals who endure major events that lead to a sense of separateness, or perhaps estrangement, from their environments. As a result, they turn inward in order to re-emerge with a created rather than an inherited sense of identity. That sense of separateness may be a necessary condition for the ability to lead. (1990: 9)

This argument is redolent of a trait approach to the study of leadership and would imply that leadership is an inherent capacity in certain individuals. Indeed, Zaleznik (1983) argues that it is necessary to identify managers and leaders and to give each group training which recognizes the strengths and capacities of the other. What is probably fruitless, in his view, is training managers to exhibit leadership.

Hickman appears agnostic about this issue and indeed uses the terms 'leadership' and 'management' fairly prolifically in his book, suggesting that these two activities are what you extract from leaders and managers respectively. On the other hand, in referring to a tension between managers and leaders, he seems to imply a set of separate personal attributes. Bennis (1989) appears not to subscribe to the view that leaders are born (and neither did the leaders he interviewed) but, like Zaleznik, he believes that leaders have often undergone a set of learning experiences that distinguishes them from managers. Moreover, leaders' learning experiences are frequently initiated by themselves. Although Bennis does not explicitly say as much, he seems to take the view that people can become leaders if organizations and other institutions create the kinds of learning experience that are conducive to the development of leaders. This position is consistent with Bennis and Nanus (1985) who argue that everyone has a capacity for leadership, which can be enhanced through education.

While it has not been feasible to review all contributors to the distinctions that make up this section, it should be apparent that it would be unwise to read too much into the precise terminology employed. Sometimes the use of the terms leader and manager imply a particular set of capacities, as in Zaleznik's discussion, but equally there are examples where the decision to write about leaders rather than leadership seems not to be laden with implications of this kind.

Conclusion

There is little doubt that there is the possibility of conceptual confusion becoming rife in this field. A number of terms are currently being used to describe what are essentially very similar phenomena. Increasingly, leadership is extolled which exhibits vision, empowers others, inspires, challenges the status quo, and adopts a proactive stance. Such actions are seen as highly motivating and as greatly enhancing people's commitment and performance. Yet different labels are given to the kind of leadership that exhibits these revered qualities. There *are* small differences between the various labels cited in Table 5.1, but they are usually a matter of emphasis. Thus, when writing about leaders or leadership *per se*, or about transformational leadership, or about visionary leadership, and so on, many authors are employing similar themes and motifs to those who write about charismatic leadership in organizations. Together, these approaches have been dubbed 'the New Leadership' to reflect the convergence of a number of recent writers on a set of themes on leadership. In the next chapter, research associated with many of the distinctions elaborated in Table 5.1 will be examined.

Notes

1 The term 'the New Leadership' is also employed by Vroom and Jago (1988) to refer to their revised contingency approach to the issue of when a leader should exercise a participative style of decision-making. However, my use of the term in this book is quite different and refers to a

number of different labels concerning leadership which share certain themes. The possibility of confusion with Vroom and Jago's use of the term is regrettable, but I wanted a phrase that would not add to the burgeoning number of labels. In an earlier article (Bryman, 1989), I referred to the approaches collectively as 'transformational leadership', but on reflection I think that it is not desirable to associate a general trend with a term that has a specific denotation.

2 Boal and Bryson (1987) have sought to elaborate House's model of charismatic leadership. I am inclined to agree with a commentator that their work is somewhat confusing (Butterfield, 1987). Consequently, their model has not been elaborated in this book. Two fairly major contributions of this article can be specified. It draws a distinction between visionary and crisis-produced charismatic leadership. In practice, this distinction may be difficult to work with, since a leader like Iacocca, who is often referred to as charismatic, achieved prominence and charismatic status through dealing with the turmoil at Chrysler, but is also regarded as a visionary leader (Westley and Mintzberg, 1988). Second, Boal and Bryson specify a number of situational factors that are likely to affect the receptivity of individuals to the two types of charismatic leader. These situational factors include: whether individuals experience job involvement and organizational commitment; personality factors like 'growth need strength'; and the degree of bureaucratization of the organization.

3 As this book was about to go to press, Iacocca appeared to be undergoing a process of decharismatization. It emerged that his decision to take a salary of just $1 a year for two years on taking over at Chrysler, which many commentators saw as having great symbolic significance, glossed over the fact that he received huge stock option grants during this period. Also, Chrysler's poor showing (losing $1 billion a year) coupled with a disastrous meeting with Japanese executives in January 1992 led Ivan Fallon to write in *The Sunday Times* (12 January 1992): 'By last week [Iacocca] had been transformed from hero to villain . . . A decade ago, Iacocca seemed to represent all that was good about American industry: blunt, honest, fiercely patriotic, devoted to his workforce and to his product. Now he represents all that is bad: demanding protection from an industry that has been exposed as second-rate and out of date, a humbug – and greedy.'

6
Research on the New Leadership and Charisma in Business Organizations

The aim of the previous chapter was to draw attention to theoretical discussions of charisma (or discussions which are similar to analyses of charisma) in the context of complex, formal organizations, with a particular accent on the business milieu. The purpose of the present chapter is to review research evidence relating to the main theoretical themes that were articulated. This means that not only will research on charismatic leadership as such be examined, but also other manifestations of the New Leadership. To some extent the themes overlap, for example, because charisma is often depicted as a component of transformational or visionary leadership, or because of certain unifying ideas, like vision, being common to charismatic and other forms of the New Leadership. Again, the point must be emphasized that it is not being suggested here that charismatic leadership is the same as trans-formational or visionary leadership, but they do share common motifs and are often treated as similar, as expressed in Bass's (1990a) use of the term 'charismalike leadership'.

Research on charismatic leadership

This section deals with research that is concerned with the investigation of charismatic leadership *per se* in formal, complex organizations.

Conger and the charismatic leader in business settings

Conger (1989) has presented data on charismatic leadership which elaborate the theoretical model mentioned in the previous chapter (see Conger and Kanungo, 1987; 1988). In large part he draws upon his doctoral research, but he also uses anecdotes and case studies based upon many well-known leaders who are regarded as charismatic (including Burr, Carlzon, Iacocca and Jobs). The research component was based on eight 'effective' business leaders, all of whom occupied very senior positions in their respective organizations. Of the eight, four were regarded as charismatic and four as non-charismatic. Conger employed a panel of experts to select business leaders on the basis of their effectiveness and whether they were charismatic. Data were collected on a variety of topics using semi-structured interviews with the executives themselves and their subordinates, periods of observation, and company documents. Of the eight executives, three were more or less universally viewed as charismatic by their subordinates (the term 'charismatic' was only used at the end of an interview session), three were deemed charismatic by between 20 and 60 per cent of subordinates, and two were never referred to as charismatic. In addition, information about prominent charismatic leaders in business, like Donald Burr (see Box 6.1), Iacocca and Jobs, is included in his book.

BOX 6.1   Don Burr: People Express

In 1980, Donald Burr, formerly president of Texas Air, started a new airline called People Express which was one of the fastest growing companies in the early 1980s. Burr is often referred to as a charismatic leader whose vision was to provide affordable, no-frills air transportation by keeping costs to a minimum. Initially, the company focused on the eastern US and operated out of Newark International, which was not used to full capacity. Burr's vision also entailed a commitment to the personal growth of the company's personnel which was built on a bedrock of minimal hierarchy, an informal structure, the opportunity to participate in the ownership of the company, and a high level of job rotation. Burr created a highly committed and motivated work force and showed a capacity to move people to new levels of effort, even when their energies had waned. But by late 1984 the company was beginning to founder, and in early 1987 it was taken over by Texas Air. Among the factors often cited as contributing to the company's demise are: excessively rapid expansion into new routes; an ill-judged takeover of an incompatible airline (Frontier); the difficulty of sustaining stressful levels of effort for more than a short period; and a failure to develop organizational structures and procedures capable of sustaining explosive growth. The immense sense of excitement and energy that Burr had created, and which had produced an immensely loyal work force, could not in the end keep the vision in the air.

Sources: Denison, 1990; Hackman, 1984; Quinn, 1988; Rhodes, 1984

Conger views charismatic leadership as essentially the product of a process of attribution, whereby certain patterns of behaviour lead some individuals to be regarded as charismatic by others, a perspective presaged in the theoretical model formulated with Kanungo. But what are the types of behaviour that lead to the attribution of charisma? Conger views the process of attribution as involving a sequence of stages. Stage one is concerned with *sensing opportunity and formulating a vision*. The leader injects a sense of purpose and unifies the disparate aspects of an organization. The formulation of a vision is often a reflection of a felt deficiency with things as they are, and the leader's vision invariably issues a challenge to the status quo. The vision gives people a sense of personal worth, since they come to view themselves as active ingredients in an organization that is vigorous and going somewhere. As a result, and also because of their greater sense of purpose, organizational members are more motivated. According to Conger, in order for the attribution of charisma to be enhanced (and perhaps to be effective), it needs to be simple, needs to express idealized goals, should challenge the status quo, will need to address members' personal aspirations, and will often involve an element of risk.

Stage two is *articulating the vision*. Organizational members must be convinced that they should commit themselves to the vision. Conger sees the way in which the message is communicated as central to this stage. Charismatic leaders are 'more effective and powerful speakers' than their non-charismatic counterparts (1989: 69). Conger sees rhetorical devices, like metaphor, as especially important. An illustration is Iacocca's use of metaphors of war and of family to get across his vision. They also have a good sense of speech rhythm, have a powerful style of speaking which lacks hesitation, and are fairly prolific in the use of gestures to convey points. They also engage in strategies for conveying a vision like value amplification (following Snow et al., 1986). With this strategy, certain values which underpin the vision, especially values that are likely to be attractive to members of an organization, are amplified (for example, free enterprise, the leading edge of technology).

The purpose of stage three, *building trust in the vision*, is self-evident. The leader must be seen as capable of bringing a vision to fruition. To this end, he or she needs to promote an image of him- or herself as an exceptional individual. Emphasizing past successes and accomplishments may be an important route. Also, Conger notes that subordinates trusted the visions of the charismatic leaders he studied, because they were perceived as having great 'strategic insight', which in many cases is the product of creating an impression of great expertise and of a capacity to see through the complexity of situations. Also, they often portray themselves as sharing fundamental values with their subordinates.

Finally, stage four involves *achieving the vision*, by which is meant empowering others so that they can feel active participants in the attainment of the vision. Empowerment is essential to the encouragement of belief that they can accomplish the vision. This self-belief is important in getting people to accomplish difficult tasks and to sustain the necessary effort for consummating the vision. Helping individuals to achieve early successes in tasks relating to the vision may have an important role here. The leader may need to become a teacher, constantly creating new learning experiences for members of the organization to give them a sense of new ideas and of what they can achieve.

Puffer (1990) has sought to explore a number of themes associated with Conger's approach. Managers and undergraduates were presented with an imaginary case study of a company and its general manager in which certain features were varied in order to determine their effects on the attribution of charisma. It was found that an intuitive decision style and the achievement of successful decision outcomes were likely to produce attributions of charisma. These factors are very consistent with Conger's findings and his broad approach, though it might be argued that Puffer's findings would suggest that he does not attach sufficient significance to personal success in generating the initial attribution of charisma.

Critical commentary on Conger's approach will be postponed until the next chapter, but in the meantime it should be apparent that his general approach draws on many themes that were encountered in Chapters 2 and 3. Indeed, the suggestion that charisma should be construed as an attributional product of certain types of behaviour is consistent with many aspects of the idea of the social formation of charisma that was outlined in Chapter 3. In fact, Conger's approach is closer to the original Weberian formulation than any of the approaches to the study of charisma that were encountered in Chapter 5. What Conger shares with so many recent writers on leadership is a preoccupation with vision, which he describes as 'the cornerstone of charismatic leadership' (1989: 36). It is entirely consistent with Weber's formulation that vision should be regarded as such a central aspect of charisma, but it should also be recognized that for Weber the perceived extraordinariness of the charismatic leader was much more central than it is to Conger. As has been demonstrated, Conger does acknowledge this aspect but only in the context of its being a device for creating a sense of trust in the leader's vision. For Weber, the belief in the extraordinary quality of the charismatic leader was much more central; it was not simply a device or artifice for getting one's mission across. Indeed, although Weber is ambiguous about this particular point, there is a sense in which he was saying that the originality or the apparent perceptiveness of the charismatic leader's mission is often what makes him or her perceived to be extraordinary. Puffer's (1990) research suggests that success, which may be the basis for being perceived as exceptional in an organization, may be much more important in the initial attribution of charisma than Conger allows. It is, of course, important not to confuse charisma with success, but there is no doubt that the latter can be a helpful route to being seen as extraordinary and exceptional. Nonetheless, Conger has provided an interesting account of the processes of charismatic leadership in organizations.

Charisma in the laboratory

Howell and Frost (1989) conducted an interesting laboratory experiment concerned with the effects of charismatic leadership. One hundred and forty-four Canadian undergraduates were randomly assigned to one of six experimental conditions. Each condition represented one of three leadership styles and either high or low group productivity norms. The three leadership styles were: charismatic, consideration and structuring. The last two are associated with the Ohio studies. Thus, each student was attached to a group led by someone exhibiting one of these three leadership styles under either high or low productivity norms. Subjects worked on a business simulation.

The 'leaders' were professional actresses who worked to precisely formulated scripts, while productivity norms were established by confederates of the experimenters who worked with the students and who were either very enthusiastic about the task or extremely bored (high and low productivity norms respectively).

Howell and Frost describe the charismatic style as exhibiting the following features:

> The leaders articulated an overarching goal, communicated high performance expectations and exhibited confidence in subordinates' ability to meet these expectations, and empathized with the needs of their subordinates . . . the leaders also projected a powerful, confident, and dynamic presence . . . Paralinguistically, the charismatic leaders were trained to have a captivating, engaging voice tone. To capture the dynamism and energy of charisma, nonverbally the leaders alternated between pacing and sitting on the edge of their desk, leaned toward the participant, maintained direct eye contact, and had a relaxed posture and animated facial expressions. (1989: 252)

The results indicate that subjects supervised by charismatic leaders generally scored higher on four measures of task peformance (including quantity and quality) than when supervised by considerate or structuring leaders. They also exhibited higher levels of task and general satisfaction, lower levels of role conflict, and better adjustment to the leader. These effects generally held irrespective of the group productivity norm, suggesting that charismatic leaders can better overcome adverse work climates.

This is a striking confirmation of the importance of charismatic leadership. Again, critical commentary will be deferred. However, one important implication of the research which can be registered at this point is that, as Howell and Frost suggest, it would appear that people can be trained to exhibit charismatic leadership. After all, these were professional actresses. This finding is of considerable importance to the issue of whether charisma is accessible only to specially gifted persons. It is not the first study about which a claim has been made that charisma was created for experimental purposes (see Naftulin et al., 1973), but its capacity to demonstrate the effects of induced charisma on the kinds of dependent variable with which organizational researchers are traditionally concerned gives it special significance.

Charisma and direct selling organizations

Biggart (1989) has examined direct selling organizations (DSOs), that is, firms which employ salespersons to sell directly and independently to customers, and has concluded from a detailed ethnographic study of many of them that there is a fairly clear charismatic element in the authority structures of many of the organizations concerned. Not all DSOs are characterized as possessing a strong charismatic component; Tupperware is an example of a DSO that could not be described as infused with charisma. On the other hand, a good many of the firms she studied could be described as exhibiting 'charismatic capitalism'. One of the chief examples is Mary Kay Cosmetics, whose founder, Mary Kay Ash, was referred to in Chapter 5.

What is it about these organizations that appears to warrant them being described as charismatic? The leaders of the firms concerned, who are usually the founders, often exhibit the kind of relationship with the distributors of the products that is discerned in social movements that are led by charismatic leaders. Biggart notes that DSOs often possess a 'cultlike character' and are run like social movements. Distributors see their work as more than just paid employment since they are frequently committed to the implicit world-view contained in the leader's mission and they form mutual support and friendship networks with each other. The leaders portray their firms as addressing fundamental values, which allows the distributors to see themselves as involved in more than selling a product. Thus, Art Williams of A.L. Williams, a life insurance DSO, presents the firm's mission as a crusade to overturn a malevolent force in the US (that is, the whole-life insurance industry). Mary Crowley of Home Interiors and Gifts presents the firm's mission as 'ensuring that no home in America is ever dull or unattractive' (cited in Biggart, 1989: 98), a theme which is reinforced by biblical references. Such leaders present their firms as being able to improve the world and to allow distributors to profit from their labours.

The CEOs themselves are perceived as special by large numbers of distributors and are viewed with a mixture of awe and reverence. Biggart quotes one of Mary Kay's devotees as saying: 'Meeting Mary Kay was quite an experience. You could just feel the power. It was a very unusual experience. You can just feel the powerful vibes and charisma' (1989: 142). This sense of the special quality of the leaders is frequently underpinned by sagas about the leaders. In Mary Kay's case, she is known to have overcome adversity in that she became a successful saleswoman even though she had to support herself and her children after her husband left her. This reputation for hard work serves as a goal for the company's distributors. Many of the chief executives of DSOs are very powerful orators and this facilitates their capacity to get their mission across and to project an image of being extraordinary. DSOs tend to have very strong organizational cultures which are infused with the leaders' missions and are constantly reinforced through special celebrations at which their oratory can be employed to great effect. Biggart notes that since the DSOs focus to such a large extent on the leader, there is a great need to routinize their charisma. Typically this tends to occur either through the designation of a successor by the charismatic leader or by presenting one or more of the leader's children as carrying on the mission once they have gone.

The very fact that DSOs possess the atmosphere of social movements provides them with a prima facie case for treatment in terms of the notion of charisma, but on top of this many of the chief executives have successfully mined a desire for work relationships that are less prone to utilitarian considerations than conventional employment contexts. They enact the role of the charismatic leader well: they give meaning to the lives of their distributors, are sensitive to the rhetorical nuances that breed commitment, and are not averse to cultivating an image of themselves as special. At the same time, they have collectively created an industry that in 1984 sold $8.6 billion in goods and services.

Research on transformational leadership

The general ideas surrounding the notion of transformational leadership were outlined in the previous chapter. Research relating to the notion will now be examined.

Bass's research on transformational leadership

Bass's programme of research has been significant because he has sought to conduct systematic research into the idea of transformational leadership employing a measurement-based framework. Central to this effort is the Multifactor Leadership Questionnaire (MLQ), which has been developed in order to provide measures of the components of transactional and trans-formational leadership that were outlined on pp. 98–100. The MLQ has undergone a number of revisions and there are slightly different versions to reflect the special characteristics of the organizations from which the various samples of leaders have been taken. The MLQ is now widely used and has achieved very quickly the kind of prominence that the Ohio State LBDQ enjoyed in the 1950s and 1960s. Although Bass's research is widely taken to have implications for business organizations, relatively few of the studies have been conducted in business firms.

In the early research undertaken with the MLQ, inspirational leadership was subsumed under charismatic leadership because of the difficulty of disentangling it; there was no measure of *laissez-faire* leadership; no distinction was made between contingent promises and rewards; and the active and passive forms of management-by-exception were not distinguished. There is a version of the MLQ in which leaders describe their own behaviour, but the most commonly used version at the time of writing is the rater form of the MLQ-5, in which the respondent ('rater') describes the behaviour of a leader, who is usually the rater's superior. Respondents are given seventy descriptions of a leader, which represent ten items for each of the seven aspects of leadership delineated by Bass and Avolio (1990a): charismatic leadership; individualized consideration; intellectual stimulation; inspirational leadership; contingent reward; management-by-exception; and *laissez-faire*. Sample MLQ items are presented in Box 6.2 along with the five-point scale on which leaders are rated. A further set of sample items can be found in Bass and Avolio (1990a). Interestingly, one of the inspirational leadership items is concerned with the question of whether the leader has a vision which urges the rater on. In view of the centrality of the notion of vision to charismatic leadership it seems strange to treat it as indicative of inspirational leadership. At the very least, this consideration would seem to point to the difficulty of treating the two as separate dimensions of leadership.

As mentioned above, the items are administered to subordinates as possible

---

BOX 6.2   Multifactor Leadership Questionnaire (MLQ)

The respondent has to decide how well each item applies to the individual being described on a five-point scale: not at all; once in a while; sometimes; fairly often; frequently. There are ten items for each of the seven dimensions.

Sample items are as follows:

Transformational leadership

Charisma   The person I am rating has my trust in his or her ability to overcome any obstacle.
Inspiration   The person I am rating uses symbols and images to focus our efforts.
Intellectual stimulation   The person I am rating enables me to think about old problems in new ways.
Individualized consideration   The person I am rating coaches me if I need it.

Transactional leadership

Contingent reward   The person I am rating makes sure there is close agreement between what he or she expects me to do and what I can get from him or her for my effort.
Management-by-exception   The person I am rating takes action only when a mistake has occurred.

Non-leadership

Laissez-faire   The person I am rating doesn't tell me where s/he stands on issues.

Source: reproduced by special permission of the publisher, Consulting Psychologists Press, Inc., Palo Alto, CA 94303, USA, from *Multifactor Leadership Questionnaire* by Bernard Bass and Bruce J. Avolio. Copyright 1989 by Consulting Psychologists Press, Inc. All rights reserved. Further reproduction is prohibited without the publisher's consent.

---

descriptions of a leader. These descriptions are then correlated with various outcomes, of which the three most prominent are: a measure of extra effort (which refers to subordinates' motivation to work harder than their jobs require); a measure of satisfaction with the leader; and a measure of the effectiveness of the leader and his/her work unit. These three measures are usually based on the same respondents' reports and often form a part of the

MLQ. Two main approaches to the measurement of leader behaviour can be discerned. First, a sample of individuals describe their superiors in terms of the MLQ and their descriptions are correlated with the foregoing outcomes. This strategy has particularly been used when general samples, like MBA students, have been the focus of the investigation (for example, Bass and Avolio, 1989; Seltzer et al., 1989; Singer, 1985). Second, focal leaders are chosen and questionnaires are completed by a number of each leader's subordinates. Subordinates' replies for each leader are then aggregated to form overall scores for each of the seven components of leadership, which are then related to the various outcomes (for example, Hater and Bass, 1988; Yammarino and Bass, 1990b). These two research approaches by no means exhaust the variety of types of study. For example, Bass (1985) reports a study of 'world-class leaders', in which undergraduates read biographies of prominent leaders and completed the MLQ for each leader as if the student was a follower or subordinate. Avolio et al. (1988) report a management simulation which spanned three months. Participants worked in teams each of which was led by a 'president' whose leadership was measured with the MLQ. The different components of transformational and transactional leadership were then correlated with financial measures of organizational effectiveness.

Some findings from published research are presented in Tables 6.1, 6.2 and 6.3, covering the relationship between measures of leadership and effectiveness, satisfaction and extra effort. In Table 6.1, studies are grouped in terms of whether they report subordinate-based measures of leader effectiveness or another type of measure (such as ratings by the leader's own superior, as in Hater and Bass, 1988). Bass (1990a) and Bass and Avolio (1990a) refer to a number of other studies, but these are not generally available at the time of writing and a decision has been made to focus largely upon readily available reports of findings. An examination of Tables 6.1 to 6.3 reveals the following tendencies:

1 Charismatic leadership (including inspirational leadership) tends to be the component that is most likely to be associated with desirable outcomes.
2 Individualized consideration and intellectual stimulation are usually the next most important correlates of outcomes, with the former usually being slightly more important than the latter; when extra effort is the outcome measure, intellectual stimulation tends to reveal the larger correlations.
3 Contingent reward usually makes a fairly important contribution to satisfaction, effectiveness and extra effort; when a distinction is made between promises and rewards, the latter seems to play a more prominent role.
4 Management-by-exception produces inconsistent results, sometimes exhibiting quite high correlations with outcomes, but these can be either positive or negative relationships; passive management-by-exception seems to be less effective than its active form.
5 *Laissez-faire* leadership is clearly highly undesirable.

Table 6.1 *Correlations between effectiveness and measures of transformational and transactional leadership, and non-leadership*

Study	CH	IC	IS	IL	CR	MBE	LF
Subordinate-based ratings of effectiveness							
Military officers (Bass, 1985)	0.85	0.70	0.47	x	0.41	0.23	x
World-class leaders (Bass, 1985)	0.58	0.40	0.34	x	0.21	–0.17	x
NZ professionals and managers (Bass, 1985)[1]	0.46	0.46	0.46	x	0.34	–0.05	x
NZ educational administrators (Bass, 1985)[1]	0.65	0.58	0.48	x	0.40	–0.34	x
NZ company managers (Singer, 1985)	0.72	0.52	0.75	x	0.71	0.47	x
Top performing managers in delivery firm (Hater and Bass, 1988)	0.81	0.75	0.71	x	0.30	0.34/–0.19[3]	x
Ordinary managers in delivery firm (Hater and Bass, 1988)	0.88	0.79	0.79	x	0.43	0.10/–0.01[3]	x
MBA students (Bass and Avolio, 1989)	0.76	0.77	0.69	x	0.68	0.22	x
MBA students (Seltzer et al., 1989)	0.81	0.76	0.71	x	0.61	–0.23	x
Navy officers (Yammarino and Bass, 1990b)	0.87	0.73	0.74	0.79	0.48/0.66[2]	0.50/0.11[3]	–0.60
Senior managers in high-technology firm (Avolio and Yammarino, 1990)	0.72	x	x	x	x	x	–0.48
Personnel managers in high-technology firm (Avolio and Yammarino, 1990)	0.66	x	x	x	x	x	–0.46
Measures of effectiveness not based on subordinate ratings							
Participants in a simulation (Avolio et al., 1988)[4]	0.39	0.44	0.48	x	0.42	0.08	x
Top performing managers in delivery firm (Hater and Bass, 1988)[5]	0.37	0.26	0.24	x	–0.17	–0.09/–0.29[3]	x

Table continues

Table 6.1 continued

	CH	IC	IS	IL	CR	MBE	LF
Ordinary managers in delivery firm (Hater and Bass, 1988)[5]	0.47	0.42	0.38	x	0.13	$-0.24/0.02^{3}$	x
Navy officers (Yammarino and Bass, 1990a)[6]	0.34	0.20	0.31	0.25	$0.17/0.21^{2}$	$0.25/0.03^{3}$	-0.29

[1] This study employed two or more measures of effectiveness, with separate coefficients being reported for each measure. The coefficients reported in this table are the mean correlations for each leadership dimension.

[2] First coefficient relates to contingent promises; second to contingent reward.

[3] First coefficient relates to active management-by-exception; second to passive management-by-exception.

[4] This study employed four financial measures of effectiveness with separate coefficients being reported for each measure. The coefficients reported in this table are the mean correlations for each leadership dimension.

[5] In this study, superiors rated the performance of leaders in terms of two criteria with separate coefficients being reported for each criterion. The coefficients reported in this table are the mean correlations for each leadership dimension.

[6] This study employed three criteria of job performance with separate coefficients being reported for each criterion. The coefficients reported in this table are the mean correlations for each leadership dimension.

NZ   New Zealand
x   no coefficient quoted in the source book or article.
Measures
CH   charismatic leadership
IC   individualized consideration
IS   intellectual stimulation
IL   inspirational leadership
CR   contingent reward
MBE   management-by-exception
LF   *laissez-faire*

Table 6.2　*Correlations between satisfaction and measures of transformational and transactional leadership, and non-leadership*

Study	CH	IC	IS	IL	CR	MBE	LF
Military officers (Bass, 1985)	0.91	0.76	0.55	x	0.45	0.29	x
World-class leaders (Bass, 1985)	0.64	0.50	0.52	x	0.28	–0.10	x
NZ professionals and managers (Bass, 1985)[1]	0.57	0.55	0.52	x	0.31	–0.11	x
NZ educational administrators (Bass, 1985)[1]	0.78	0.61	0.57	x	0.53	–0.21	x
NZ company managers (Singer, 1985)	0.81	0.70	0.72	x	0.55	0.17	x
MBA students (Bass and Avolio, 1989)	0.88	0.82	0.70	x	0.64	0.13	x
MBA students (Seltzer et al., 1989)	0.86	0.77	0.70	x	0.64	–0.24	x
Navy officers (Yammarino and Bass, 1990b)	0.89	0.81	0.73	0.82	0.53/0.72[2]	0.44/0.19[3]	–0.55
NZ police officers (Singer and Singer, 1990)	0.59	0.51	0.53	x	0.17	–0.05	x
Taiwanese managers in a commercial organization (Singer and Singer, 1990)	0.62	0.58	0.43	x	0.54	0.25	x

[1] This study employed two measures of satisfaction with the leader, with separate coefficients being reported for each measure. The coefficients reported in this table are the mean corelations for each leadership dimension.

[2] First coefficient relates to contingent promises; second to contingent reward.

[3] First coefficient relates to active management-by-exception; second to passive management-by-exception.

All of the coefficients refer to the correlation between each dimension of leader behaviour and satisfaction with the leader, except Singer (1985) which is in relation to a measure of subordinate job satisfaction.

See Table 6.1 for explanation of abbreviations.

Table 6.3 *Correlations between extra effort and measures of transformational and transactional leadership, and non-leadership*

Study	CH	IC	IS	IL	CR	MBE	LF
NZ professionals and managers (Bass, 1985)	0.50	0.25	0.49	x	0.38	−0.28	x
NZ educational administrators (Bass, 1985)	0.72	0.60	0.76	x	0.44	−0.42	x
Supervisors and managers in manufacturing firm (Bass, 1985)	0.88	0.79	0.80	x	0.76	−0.24	x
MBA students (Seltzer et al., 1989)	0.79	0.73	0.76	x	0.62	−0.19	x
Navy officers (Yammarino and Bass, 1990b)	0.17	0.27	0.24	0.22	0.04/0.22[1]	0.25/0.03[2]	−0.35
One general manager in defence contractor (Ehrlich et al., 1990)	0.65	0.34	0.44	x	0.58	0.31	x

[1] First coefficient relates to contingent promises; second to contingent reward.
[2] First coefficient relates to active management-by-exception; second to passive management-by-exception.

See Table 6.1 for explanation of abbreviations.

In addition, a number of other correlates of transformational and transactional leadership have been demonstrated by various studies. For example, a study of MBA students by Seltzer et al. (1989) has shown that charisma, individualized consideration and contingent reward reduce burnout and stress symptoms. Intellectual stimulation and management-by-exception seem to be positively associated with these outcomes. In a study of US retail chain workers, Peterson et al. (1989) examined the effects of the MLQ charismatic leadership subscale in conjunction with other leadership- and work-related variables (none of the other MLQ measures was employed). It was found to have the most pronounced impact of all the independent variables on store effectiveness and even more strikingly on organizational commitment. Howell and Higgins (1990a) have examined the role of transformational (but not transactional) leadership in the propensity of individuals in organizations to act as 'champions' of information technology innovations in Canadian companies. Champions were more likely than non-champions to exhibit transformational leadership. They were especially more likely to exhibit inspiration and to a lesser extent intellectual stimulation. Charisma was relevant to the prediction of promoting innovation, but its effect was not great, while individualized consideration barely figured. This study employed a version of the MLQ through which individuals reported about leader behaviour in respect of themselves. The study is of extra interest because it addressed transformational leadership among informal leaders, rather than the designated leaders who are usually the focus of inquiries in which the MLQ is employed. However, in view of the fact that charisma is often associated with innovation and change, it is slightly disconcerting that its impact on the championing of technological innovations was not more pronounced. On the other hand, another study conducted by these authors, which did not employ the MLQ, did find that individuals who exhibited charismatic leadership were more likely than others to be champions of technological innovations (Howell and Higgins, 1990b). In this second study, charismatic leadership was gauged in terms of: demonstration of self-confidence; great certainty about ideological goals; individualized considera-tion; confidence in the capacity of others to carry out tasks; unconventional behaviour; and appraisal of environmental circumstances for the prospects of change.

Bass's framework for examining transformational and transactional leadership has produced an impressive array of findings which possess a good deal in common. The body of evidence points to charismatic leadership playing a very important part in many of the outcomes that have traditionally been of interest to organizational researchers, but it is also apparent that it is not sufficient on its own for promoting 'performance beyond expectations', since other aspects of leadership have a significant role.

It will be recalled from Chapter 1 that one contributory factor to the loss of support for the Ohio State instruments was the recognition that they contained measurement defects, such as contamination by implicit leadership theories. The MLQ is extremely similar to the LBDQ in the way in which the measurement of leader behaviour is conducted. In particular, the reliance on subordinates' reports for measures of leaders' behaviour (as well as for measures of many outcomes) in both the LBDQ and the rater form of the MLQ is very striking. This similarity could be taken to suggest that the MLQ suffers from the same measurement problems as the Ohio questionnaires. Bass and Avolio (1989) have explored a number of aspects of the measurement properties of the MLQ subscales. However, their research only partly addresses the potentially damaging effects of subordinates' implicit leadership theories on how they describe their superiors when answering MLQ questions. Bass and Avolio found that respondents saw transformational leadership (and especially the charisma component) as closer than transactional leadership to their image of the 'ideal' leader. This finding confirms the possibility of biases in respondents' perceptions of the kind mentioned in Chapter 1. However, the MLQ measures could be more problematic if it were shown (as it was in the case of measures of initiating structure and consideration in the Ohio questionnaires) that respondents' ratings of their superiors' behaviour were affected by such things as their knowledge of the effectiveness of those superiors. If this were true, as it was with the Ohio research, the MLQ measures would be flawed. It would mean that the high correlations that have been found between various outcomes and charisma, individualized consideration and intellectual stimulation could be a product of respondents' models of how effective leaders behave. On the other hand, since it might be legitimately argued that the attribution of charisma is at least in part a product of the perceived effectiveness of leaders, it would be expected that the MLQ charismatic leadership subscale would be influenced by the performance of leaders. However, this suggestion makes the correlations in Table 6.1 rather difficult to interpret, since it is not obvious whether effectiveness causes the attribution of charismatic leadership or whether charismatic leaders engender greater effectiveness or even whether each is true. The static nature of the cross-sectional designs that underpin most of the MLQ-based research makes it difficult to discriminate between the different possibilities. The research conducted by Avolio and Yammarino (1990), which is discussed below, has some bearing on the influence of implicit leadership theories on the MLQ.

Some other problems with the research can be identified. There is a relative absence, as in the Ohio research, of situational analysis. Although the data in Tables 6.1 to 6.3 point to a high level of consistency in the results that have been obtained, there are differences from study to study, so that the implications of different situational contexts for the effectiveness of the various types of leader behaviour are largely unexplored. The bulk of the studies employ correlational research designs so that the direction of causality is not beyond reasonable doubt. A further difficulty derives from the frequent use of respondents for reports of both leader behaviour and outcomes. When this occurs, there is the possibility of 'common method variance', whereby correlations are artificially inflated *inter alia* by respondents' proclivity for consistency in answering questions. However, not all of the relevant research exhibits this tendency towards single-source bias. As can be seen in Table 6.1, Hater and Bass (1988) and Yammarino and Bass (1990a) used both a subordinate-based measure of effectiveness and other types of measure. Correlations involving the former type of measure would be prone to common method variance (since respondents are the source of both leadership and effectiveness data when completing the MLQ), but correlations involving the other types of measure would not be affected by this problem. In both cases, the general pattern of findings was similar to that reported for this study in Table 6.1, but the correlations tended to be quite a lot smaller. For example, in Yammarino and Bass (1990a) the mean correlation between charisma and three measures of job performance was 0.34, as against 0.87 for the subordinate-based measure of performance. In the Hater and Bass (1988) study of top performing managers the corresponding correlations were 0.81 and 0.37; for ordinary managers in the same study they were 0.88 and 0.47. A further possible limitation of the MLQ approach is that with the exception of the Howell and Higgins (1990a) study, like the bulk of the Ohio studies, there is a preoccupation with leader behaviour among designated leaders.

Avolio and Yammarino (1990) have addressed a further problem thrown up by the Ohio measures: could those MLQ-based studies which aggregate individuals' depictions of leaders to form group-level descriptions of those leaders be masking important differences in leader–subordinate relationships? This is the issue raised by the vertical dyad linkage (VDL) approach that was mentioned in Chapter 1. The authors addressed this issue in a large high-technology firm, taking two sets of upper-level managers as the focus of attention: line managers and personnel managers. They examined the relationships between charismatic leadership, *laissez-faire* and effectiveness. They found that correlations between effectiveness and averaged descriptions of the two types of leader behaviour were generally marginally larger than when differences in leader–subordinate relationships were taken into account in the manner suggested by the VDL approach. Moreover, averaged descriptions of leader behaviour seemed to represent raters' depictions of their focal leader for line managers much better than for the personnel managers. Avolio and Yammarino suggest that accounts of the personnel managers seemed to be affected by raters' implicit leadership theories in that depictions of charismatic leadership were profoundly affected by differences in perception by raters (that is, subordinates). If a personnel manager is perceived in contrasting ways by his or her subordinates, the implicit leadership theories of the latter must be playing a significant role in how these leaders are being rated. For neither group of managers did the VDL approach represent a useful framework. This study is important for its rejection of the potential relevance of the VDL approach and for its demonstration of the role of implicit leadership theories in the measurement of charismatic leadership. Also, the different findings for line and personnel managers may point to differences in their jobs which would form the basis for the specification of situational factors which may have an impact on the effects of transactional and transformational leadership.

Smith and Peterson (1988) have questioned the degree to which the measures of transformational leadership really reflect Burns's (1978) conception. They argue that the questionnaire items generally do not represent the notion of transformational leadership being a two-way process that can be discerned in Burns's conceptualization. Instead, many of the items tend to be concerned with the effects of leaders on followers.

What of the measure of charisma itself? The charisma subscale seems to encapsulate many of the chief elements of charismatic leadership that have been identified in previous chapters. However, as suggested above, the tendency to treat the item concerned with vision as indicative of inspirational, rather than charismatic, leadership is disconcerting. Another element that was central to Weber's depiction was the notion of the charismatic leader as someone who is seen as exceptional. However, only two items out of the ten which measure charisma in the MLQ could be viewed as tapping this aspect of it, and one of these is presented in Box 6.2. Yet if Weber's definitions of charisma are examined, the sense of the charismatic leader as someone who is deemed extraordinary is absolutely central. In the MLQ, however, it is treated as a fairly minor element. In fact, the very treatment of charisma as a *variable* is conducive to less emphasis being placed upon the notion of the charismatic leader as someone who commands loyalty by virtue of his or her extra-ordinariness. When treated as a variable, charisma becomes a matter of degree and the image of the charismatic leader as exceptional becomes less tenable.

There is also a slight ambiguity about the nature of charisma in the MLQ. Contingent reward, intellectual stimulation, management-by-exception and so on are all types of leader behaviour. In the earlier writings, Bass seemed to construe charisma in a similar way to the other components of leader behaviour, for example, when using the phrase 'charismatic leadership behavior' (1985: 209). However, Bass and Avolio write: 'Transformational leaders are likely to become charismatic in the eyes of their followers' (1990a: 242). This statement seems to imply that charisma is a *product* of transformational leadership. But since charisma is a component of transformational leadership it is difficult to see how it can be a product as well. Some light may be shed on this issue when Seltzer et al. write that 'attaining charisma in the eyes of their followers' (1989: 175) is one of the ways in which transformational leaders engender high performance levels (that is, along with intellectual stimulation and individualized consideration). It would seem that when responding to a questionnaire about their superiors, subordinates are not being asked about behaviour that is indicative of charismatic leadership, but about behaviour that produces charisma. By contrast, the questionnaire items that purport to measure, for example, individualized consideration indicate how the leader behaves in terms of that component. It is consistent with Weber's account to view charisma as an attribution made by followers, but the chief purpose of this discussion has been to point to a possible ambiguity in the nature of charisma as compared with the other aspects of transformational leadership in Bass's writings. Nonetheless, the development of the MLQ represents an extremely important and impressive exercise in the measurement of leader behaviour.

Podsakoff et al. (1990) have also adopted a quantitative approach to transformational and transactional leadership. Drawing on a number of New Leadership approaches they conceptualized transformational leadership as comprising six dimensions each of which was measured by a multiple-item scale: identifying and articulating a vision; providing an appropriate model; fostering the acceptance of group goals; high performance expectations; providing individualized support; intellectual stimulation. The first three were found to be highly interrelated in their research and were collectively dubbed a 'core' dimension of transformational leadership. Transactional leadership was measured by one scale alone – contingent reward behaviour. The authors were concerned with the impact of the two forms of leadership on organizational citizenship behaviour (OCB), which refers to behaviour that goes beyond the requirements of a formal role and that also contributes to organizational effectiveness. Podsakoff et al. expected that the effect on OCB would be part indirect, in that trust in the leader and employee satisfaction would act as intervening variables which mediate the effects on subordinate behaviour.

Data were collected from employees and their supervisors in a US petrochemical company. The six types of leader behaviour (as a group) had an effect on OCB, but the effect was indirect, that is, it was mediated by trust and satisfaction (the former to a far greater degree than the latter). Trust was found to be affected positively by 'core' transformational leadership and individualized support, negatively by high performance expectations and intellectual stimulation, but not at all by contingent reward behaviour. This research suggests that the extent to which leaders are able to create trust in themselves through transformational leadership plays an important part in the preparedness of their subordinates to put more into their work than is strictly required by their formal role obligations. The research also implies that there would be some virtue in examining the extent to which the effects of the forms of leader behaviour measured by the MLQ on such outcomes as extra effort and effectiveness are mediated by potential intervening variables like trust.

Tichy and Devanna's research on twelve CEOs

Tichy and Devanna (1990) have carried out research on twelve CEOs, including Iacocca, Welch and John Harvey-Jones of ICI. With the exception of Iacocca, the data were gleaned from in-depth interviews. In the case of Iacocca, secondary sources and current and past co-workers provided data. The authors acknowledge an intellectual debt to both Burns (1978) and Zaleznik (1977) for the distinctions that they proffered (see Table 5.1). They believe that there is an urgent need for transformational leadership in order to cope with the complex and changeable environment that firms face nowadays. This environment embraces vastly greater competitiveness and technological change than in previous eras, along with rapid social change. An organization that fails to transform itself in response to these changes risks failure.

How did the twelve leaders go about the task of organizational transformation? Tichy and Devanna conceive of the process in terms of three 'acts'. Act 1 entails a *recognition of the need to revitalize the organization* as environmental pressures trigger a need for change. But people working in organizations tend to resist change, so the leader must create dissatisfaction with the status quo. This is easier when the organization is manifestly in a state of crisis, as was the case at Chrysler when Iacocca took over, than when it is doing quite well, as was GE when Welch desired to anticipate greater foreign competition and its adverse effects. Tichy and Devanna recommend such strategies as getting people to visit other organizations so that they can examine alternative ways of doing things, or changing people's ways of thinking about organizational performance by getting them to measure it against competitors, rather than previous years' results. Once the leader succeeds in creating dissatisfaction, he or she will need to dismantle the old values and ways of doing things. Simultaneously, the leader must deal with people's anxieties about loss of power or status and generally help them to feel sanguine about the transformation.

An important component of the management of transition is Act 2, which entails the *creation of a vision*. The vision is rarely the product of an individual's thinking alone, but incorporates disparate views from within the organization and as such is often an amalgam of a variety of elements. A vision motivates organizational members because it provides them with a challenge and 'a conceptual roadmap or set of blueprints for what the organization will look like in the future' (1990: 128). People come to identify with what the organizations will become, rather than with what it looks like now. Central to the vision is a mission statement which provides a sense of direction and establishes values for the organization and its members. In order to get the new vision and mission accepted, the transformational leader must market the ideas that he or she holds dear, which is likely to entail instilling new values so that the organizational culture facilitates rather than acts as a barrier to the vision and its associated strategy. People may need to be educated to understand what advantages the new vision holds for them. They must be allowed to have responsibility for implementing change in line with the vision. It may be necessary to change certain key personnel since the CEO's executive team must be fully committed to the vision. In order not to appear totally iconoclastic, the leader may need to retain aspects of the organization's past (for example, certain practices, elements of its culture).

Act 3 involves *institutionalizing changes*, which in essence means that the leader must design structures which will smooth the way for the vision to be accomplished. Among other things, the leader must 'creatively destroy' (1990: 188) and then reassemble the old and the new, with an emphasis on the latter. Thus, both Welch at GE and Akers at IBM (not one of the twelve leaders in the study; see Box 6.3) are cited as transformational leaders who sought to break down the bureaucratic elements of their respective organizations in order to create structures that were more in keeping with their visions of leaner organizations that were responsive to change. In place of bureaucracy, they aimed to establish independent business units that would be more capable of responding to the pressures of the market place. In order to effect the necessary cultural changes, a variety of strategies will need to be involved, including: greater control over the selection of new personnel; workshops; and attention to appraisal and reward systems.

BOX 6.3 John Akers: IBM

IBM was eulogized by Peters and Waterman (1982) as the quintessential customer-oriented company and, indeed, service to the customer has always been a prominent ingredient of its strong corporate culture. The then chief executive, John Opel, saw himself as the custodian of the company's culture which he viewed as a kind of *sine qua non*. He was succeeded in February 1985 by John Akers who had come through the ranks at IBM and had an enviable reputation in marketing. Akers's arrival seems to have coincided with a sharp deterioration in IBM's trading position. This can be attributed to a number of factors, but a prominent one in Akers's view was that his company had taken its eye off the customer. As a result, other computer firms were able to steal a march on IBM by supplying products which met customer needs more directly. In response to this trend, Akers took great strides to refocus his company's energies on customers. A major aspect of the transformation was that he waged war on IBM's bureaucracy in order to make it more entrepreneurial and sensitive to customers' requirements. This entailed pushing responsibility down the line to newly created autonomous business units. The year 1987 was designated 'the year of the customer'. In addition, sales staff were given special training in handling customer needs rather than simply selling pre-existing products. However, in March 1991 it was reported that IBM was encountering difficulties in the market and its profits were declining quickly. In response, it announced 14,000 redundancies in the US and Europe. Two months later, Akers was publicly scathing about the complacency of his employees, saying that there were 'too many standing around the water cooler waiting to be told what to do' (*The Independent*, 30 May 1991). Does this mean that the new vision and the cultural change had failed to take effect and to impress and empower employees?

Sources: Dreyfuss, 1989; Loomis, 1989; Taylor, 1983; Tichy and Devanna, 1990; Warner and Fagan, 1991

Tichy and Devanna identify a number of factors that distinguish transformational from transactional leaders: they see themselves as change agents; they are courageous; they believe in people; they are concerned to articulate core values which steer their behaviour; they never stop learning; they are able to cope with complexity, ambiguity and uncertainty; and they are visionaries. Transformational leadership can be learned and 'is not something that occurs solely through the behavior of charismatic geniuses' (1990: xii). It is clear that transformational leadership is no guarantee for organizational survival, let alone success. In an update on the twelve leaders in the second edition, they note that four years later, some of the companies have put in less than impressive performances. The two CEOs who led computer companies have struggled in the face of a poor competitive environment. Even Iacocca's golden touch is reported as having deserted Chrysler, which was slipping behind in market share (see Box 5.1).

While replete with interesting ideas, Tichy and Devanna's book is flawed as research. As the follow-up suggests, it has a limited time horizon, which makes generalizations hazardous. If a cursory analysis of the position for these transformational leaders a mere four years later suggests that transformational leadership has had mixed results, it is difficult to know what should be made of the strident acclaim that such leadership receives. There is no comparison group of transactional leaders to show what they are doing wrong, although there is plenty of innuendo about their flaws. This contrasts with Bass's view that transactional leadership has an important role to play in organizations.

Transformational leadership as romanticized leadership

In a series of studies, Meindl et al. (1985) showed that the degree to which individuals make leadership attributions (that is, explaining organizational events by reference to leadership) is profoundly affected by organizational performance. In particular, people are likely to see organizational performance as due to leadership factors when that performance is either strong or weak; they are less likely to see organizational performance as a function of leadership when it is moderate. Meindl et al. concluded that individuals are inclined to exaggerate the significance of leadership, especially when performance levels are at extremes. This conclusion in turn led them to suggest that people tend to 'romanticize' leadership, that is, they tend to see leaders as more significant than they probably are or can be.

Meindl (1989) has suggested that the recent preoccupation with transformational leadership and with charisma in particular is indicative of 'hyper-romanticism'. This implies that in the recent writings on the New Leadership, charismatic and transformational leadership have been accorded an especially inflated significance. In order to test these ideas, business students were asked to complete the MLQ in respect of Ronald Reagan and Lee Iacocca. They also completed the Romance of Leadership Scale (RLS) which measures the individual's propensity to see leadership as a highly significant factor in determining organizational outcomes. Meindl found that the higher an individual's RLS score, the more likely he or she was to see Reagan and Iacocca as transformational leaders. This tendency was particularly apparent with charisma: the RLS–charisma subscale correlations were 0.44 and 0.53 for Reagan and Iacocca respectively. Thus, individuals who romanticize leadership are more likely to describe leaders as transformational, and as charismatic in particular. Meindl also formulated a model of charisma as a process of social contagion.

In another study, Ehrlich et al. (1990) investigated the perceptions of a general manager of a small, high-technology defence contractor who is generally believed to have been responsible for a radical transformation of the company's fortunes. Along with a number of measures, the MLQ, the RLS and the measure of extra effort were administered to employees. The manager emerged with high scores on charisma and individualized consideration. A pattern of correlations between extra effort and transactional and transformational leadership that was broadly similar to other studies was found (see Table 6.3). The correlation between charisma and RLS was quite high (0.32), but non-significant. This latter finding is somewhat at odds with the notion of charisma as romanticization. However, the research is of further interest because it sheds some light on the circumstances in which an attribution of charisma is made. It was found that employees who knew the manager very directly were less likely to describe him as charismatic than others. This finding suggests that the separation of leaders from subordinates may contribute to a perception of the leader as charismatic and builds on the understanding of charismatic leadership as an attributional process (Conger and Kanungo, 1987).

Meindl's general romanticization hypothesis has been derided by Bass (1990c) for going too far in an opposite direction in that his views seem to relegate leadership to a very minor role in human affairs. Bass argues that even a cursory glance at military, political and business history would suggest that the effects of leadership are real and not, as implied by Meindl, in the mind. On the other hand, it could be argued that Meindl's analyses relate to the tendency to exaggerate the effects of leadership, rather than to the question of whether it has consequences. In a sense, we could turn Meindl's (1989) examination of charisma on its head by suggesting that it has always been recognized by writers in the Weberian tradition that charisma is in the eyes of the follower (see Chapter 2) and that it is precisely because many leaders recognize this fact and the power of being seen as charismatic that they seek to create the groundwork for being seen as such, as the discussion of the social formation of charisma in Chapter 3 implies.

Research on leadership

In this section we will be concerned with research that has explicitly examined the concept of leadership as distinguished from management. Such research follows in the path of the ideas promulgated by Zaleznik (1977).

Bennis and Nanus on leadership

Bennis and Nanus (1985) carried out a detailed study of ninety prominent and successful leaders, of whom sixty were CEOs in the private sector and the remaining thirty were distinguished individuals from the public sector. Each leader was subjected to long unstructured interviews of three to four hours' duration, and ten were observed for around five days.

The research suggests that the leaders had developed four strategies which distilled the essence of leadership. First, there is *attention through vision*. Each interviewee had a compelling vision for the future that provided both the leader and others with a way forward that guided their action. The vision 'articulates a view of a realistic, credible, attractive future for the organization, a condition that is better in some important ways than what now exists' (1985: 89). The vision 'may be as vague as a dream or as precise as a goal or mission statement' (1985: 89). When the vision is shared by others in the organization they have a sense of direction and can locate their own position in relation to where the organization is going. Members of the organization come to feel empowered because an attractive vision of the future energizes and motivates as they come to identify with the future that the leader outlines. The vision itself derives from the leader's past experiences, an assessment of current strengths and weaknesses, and an appraisal of likely trends. Failure to articulate a vision will lead to lack of direction for the organization, and confusion and lack of self-confidence for members of the organization. But the vision must be effectively communicated throughout the organization.

The leader must persuade others of the vision's good sense and must ensure that it permeates the organization, for example by incorporating its key tenets into the organization's strategy and culture. Thus, the leader must create *meaning through communication*. Leaders must constantly reiterate the vision and its desirability. They are in the business of moulding the organization's understanding of itself so that the vision can be both accepted and made to work. Training may be used as a method for inculcating the new values which are necessary for gaining support for and understanding of the new vision, while the deployment of symbols which signal a change of direction may have a powerful effect. It will also be necessary to underpin the change of direction by altering the organization's structure in line with the vision and the attendant values. There would be little point in promulgating a vision of a more market-led and entrepreneurial organization if a cumbersome bureaucracy which is resistant to change is left intact.

The leader must create a climate of mutual *trust*, since without this commodity change will be viewed with suspicion and hence the vision will not mobilize and empower. Bennis and Nanus say that not only must the vision be 'clear, attractive, and attainable' (1985: 154), but also the leader must be seen as someone who is predictable and does not vacillate all the time. The leader's own actions must be consistent with the vision and its attendant values.

The fourth strategy identified by Bennis and Nanus is *deployment of self*. The leaders were good at knowing their strengths and weaknesses and using the former to good effect. They were constantly learning and reflecting on their experiences. Moreover, they encouraged members of the organization to learn through a number of schemes such as conducting experiments to examine the effects of possible changes, urging comparisons with other organizations, constantly monitoring environmental change, and instigating training programmes.

Vision is undoubtedly the fulcrum for Bennis and Nanus's consideration of leadership, while the main effect of leadership is to empower organizational members. Whereas management creates compliance, leadership creates empowerment. Where, if at all, does charisma figure in all this? Bennis and Nanus report that none of their interviewees mentioned charisma as a factor in their leadership and that only a few of them corresponded to the researchers' image of the divinely inspired charismatic leader. However, they make an interesting observation when they remark that 'charisma is the result of effective leadership, not the other way around' (1985: 224). This point recalls Weber's emphasis upon charismatic leaders being viewed as exceptional by their followers and is an issue to which we will return below.

This study suffers from the same kind of problem identified in relation to Tichy and Devanna's research, namely, that there is no comparison group of managers against whom the ninety leaders can be directly compared. There is a risk that one ends up glorifying the leader or transformational leader, without systematic attention to what management or transactional leadership comprises. As a result, there is a further risk that management or transactional leadership is treated in a somewhat stereotypical manner (or at worst caricatured) in an attempt to etch the distinguishing and often venerated features of leadership or transformational leadership. It is also slightly disconcerting that in both studies we have to rely to such a large degree on leaders' reports about themselves and their effects on their followers.

Kouzes and Posner on leadership

Kouzes and Posner (1987) distinguish between leaders and managers, whom they see as playing different roles. The former are associated with change and innovation; the latter with stability and control. Each is associated with different times: managers with periods of constancy; leaders with periods of turbulence. Both are needed, but leaders seem to merit special attention because they take us in new directions which are required by the newer circumstances of upheaval and change that confront the modern business organization. The precise nature of the connection between the ideas presented in their book and research which they have carried out is not entirely clear. Kouzes and Posner have developed two research instruments for investigating leadership. The Personal Best Questionnaire asks leaders to describe their 'personal best leadership experience'. They are then asked a number of open-ended questions about this experience. The leadership practices that are discussed in their book stem from an analysis of data deriving from this instrument which has been administered to a variety of managers. In-depth interviews have also been carried out with forty-two managers. From this questionnaire the Leadership Practices Inventory (LPI) was derived to tap subordinates' ratings of the extent to which their superiors exhibit the five leadership practices that were identified at the earlier stage in their work. There is also a version in which managers report on their own behaviour using the LPI. There are thirty items (six per leadership practice) which are statements about leader behaviour, and respondents have to answer how far the item applies to their superior (or to themselves if respondents are being asked about their own leader behaviour).

The five practices that were identified as contributing to successful leadership can now be examined. First, leaders *challenge the process*. They are constantly in search of new opportunities and are prepared to take risks and to experiment. They are both receptive to and a source of new ideas. Second, they *inspire a shared vision*. A vision for Kouzes and Posner is an image of the future which allows the leader to give a sense of direction to the organization and to provide ideals and a feeling of what is special about the organization. The vision itself derives from the leader's past experiences which are applied to an analysis of present circumstances. It is then necessary to attract others to the vision. An important component of this process will be the language within which the vision is couched, such as military metaphors ('to rally the troops') and a positive approach to the communication of the vision. Following research by Friedman et al. (1980), Kouzes and Posner suggest that charisma, in the form of a high level of non-verbal expressiveness (such as a lot of body movement, smiling, touching), can contribute to the effective communication of the vision.

The leader must *enable others to act*. This means that the leader has to promote cooperation and collaboration between people so that they will jointly implement the vision. To do this, cooperative goals and trust must be established. People will need to be empowered by removing impediments to a sense of powerlessness, such as rules and regulations and limited participation. Empowerment can be further enhanced by giving people tasks which are central to the vision, by allowing them autonomy, and by giving recognition for successes. Fourth, the successful leader *models the way*. The leader inculcates values that underpin the vision and must behave in ways that are consistent with the vision. He or she must also recognize that it is better to view the substantial organizational change that is required for installing a new vision as a series of 'small wins' rather than a single, all-embracing transformation. By breaking down change into small packets it comes to be seen as less overwhelming, and the confidence of organizational members can be built up through the recognition and celebration of small successes which are associated with the vision. Finally, the successful leader *encourages the heart* of organizational members to persist with the vision. This can take a number of forms such as exhibiting high expectations and rewarding individuals for success in a variety of ways. Kouzes and Posner recommend celebrating accomplishments whenever possible.

Posner and Kouzes (1990) report a study which shows that the five leadership practices measured by the LPI collectively explain 55 per cent of the variance in subordinates' assessments of their superiors' effectiveness. They also report a study which demonstrates that LPI scores can discriminate between successful and unsuccessful managers.

Issues in New Leadership theory and research

In this section, a number of questions that are generated by the New Leadership are examined. No claim is being made to suggest that the list is exhaustive: the questions simply represent this author's perspective on a number of issues that require more detailed attention than was feasible when considering the work of the different theorists and research programmes examined in this and the previous chapter. To a certain extent, the considerations that follow represent something of a precursor to the more critical stance taken in Chapter 7, since in many cases the issues to be explored reflect ambiguities, inconsistencies, or matters that require clarification in New Leadership theory and research.

Can people be trained in the New Leadership approach?

One area of potential controversy is whether New Leadership in any of its guises can be cultivated. The Howell and Frost (1989) experiment is interesting in this regard because professional actresses were trained to exhibit charismatic leadership. By contrast, the Avolio and Gibbons (1988) research, which was cited in Chapter 5, suggests that the opportunity for cultivating transformational leaders may be limited unless an attempt is made to develop individuals at an early juncture in their careers. Drawing on their research on a school superintendent in the USA, Roberts and Bradley (1988) conclude that the ability to develop charismatic leaders is substantially constrained by the situation in which leaders find themselves. Most writers who consider this issue recognize the limits to the development of New Leadership in individuals but suggest that there are areas where it can be cultivated.

Many authors observe that it is unlikely that *anyone* can become an exceptional leader. Kouzes and Posner reckon that at least 50 per cent of the variance in leadership ability is explained by genetic factors, so there may be ample room for developing leadership. Even though Bass has documented the personal traits that are associated with transformational leaders (Bass, 1985), he has developed a programme for training and developing transformational leadership. Indeed, he and Avolio received financial help to the tune of $1,396,691 to train and develop transformational leadership in 400 leaders from a variety of spheres.[1] Bass and Avolio (1990a) have proposed a number of strategies for promoting transformational leadership and the better aspects of transactional leadership. For example, there are training workshops of three to five days' duration, which are then followed up. Initially, leaders are given an explanation of the types of leadership involved and are given feedback on their MLQ scores, as rated by themselves and others. Areas for improvement can then be examined with the leaders, and the ways in which changes to behaviour can be implemented are discussed. The function of this stage is to create an appreciation that the development of leadership potential in oneself holds the key to developing the potential of others. Over the following months, leaders elaborate 'personal development goals and plans' (1990a: 259), which may include counselling, observation of other leaders, or attending specific workshops. The leader's development is assessed on a number of occasions through a number of possible strategies: observation, interviews with subordinates, and readministration of the MLQ. Bass and Avolio report two studies which demonstrate that this leadership training package has beneficial effects on leadership performance and on a range of subordinate outcomes, like productivity and absenteeism.

Bass and Avolio (1990a) also conduct development programmes for teams within organizations. These programmes adopt a broadly similar approach to the individual training sessions, but involve much closer relationships with the host organizations, coupled with such devices as off-site retreats. Bass and Avolio (1990b) also refer to training programmes for companies which are tailored to the specific needs and orientations of the companies concerned. These programmes entail fourteen modules, of which the first eight make up a basic workshop and the other six form an advanced workshop, usually three months later. The basic workshop has a similar content to the individual workshops described above. The aim of the advanced workshop is to allow trainees to assess their progress with their personal plans and to receive feedback on how their leadership is perceived (in terms of the MLQ) by peers and bosses. They are then introduced to new topics to further their leadership abilities, such as how to ehance their capacity to be intellectually stimulating and how to overcome organizational constraints. Towards the end of the programme, which is a module on inspirational leadership, a team of trainees work on an organizational simulation of a firm which has to be pointed towards expansion and create a vision which has to be sold to the board of directors in the form of a plenary session of co-trainees.

However, Bass clearly sees his framework as also having implications for such areas as selection and placement of managers. Individuals' MLQ scores can be employed as part of management assessment and selection programmes. Alternatively, individuals could be measured in terms of known personal correlates of transformational leadership factors. Thus, Bass suggests that since charismatic leaders 'are characterized by energy, self-confidence, determination, intellect, verbal skills, and strong ego ideals' (1990b: 26), these traits can be employed as part of firms' selection and placement activities.[2]

Conger and Kanungo (1988) propose that charismatic leadership can be developed by cultivating five competencies. First, leaders must be trained in 'critical evaluation and problem detection skills', so that they become sensitive to the kinds of context within which charismatic leadership can most readily take root, such as crisis situations. Second, 'visioning skills' can be fostered in a number of ways. They recommend courses in creative thinking to induce a capacity both to unlearn and to contemplate profound change. The Quick Environmental Scanning Technique (QUEST), recommended by Bennis and Nanus (1985), is also advocated. The sessions associated with this approach entail managers meeting in brainstorming groups in which they reflect on their company's environmental circumstances and move towards devising strategies for dealing with potential scope for change and with potential hazards. Third, communication skills for conveying a vision need to be honed by developing linguistic skills. Fourth, leaders must cultivate impression management skills which reinforce the bases of their charisma. Conger and Kanungo write: 'In order to present a charismatic image, they should be trained in four areas: modeling (the use of exemplary behavior), appearance, body language, and verbal skills' (1988: 317). Finally, empowering skills need to be fostered in order to enable members of the organization to bring the leader's mission to fruition. Empowerment can be enhanced through a variety of techniques: communicating high performance expectations; improving participation in decision-making; divesting subordinates of the constraints imposed by bureaucratic arrangements (such as an excessive emphasis upon rules, routine and regulations); setting meaningful goals; and backing up the foregoing by appropriate reward systems.

Bennis and Nanus (1985) do not allocate much space to training, except to decry much conventional management education and to recommend greater attention to *leadership* education. They argue that the former encourages excessively linear thinking and is focused upon situations that are stable and simple, which are not appropriate to the requirements of leadership in today's organizations. This point is echoed by Morgan (1988a) who argues that conventional MBAs tend to create a bureaucratic mentality that is inimical to the contemplation of radical alternatives. Taking a case study of a company referred to as Eagle Smelting, he shows how MBA students typically diagnose the firm's problems in terms of factors which are important but unlikely to provide a springboard for fundamental change. By encouraging them to consider alternative ways of examining the company's problems, an appreciation of the prerequisites for organizational transformation can be instilled.

While there is an acknowledgement that there can be barriers to the capacity of individuals to be trained in the New Leadership such as personal abilities and experiences, the majority of writers seem to take the view that it is possible to develop the necessary skills. There is also a consensus that such training should be viewed as essentially different in orientation from conventional management training contexts, which are appropriate for a different set of concerns.

Do the ideas associated with the New Leadership apply just to the top of the organization?

It is easy to develop an impression that the New Leadership is to do with leaders at the very apex of the organization, such as CEOs, company presidents and so on. Two factors conspire to provide this impression. First, the idea of vision that the leader is supposed to impress upon the organization is something that is normally perceived as the prerogative of the most senior individuals in an organization. Second, the majority of the studies conducted on New Leadership have tended to focus upon leaders at the very top of the organization and to employ such leaders to illustrate the ideas that are being proposed. The leaders studied by Bennis and Nanus (1985), Conger (1989) and Tichy and Devanna (1990), for example, were all at the very apex of their organizations. A similar point could also be made about the leaders of DSOs studied by Biggart (1989). Also, the leaders who are invariably used to illustrate the New Leadership – Watson Senior of IBM, Iacocca, Welch, Jobs – are individuals who are or were at the helm of the organization as a whole. The language of the New Leadership writers tends to underscore this impression with reference to the transformation of the organization, changing the organizational culture, supplying the organization with a new set of values, and so on.

It may appear surprising, therefore, that the majority of these writers subscribe to the view that the New Leadership can and should be disseminated throughout the organization, and at the very least should touch a company's middle managers. Tichy and Devanna write:

> Even though most of what is written about transformational leadership focuses at the top of the organization, we feel that the challenge is for transformational leadership at all levels in an organization. (1990: xiv)

Bennis and Nanus (1985: 224) similarly note that they may have inadvertently perpetuated the view that the kind of leadership that they advocate exists only at the top of the organization because of their focus upon very senior leaders. They write that this was not their intention.

Even when top leaders are not the focus of attention, there tends to be an emphasis upon seniority. As an example of a leader (as against a manager), Kotter (1990) provides such figures as Jim Adamson who, as general manager of a problem National Cash Register plant in Dundee, gradually transformed the plant into a successful enterprise in large part through the implementation of his vision that it could become a world leader in the production of automatic teller machines through an emphasis upon quality and reliability (attributes that had previously been emphatically absent from the plant's products). Another is Lou Gerstner, who moved from McKinsey to become executive vice-president in 1978 (and a year later president) of the Travel Related Services division of American Express and who, following strategy meetings, formulated a vision 'of a dynamic and growing enterprise that was economically prosperous' (Kotter, 1990: 41). While these leaders are not in the same position of seniority as figures like Iacocca or Welch, they nonetheless have considerable authority and autonomy within their spheres, and it is by no means irrelevant that each was called in to deal with segments of large companies that were underperforming. Consequently, even when top leaders have not been the focus of attention, the leaders concerned have often been prominent individuals with a good deal of seniority and often autonomy.

Although Bass tends to employ illustrations of very senior or prominent leaders, he clearly regards transformational leadership as fairly widely distributed and hence not an exclusive preserve of the few. This tendency is evident in his belief that transformational leadership can be fostered at a variety of levels in an organization and in his use of the MLQ, which creates a sense of transformational leadership being a set of dimensions of leader behaviour that are spread throughout the organization, albeit differentially.

With the exception of writers like Bass, there is a tendency to emphasize top executives in the literature on the New Leadership in business and other complex organizations. In part, this occurs because it is easier to see their role in relation to the process of setting direction for the organization as a whole (or a division of it) at the upper echelons. It is also possible that many of the illustrations are of leaders who have implemented successful turnarounds and who are therefore more prepared to conspire in publicizing the view that the success was due to them. As such, the emphasis upon the top layer of organizations may have strong affinities with Meindl's (1989) suggestion that the preoccupation with transformational leadership can be considered hyper-romanticism. Equally, since there is a distinct tendency to highlight the upper reaches of organizations, the suggestion that the New Leadership is not the exclusive preserve of a few distinguished individuals has to be taken on trust, since little or no evidence to confirm this proposition is provided.

Is the New Leadership really different from the old leadership?

Table 1.1 implies that the various approaches that can be subsumed under the rubric 'New Leadership' represent a substantial change in the basic approach to the understanding of leadership. Sashkin and Burke (1990), for example, suggest that what we are witnessing is no less than a paradigm shift, a term which derives from Kuhn's (1970) examination of scientific revolutions. How accurate is the notion that the New Leadership approaches constitute a totally different approach? After all, charismatic, transformational or visionary leadership could be construed as different leadership styles in the manner of the Ohio State or path-goal studies.

It is probably not too melodramatic to treat the New Leadership as a totally new approach. There is much greater attention paid to the issue of exactly what leadership is than in the earlier approaches, although there is still probably an excessive tendency to emphasize designated leaders. Second, the leitmotif of the New Leadership writers – vision – was not evident among the earlier approaches and represents something more than merely a form of leader behaviour. Third, the idea that earlier approaches were solely concerned with management or transactional leadership, which rarely motivate to the same degree as leadership or transformational leadership, suggests that the New Leadership writers are sailing in previously uncharted waters. Fourth, the New Leadership writers view leadership as a complex amalgam of personal and behavioural factors, thereby superseding the old question of whether leadership is a matter of traits or behaviour that can be learned. Fifth, it has been suggested that New Leadership writers employ different dependent variables from those found in old leadership research. House et al. have asserted:

> [In] contrast to transactional theories, which focus on the effects of leader behaviors on follower cognitions, motivation, and performance, charismatic or transformational leadership theories take as their dependent variables followers' emotional responses to work-related stimuli, as well as their values, self-esteem, trust and confidence in the leader, and motivation to perform above and beyond the call of duty. (1988: 100)

Sixth, there is widespread use of qualitative case studies; these were rarely used in research from the previous eras, which was rooted in the tradition of quantitative research.[3]

However, following on from the last point, when New Leadership research is quantitative, as in the work of Bass and of Howell and Frost, it begins to take on the appearance of older leadership approaches. One could be forgiven for interpreting the Howell and Frost research as an experiment which manipulates three different leadership styles. It may be that if qualitative studies drawing on New Leadership ideas gradually give way to quantitative research, a fairly common development in research fields in the social sciences, the distinctiveness of the new approaches will become less apparent. Also, it is striking that, with the exception of the notion of extra effort, the dependent variables typically examined in Bass's MLQ-based research and in other quantitative studies of the New Leadership are very similar to those usually employed in relation to the Ohio and path-goal studies. The same could also be said of the Howell and Frost experiment. It may be that quantitative studies of leadership are restricted in terms of the range of dependent variables that lend themselves to being measured.

Is New Leadership sufficient?

Writers differ somewhat regarding the importance of, for example, trans-actional leadership and management, for organizations. Bass's work makes it clear that transactional leadership is an essential aspect of any leader's job, although the results cited earlier suggest that contingent reward behaviour is more likely than management-by-exception to produce favourable outcomes. Hickman (1990) and Kotter (1990) both extol the virtues of leadership, but see management as an essential aspect of organizational functioning. As Kotter puts it: 'Any combination other than strong management and strong leadership has the potential for producing highly unsatisfactory results' (1990: 7). Likewise, Nadler and Tushman (1990) argue that charismatic leadership is not sufficient on its own and that it must be complemented by instrumental leadership. This term, as Nadler and Tushman recognize, has been used in the context of path-goal theory (see Chapter 1), but their use of it seems somewhat broader. For them, instrumental leadership involves: structuring (building teams, setting goals, defining responsibilities); controlling (monitoring, assessing performance); and rewarding (administering rewards and punish-ments in response to performance levels). Without the support of instrumental leadership, the radical change that charismatic leadership can engender may run into the sand, a theme that can also be found in both Hickman's and Kotter's expositions of the management versus leadership themes.

Bolman and Deal (1991) have adopted a somewhat different approach to this issue but one which is broadly in sympathy with the views expressed in the previous paragraph. They use the term 'symbolic leadership' to refer to an approach to leadership that is broadly similar to the New Leadership. It involves the deployment of symbols and stories to disseminate a vision that engenders loyalty among members of the organization and others. However, they also distinguish three other types of leadership: structural leader-ship, which is preoccupied with organizational design; human resource leadership, which is oriented to providing support for employees; and political leadership, which involves having a grasp of political realities both within and outside the organization and how these can be made to work for the benefit of the organization. Structural and human resource leadership seem to overlap substantially with old leadership conceptions (Tables 5.1 and 5.2), while political leadership appears to be independent of the old/New Leadership pairings. Each approach to leadership is depicted as a 'frame', that is, a framework within which organizational reality is interpreted. Each form of leadership has its disadvantages and advantages, so Bolman and Deal recommend multiframe thinking, whereby leaders take a broader view of organizations and from a number of perspectives. The implication of these ideas is also that the New Leadership, in the form of symbolic leadership, is not sufficient on its own.

On the other hand, Bennis and Nanus are very dismissive of individuals who function more or less exclusively as managers. This stance has been carried forward into Bennis's more recent work, where he proposes that an important difference between leaders and managers is that the former 'master the context' whereas the latter 'surrender to it' (Bennis, 1989: 44). Tichy and Devanna seem to decry transactional leadership, seeing it as a relic of 'an earlier era of expanding markets and nonexistent competition' (1990: xii), whereas transformational leadership is what is needed for the new environmental conditions. Kouzes and Posner (1987) say that we need both managers and leaders, but virtually the whole book is on the latter and there is only the barest outline of where management fits into the picture. Their emphasis strongly suggests that they see leaders as far more important than managers.

There is a lack of clarity about whether old and new forms of leader behaviour can or should be exhibited by the same people. Can someone be both a manager and a leader or do people have different proclivities which propel them in one direction or another? If the latter were the case, then there might be limited advantage to be gained from training managers in behaviour associated with the New Leadership. After all, if management and transactional leadership are both needed, as at least some writers suggest, and if some people are inclined to be managers rather than leaders, the grounds for training some individuals to foster New Leadership practices may be pointless. However, as suggested in Chapter 5, writers vary considerably over whether they see management or transactional leadership and leadership or transformational leadership as different types of person (for example, Zaleznik; Bennis and Nanus) or as activities which need to be displayed jointly, albeit not in equal measure (for example, Bass; Hickman; Kotter).

Overview

If we review the ideas and research that have been explored in this and the previous chapter, we find that there are a number of common themes. First, *vision* is central to all of the writers that have been mentioned. The theme of vision can also be found among writers who refer to 'visionary leadership' (for example, Sashkin, 1988; Sashkin and Burke, 1990; Westley and Mintzberg, 1989), as well as various other contributors to work on management and leadership issues (for example, Morgan 1988b; Levinson and Rosenthal, 1984; Gluck, 1984). Not all writers conceive of vision in exactly the same way. In some cases, it is barely distinguishable from kindred terms like goal and mission (for example, Bennis and Nanus, 1985), whereas other writers see a clear difference between such terms. Kotter (1990), for example, views goals as products of visions. Writers also differ in the character of visions: Kouzes and Posner (1987) suggest that vision has a pronounced element of intuition, whereas for Bennis and Nanus it is much more rational, involving a preparedness to assemble and reflect on a wealth of diverse information, in which intuition plays a more minor role.

Second, the importance of *communicating the vision*, so that it is fully understood and can be a focus for people's commitment, is mentioned by most writers. The vision will be useless if it is not shared with others. A number of factors are seen as playing an important part in the vision's dissemination. Kouzes and Posner, and Tichy and Devanna, refer to education and training as providing dissemination mechanisms. Conger, and Kouzes and Posner, mention the manner in which the vision is communicated as crucial, such as the use of rhetorical strategies like metaphor in conveying ideas. The leader can also signal the vision through actions which reinforce its basic premises. Kouzes and Posner's idea of celebrating small successes is an illustration of the kind of symbolic leadership in which the leader must engage in order to get the ideas behind the vision across. John Thorbeck describes a number of such celebrations when he was CEO at G.H. Bass & Co., a US shoe manufacturer. In order to get across his initially rather implicit vision of a more market-oriented company, he 'focused hard on little victories . . . [like] a report from sales that a particular account had accepted the $100 shoes, even if they'd taken only a hundred pairs' (Thorbeck, 1991: 56).

Third, many of the writers observe that *empowerment* of organizational members is often enhanced by the inculcation of a vision, but there is less agreement about how it materializes. Conger views empowerment as an almost inevitable consequence of charismatic leadership. This suggestion makes sense in the light of the fact that Conger's focus is on charismatic leadership, which can be depicted as an exchange relationship in which followers gain a greater sense of power (see Chapter 3). However, in organizations there may be profound impediments to the employee's sense of empowerment in the form of structures that inhibit autonomy (Kanter, 1979), so that it may be inadvisable to depict empowerment as a direct consequence of New Leadership practices and of vision in particular. By contrast, other writers like Kouzes and Posner imply that empowerment is something that must be facilitated in order for the vision to come to fruition.

Fourth, the role of the leader in relation to *organizational culture* occasionally appears as a theme, usually in connection with the idea that the leader has to create a culture that is consistent with the vision and which will therefore facilitate its broad acceptance. This notion is especially visible in Peters and Waterman (1982) and Tichy and Devanna (1990). Similarly, a number of writers refer to the need to *change organizational structures* in line with the vision. A common theme in this connection is that in order to pursue a vision of a more competitive company, bureaucracy will have to be dismantled, and greater autonomy given to and fewer restrictions placed on business lines, so that a more entrepreneurial spirit may be engendered and greater empowerment fostered. This idea lies behind many of the changes that Welch has sought to inaugurate at GE (see Box 5.3).

Fifth, the capacity of leaders to implement their visions will be impaired if they do not have the *trust* of those with whom they work. This theme is especially pronounced in Bennis and Nanus's book, but is implicit in some other works. Following Howell's (1988) distinction between personalized and socialized charismatic leaders, we might anticipate that the former will be less likely than the latter to achieve the levels of trust that are necessary to implement radical change. Leaders who fail to lead by example when projecting their vision to others are also less likely to achieve the levels of trust that are required. Also, as Bennis and Nanus suggest, the leader needs to be predictable. Too many changes, for example, can destroy that kind of trust. When David Kearns, CEO at Xerox for most of the 1980s, sought to inject a new vision of a focus on quality in order to regain market share that had been lost to the Japanese, he had to overcome a belief among employees that this was the latest 'flavor of the month' to get them out of their difficulties, and that therefore it would fade from the scene with little or no impact on them or the company's problems (Jacobson and Hillkirk, 1986). In the end Kearns was successful, but such cynicism, which is indicative of an absence of trust, can be very damaging to the leader's quest for the implementation of a vision.

In a sense, vision is pivotal to all of these themes because they represent factors which may obstruct the capacity of leaders to implement their visions. General Motors can be employed as an illustration of this point. During the 1980s, with Roger Smith as chairman, the company was portrayed by many commentators as lacking a clear direction. Miller (1990), for example, describes it as a 'drifter' during this period. But this tendency cannot be attributed directly to an absence of vision on Smith's part, because he is often described as a visionary executive (for example, M. Keller, 1989; Moore, 1988). Instead, it has been suggested that he failed to communicate his vision of a transformed company capable of competing at the start of 2000. As M. Keller has put it: 'His loner's stance reflects an attitude that "*I* have the vision, *you* do the work"' (1989: 64). He failed to make great inroads into the elimination of the corporate bureaucracy, so that the organizational structure acted as a hindrance to the implementation of his vision. He also moved on too many fronts too quickly – 'new models, new plants, and new organizations' (Moore, 1988) – so that not only did the broad vision lack concrete direction, but also employees had little trust in the changes that were being heaped on them. These factors only constitute part of the problematic picture that the company presented to some analysts at the end of the 1980s, but it does help the appreciation of the significance of some of the factors that have been covered in this section.

The position of charisma in relation to the various conceptions of New Leadership varies greatly from virtual insignificance (for example, Kotter; Tichy and Devanna), in spite of the presence of common themes, to a central focus (for example, Conger; Howell and Frost). Bass's research occupies an intermediate position.

In this section, some possible problems with the New Leadership approach were becoming apparent. This critical spirit will be an emphasis in the next chapter.

Notes

1 Reported in *Academy of Management News*, vol. 20, no. 2 (March), 1990.

2 Interestingly, these same words are employed in Bass and Avolio (1990a: 268) to describe the personal characteristics of *transformational* leaders.

3 The distinction between quantitative and qualitative research has been explored in Bryman (1988).

7
The New Leadership and Charisma: an Evaluation

Criticisms of the literature on the New Leadership and charismatic leadership in particular have been made on a number of occasions in this book, but the purpose of this chapter is to concentrate on a critical assessment of many core themes. We will also return to the specific theme of charismatic leadership for an examination of the differences between it and other manifestations of the New Leadership and for an assessment of what an emphasis on charisma has to offer. The New Leadership seems to have become established as a new orthodoxy, and so it is timely to launch such an evaluation, though other writers have also begun to infuse a critical element into their discussions (for example, Conger, 1989: Chapter 8; Hogan et al., 1990; Murphy, 1988). Nor are management practitioners themselves always convinced of the New Leadership's tenets. Harvey-Jones, formerly of ICI and one of the twelve transformational leaders in Tichy and Devanna's (1990) study, has commented: 'I do not believe in the myth of the great leader who can suddenly engender in his people a vision and lead them to an entirely new world. I believe that reality is more traumatic and demanding' (1991: 35).

An evaluation of the New Leadership

In this section, the chief emphasis will be upon the New Leadership as a whole. Inevitably, this will involve making incursions into charismatic leadership, but as far as possible the specific evaluation of the literature on charismatic leadership in business organizations will be postponed until the next section.

Is vision good for organizations?

It is very important that vision is a central theme in the approaches associated with the New Leadership. Vision is somewhat less prominent in Bass's (1985; 1990b) quantitative research on transformational leadership than it is in the work of other authors. In the bulk of theory and research concerned with the New Leadership, the true leaders or the leaders who are most likely to be effective are those who envision an image of the future for their organizations and relentlessly persevere with this mental picture, often in the face of considerable resistance. Such leaders are individuals who deal in values in that an important component of the process of creating a vision is one of instilling new principles which will both guide organizational members to the new future that the vision reflects and mobilize their energies behind the new way forward. The leader facilitates the process by creating a climate of trust which will help the vision to gain acceptance, by empowering people so that they have the opportunity to make the vision work for themselves, and by tirelessly reiterating the vision and its underlying values through as many media as possible within the organization. The leader comes across as an 'environment watcher' who makes judgements about environmental trends and orients his or her vision to feelings about likely developments. Organizational structures and culture are then dovetailed with the vision, while plans, budgets, strategies and so on are reflections of that vision. However one looks at it, vision is a fulcrum around which the activities of the new leader revolve.

But is it sufficient just to have a vision, or does the content of the vision matter? Clearly, leaders can get things wrong. Conger (1989) cites the case of Robert Lipp, the former president of Chemical Bank in the USA, whose vision of a population of individuals who bank at home floundered when there was a poor take-up of the facility. Home banking did not appeal because people did not like the initial costs, were not convinced that writing a cheque to pay a bill was all that onerous, and were disinclined to lose the period between writing a cheque and its being cashed at the bank. Although it seems an obvious point, the content of a vision will have a profound influence upon the leader's success. It is not simply the creation and dissemination of a vision that have been responsible for some of the success stories that have been encountered, but the content of the vision as well. Kotter (1990) has proposed that a good vision is one which is both desirable and feasible. To be desirable, the vision must benefit such groups as customers, shareholders and employees. A realistic vision is one which can simply be shown to stand a chance of success. Lipp's vision seems to have failed the test of desirability from the point of view of customers, though it was feasible in terms of the available technology. However, it is difficult to anticipate the degree to which visions are desirable, although the foregoing example points to the desirability of prior research.

It is noticeable that the more striking visions that have been examined often entail a strong market orientation, combining a concern for customers with an acute awareness of competitors, or the inculcation of an entrepreneurial spirit through the creation of relatively autonomous business lines within the organization (for example, Welch and Carlzon; see also Sabin, Box 7.1). Sometimes elements of both approaches within a single vision can be discerned. But it may well be that the key factor is that these components of the vision were the critical factor and not the mere fact of a vision. By contrast, General Motors in the late 1970s and in the 1980s has been characterized as insensitive to the significance of foreign competition, insensitive to its customers' needs, and exhibiting a cumbersome bureaucracy that stifled initiative (Miller, 1990; Moore, 1988). Thus, much more significant in many instances than the mere possession of a vision is the question of whether that vision points the company in a particular direction that is in tune with the times. This point may appear trite, but in view of the prominence of vision in much of the leadership literature, it seems to require explicit expression.

BOX 7.1   Paul Sabin: KCC

Paul Sabin has been chief executive of KCC (formerly Kent County Council) since 1986. It may seem perverse to use him as an illustration in the context of a discussion of business organizations, but in fact he is highly appropriate, for Sabin's vision was of a local government organization that was also a business organization. Consequently, the changes that he has inaugurated have resulted in an organization with a strong business orientation. For example, its eighteen departments are referred to as businesses and their heads as business managers. When he arrived he found the traditional local government bureaucracy, replete with formalized procedures, a predilection for consensus management, and a reactive approach to its environment, but a highly committed professional staff. Sabin set about replacing this framework with a managerial approach that created a greater inclination to take risks and a more pronounced emphasis on individual accountability in order to get closer to customers (note the terminology – not *clients*). He got many of these ideas across through a video entitled *Making Kent a Better Place*. To change the culture in order to facilitate the implementation of the vision, staff were brought together in groups to explain the changes. In addition, managers were trained in the operation of resources. He replaced many members of the managerial team with people who were more in tune with his thinking, that is, managers with a more pronounced entrepreneurial inclination. Sabin believes that the organization has become more effective and efficient, and feels that this view is shared by KCC's elected members.

Source: Hegarty, 1991

One possible consequence of vision is that it turns into obsession and as a result the leader's and others' judgement is adversely affected. A number of writers have noted that decision-makers often escalate their commitment to chosen lines of action in spite of evidence that their initiatives are not working (for example, Staw, 1976; Staw and Ross, 1987). This tendency might be all the more likely to occur when the leader is in the midst of working through initiatives associated with a deeply held vision which is plainly not working. If the leader has convinced others of the virtue of his or her vision, or if they are reluctant to go against the leader out of either personal affection or fear (Janis, 1972), the potential for the vision going increasingly sour is considerable.

Equally, if a vision is accompanied by inappropriate management and leadership practices, it may well founder. This recalls the suggestion that a number of writers have made to the effect that leadership needs to be accompanied by management (for example, Kotter, 1990) or that charismatic leadership needs to be tempered by instrumental leadership (Nadler and Tushman, 1990). Such views were encountered in Chapters 5 and 6. Jim Dutt's vision as chairman of Beatrice Foods was of a 'tautly run, tightly focused multinational that would be a world leader in food and consumer products' (Dreyfack, 1985: 20) which he pursued with quasi-religious zeal. However, in 1985 he was ousted just six years after he became chairman, but not because his vision was viewed as wrong; both the board and a stock analyst are cited by Dreyfack (1985) as viewing it as fundamentally correct. Instead, his authoritarian and punitive approach to handling his managers led to a huge drop in morale and a large number of departures, both of which were seen as extremely detrimental to the company's position.

Thus, a preoccupation with a vision may engender a loss of grip on other aspects of organizational reality. This seems to have occurred in the cases of Burr and Jobs, whose single-minded visions were associated with a lack of concern for organizational issues which loomed larger and larger as their respective companies grew at a very rapid rate. This point recalls the issue raised in the previous chapter where the question of whether New Leadership on its own is sufficient. In Jobs's case, the decision to bring in Sculley to deal with organizational and managerial matters was only partially successful from his point of view, since he did not like the actions that were taken and eventually left. In Burr's case, the preoccupation with growth in order to realize his vision engendered a lack of attention to the management and organization of the company which led to its downfall. Burr became increasingly unable to brook dissent, and as the People Express flew into a period of greater turbulence, its flat hierarchy coupled with its innovative human resources strategy began to dissipate. It was clear that in spite of the participative climate that Burr had sought to create, he saw his vision as paramount. Rhodes (1984: 51) quotes him as saying: 'If you don't agree with that direction . . . you shouldn't be here.' By the end of the following year, it was reported that Burr's style had become increasingly dictatorial and those who dared to question him ended up either leaving or being fired. Byrne (1985: 59) quotes a former top executive as saying:

> Employees aren't allowed to ask questions anymore. Fear pervades the place. The sense is you don't cross Burr. It's become a one-man show, and it wasn't like that before.

In November 1984, Burr fired Lori Dubose, a managing officer who had been highly instrumental in developing People's human resources approach, for challenging and questioning him on certain key issues (Byrne, 1985).

It would be pointless to condemn all visions and their exponents simply because of extremes like this, but equally the rosy picture that is sometimes presented of visionary leaders is also to be questioned. The management literature is notorious for its predilection for fads and fashions which offer nostrums for complex problems. They have all contained germs of truth, but they have never been panaceas. Vision is no different.

One of the problems with the proliferation of success stories about individuals like Iacocca and Jobs's early years at Apple is that this nascent hagiography does not tell us enough about the circumstances associated with failure. The impression could easily be gleaned that simply being a manager or transactional leader, and therefore not having vision, is enough to guarantee failure, when in fact visionary leaders have probably made a fair contribution to organizational failure.

What about the team?

It would be easy to gain an impression from the New Leadership theory and research of a cadre of outstanding individuals who single-handedly invent innovative new companies or turn ailing ones around by dint of their vision. One of the reasons for the interest in charisma is precisely that it seems to fit this focus on the individual leader. The business hagiography associated with figures like Iacocca and Carlzon perpetuates this impression since they are often willing conspirators in conveying a sense of their special role. However, there is a risk that the New Leadership may actually overstate the importance of individual leaders. There *is* a recognition of the role of teams in effecting change. The leader is depicted as needing to collect like-minded individuals who will help to implement his/her vision. This process can be seen with the school superintendent who was referred to in Chapter 4 as well as with Paul Sabin of KCC (see Box 7.1). Iacocca also recognized the need to build a team: he recruited Greenwald from Ford to set up much-needed financial controls at Chrysler; he promoted Sperlich to take charge of product planning; he recruited Laux to take over sales and marketing; Matthias, a former Ford employee, was brought out of retirement to enhance quality; and so on. Reich (1987) implies that as a result there may be a tendency to exaggerate Iacocca's role and that the turnaround at Chrysler is mistakenly attributed to him alone.[1] However, this kind of point is not the reason for raising issues about the role of teams; in any case, it would not be unreasonable to argue that Iacocca's influence was paramount since it was he who welded together a team for the daunting task ahead.

Instead, the chief purpose of this section is to suggest that teams can be instrumental in turnarounds in a manner that is to a significant degree independent of a focal leader. Greiner and Bhambri (1989) use a case study of a pseudonymously named US distributor of liquefied propane gas – Mega – which shows how the kind of organizational transformation that is often attributed to individual leaders may be the product of a broader constituency of executives. The chairman of Mega's holding company – Alpha Industries – was dissatisfied with its performance and recruited a new CEO who is referred to as Tom Rice. Rice took a number of initial steps to ease some of Mega's immediate difficulties, but he also initiated some longer-term steps. Following the advice of a consultant, Rice took his top management team off to a retreat to discuss strategy and other issues. The executives formed subgroups and reported back with surprisingly similar views which resemble a vision for the company:

> Both groups agreed that Mega should concentrate exclusively on the propane industry, become more marketing-oriented, make propane-related acquisitions, and set high financial goals. Their analysis had determined that despite being in a mature industry, there was still 'room for Mega to clean up'. (1989: 73)

Rice encouraged the team to move towards a consensus over and a commitment towards the new strategy, and in the process they became empowered. Further retreats followed. At the second, a strategy statement was finalized:

> Mega is a leading marketer and distributor of LPG and related services. We set aggressive financial goals and achieve growth through market development and acquisitions. Our people establish a competitive advantage in selected market segments through a unified effort that demands:
>
> 1   a strong marketing orientation
> 2   high standards of safety
> 3   outstanding service 'before our customers need us'. (1989: 74)

Subsequently, a new organizational structure was created to blend with this vision and the strategic direction that the company was taking. The vision was then successfully transmitted to Mega's middle managers who exhibited 'a sustained burst of energy and activity' (1989: 79).

This case study is striking because the turnaround cannot be solely attributed to the new CEO. It was not *his* vision that led to a change in the company's fortunes; his influence was far more indirect in that he acted mainly as a catalyst and an enabler. It was the team that was responsible for what happened and, perhaps because of this, their enthusiasm was considerable. Nor is this an isolated instance. Child and Smith's (1987) examination of organizational transformation at Cadbury does not convey the impression of a single individual acting as the motor of change. Their study shows how, over a period of many years, Cadbury moved further and further away from the paternalism and organizational practices associated with its Quaker past and towards the 'Mars model', which is much more in tune with contemporary business methods. As with so many of the cases that have been encountered, the stimulus for organizational transformation derived from a sharp deterioration in performance (in the 1970s) following increased competition. The impression that one gleans from Child and Smith's account is that the impetus for change did not stem from a single individual. Instead, there appears to have developed a common perspective among a number of key actors at Cadbury who were able to envision new directions which allowed them to break out of ways of operating that were both peculiar to the company and pervaded the sector as a whole. The company's deteriorating financial position lent legitimacy to the prospective change advocates. These individuals, who were all very senior figures in the company, were in a position to appreciate the need for change and the directions it should take because they had prior experience as change agents or were in touch with other organizations which provided models for new ways of thinking about Cadbury and its environment. By virtue of their position power and the successful creation of a feeling that change was urgently needed, they both created and pushed through a vision of a rationalized, decentralized and more competitive organization. They did employ symbols to effect a gradual reorientation among company employees (such as through catch phrases which crystallized the change of direction), but they were not adverse to pushing change through by dint of their positions or offering rewards for acceptance of changes. In the end, the transformation proceeded in a relatively trouble-free way.

In both of these cases, we see the team as the chief fount of the kind of change that is normally attributed to transformational or visionary leaders. Particular actors may have had a special role in galvanizing the team, as in the Mega case, but it would be spurious to see dramatic turnarounds in fortune as originating in such persons. While writers on the New Leadership fully recognize the importance of building teams to implement change and needing to work through others, it is always the leader who resides at the centre of their thinking. All that is being said here is that the role of such leaders is easily prone to exaggeration and that the position of teams in creating visions and implementing organizational transformations should not be underestimated.

Problems with an emphasis on top executives

It was observed in the previous chapter that there is a tendency for many New Leadership writers to emphasize senior leaders in the organization. This tendency is much less apparent in the quantitative investigations (for example, Bass; Howell and Frost), but in spite of protestations to the contrary, writers on transformational or charismatic leadership have tended to focus on the apex of the organizational hierarchy. As we have noted, either the leaders studied by such writers have been senior leaders or there has been a tendency to use well-known figures as illustrations, and these are usually senior individuals. In taking leaders like Jobs, Burr, Iacocca and so on to illustrate many points, the present book could be viewed as sharing in this tendency. However, in the absence of well-documented case studies of less prominent figures who exhibit the kinds of behaviour pattern associated with the New Leadership, this tendency is likely to continue.

It is also worthwhile examining whether it is feasible for an organization to contain a plethora of transformational or charismatic leaders. For all the talk of empowering subordinates or converting followers into leaders, very little serious discussion seems to have arisen about how an organization would be pulled together if it had many leaders pursuing their personal visions. It has already been shown that Burr was not inclined to brook competing views, and one would guess that few of the other leaders that have been discussed in this and the previous two chapters would easily embrace the tumult that could be involved. Carlzon (1987: 37, 69) clearly sees the vision and strategy of an organization as being the concerns of a company's most senior leaders, although they may draw on ideas from many levels. By contrast, Peters and Austin (1985: 287) are enthusiastic about the fact that they often find 'pockets of excellence' in even poorly run companies. This occurs typically when there is a visionary leader running a plant, restaurant, department or whatever. These pockets can sometimes be held up as models for other spheres of the organization. However, whether an organization can tolerate a profusion of visions is questionable, although some organizations can probably do so better than others. One need only look to the difficulties John DeLorean encountered at General Motors (GM) as a result of his predisposition to doing things differently from the manner prescribed by the dominant culture to gain an insight into the problems that a vision which clashes with the prevailing ways of operating can engender (Martin and Siehl, 1983). DeLorean ridiculed many of the core values, and in his division a counterculture emerged in contradistinction to the dominant culture's emphases (such as the GM preference for loyalty and deference to authority). In the end, DeLorean left GM to found his own company. Of course, vision and culture should not be equated, although the latter invariably follows on from the former, but this illustration gives an insight into the difficulty of sustaining enclaves of non-conformity. It might be argued that there is a need to distinguish the 'master' vision of an organization (or in a large organization, of each of its major divisions) from the 'secondary' visions that might arise in various quarters. However, this is a rather diluted portrayal of vision and would be difficult to distinguish from goals and aims. Parenthetically, it is worth observing that precisely because vision is often depicted as setting the direction of the organization, it is becoming increasingly difficult to distinguish it from strategy. The use of the term 'strategic vision' (for example, Westley and Mintzberg, 1988) is likely to reinforce this tendency. Because of this level of analysis in the New Leadership literature it is becoming increasingly difficult to know where leadership theory and research finishes and strategic management theory and research starts.

If the New Leadership does relate better to the apex of the organizational hierarchy, it might legitimately be questioned what it has to offer the many people in organizations who occupy positions in which they are responsible for motivating and directing the work of others. It has been observed that earlier approaches to leadership concentrated too much on leadership *in* organizations and too little on leadership *of* organizations (Bryman, 1986; Dubin, 1979). It would be ironic if the New Leadership suffered from the opposite problem: strong on leadership *of* organizations, but weak on leadership *in* organizations. In fact, there is a risk that the New Leadership would not even view the activities of supervisors and foremen as leadership, in that for some writers the more mundane tasks that such personnel carry out might be treated as 'management'. The quantitative work of Bass and of Howell and Frost is less open to this charge, but this is probably due to the fact that the visionary responsibilities of transformational leaders in their research is much less prominent than it is in the more discursive and qualitative investigations that have been examined. Perhaps what is needed is a language that spans all levels of the organizational hierarchy, or for many New

Leadership writers to be more convincing in their claim that transformational leadership can occur at any level.

Lack of situational analysis

One of the most surprising features of the New Leadership is that it heralds a return to the 'one best way' approach to thinking about leadership that was characteristic of most trait and style research. The various contingency approaches to leadership that emerged in the late 1960s and early 1970s participated in a general trend in organization theory towards an emphasis on the need to embrace situational exigencies. During this period, leadership researchers took it as axiomatic that it was necessary to examine the situational factors which might condition the effectiveness (and hence appropriateness) of particular leadership styles. While the contingency perspective undoubtedly had fallen into disfavour in many quarters by the early 1980s, this was not due to a conviction that contingency approaches to leadership were misguided in principle. Instead, the lack of consistent evidence, the atheoretical nature of much research, and the ambiguous implications of some of the contingency approaches for developing leaders contributed to its unpopularity. During the 1980s, there was something of a vacuum in that a number of theoretical approaches competed for attention (see the volumes edited by Hunt et al., 1982; 1987). It was in this context that the New Leadership emerged as a focus for a large number of writers, though a good deal of theory and research in the field is carried out independently of the New Leadership. However, the chief point that is being made at this juncture is that the general principle associated with contingency approaches, namely that there is no one best way of leading, met with broad support and was never specifically rejected.

Nonetheless, most of the New Leadership theory and research smacks of 'one best way' thinking. In large part, this tendency can be attributed to the Peters and Waterman (1982) 'excellence' mode of presenting ideas which prompted a great deal of the interest in transformational leaders with vision. As in Peters's later books, Peters and Waterman presented their ideas as universal principles. This predilection for general propositions explains much of the popularity of their book, for its ideas were not hedged with the ifs and buts that tended to pervade the contingency leadership approach.[2]

On the other hand, it is necessary to be guarded about taking the view that the effects of leader behaviour are always situationally contingent. Podsakoff et al. (1984) studied the effects of leader reward behaviour among samples of US local government workers, hospital pharmacists and state government employees. They found that contingent reward behaviour (responding to good performance with praise and rewards) by leaders was consistently and positively related to measures of subordinate satisfaction and performance regardless of a host of moderator variables, such as task routineness, locus of control, organizational formalization and job autonomy. However, in view of the fact that many other findings suggest that the effects of leader behaviour are situationally contingent, it might have been anticipated that situational factors would be relevant to considerations of the effectiveness of transformational or charismatic leaders in organizations, and it is to this issue that we now turn.

There is an occasional indication that situational factors at a broad 'macro' level are relevant. Tichy and Devanna (1990), for example, see the transformational leader as increasingly necessary because of the unstable, competitive environments that most business organizations face nowadays. Transactional leadership was appropriate during 'the earlier era of expanding markets and nonexistent competition' (1990: xii). Woycke (1990), drawing on data about leaders like Castro and Nkrumah, has suggested that charismatic leadership may be especially appropriate to organizations in developing countries. However, the contingency approach would suggest that it is necessary to probe more deeply to ask whether its chief tenets of good leadership are appropriate to some organizations or divisions within organizations but not others.

The vast majority of the writers who were cited in the previous two chapters have not addressed this issue at all. When reading Bennis and Nanus (1985), Conger (1989) or Tichy and Devanna (1990) we get virtually no sense of the leader (as against the manager) or the charismatic leader or the transformational leader being more effective in some situations than others. There is occasional recognition that situational factors may affect the emergence of transformational leaders. House (1977) suggests that charismatic leaders are more likely to appear when conditions are stressful. Similarly, Bass and Avolio propose that such leaders 'are more likely to emerge in times of growth, change and crisis' (1990a: 245). This could mean either of two things, when one bears in mind the connection between crisis and charisma that was examined in Chapter 3. It could mean either that periods of turbulence prompt a transformational leader to emerge, possibly implying that there is a longing for a saviour and that an individual emerges who feels 'called' to do what is necessary; or that the transformational leader finds it easier to promulgate a revolutionary new vision during periods of uncertainty. In fact, it is the latter interpretation that is plumped for, in that Bass and Avolio write that such a leader 'is likely to find more ready acceptance in organizations facing rapidly changing technologies and markets' and in 'organically structured organizations' (1990a: 245). These two factors are likely to be connected, since all things being equal it should be expected that organic organizations will be associated with turbulent environments (Burns and Stalker, 1961). On the other hand, Bass and Avolio (1990a: 245) suggest that mechanistic organizations 'may inhibit transformational leaders and be resistent to their influence'. Unfortunately, there has been virtually no attempt to examine these suggestions empirically. Singer and Singer's (1990) research suggests that, if anything, leaders in a mechanistic organization are somewhat more likely to exhibit transformational than transactional leadership, which would appear to go against the grain of Bass and Avolio's suggestion. However, this research does not allow any conclusions to be drawn about whether transformational leadership works better in mechanistic or in organic organizations, which is the more important aspect of Bass and Avolio's speculation from the point of view of developing a situational understanding.

In Howell and Frost's (1989) laboratory experiment, the effects of three leadership approaches – charismatic, structuring and consideration – were examined under high and low productivity norms. This design proffered the opportunity of establishing whether productivity norms moderate the effects of charismatic leadership. Their data suggest that charismatic leadership was more likely to have a positive impact on two out of four measures of task performance under high productivity norms and was much more likely to enhance adjustment to the group under these same conditions. However, productivity norms made virtually no difference to the impact of charismatic leadership on the other two measures of task performance, all five measures of task adjustment, and adjustment to the leader. These findings do provide a modicum of evidence to suggest that charismatic leadership may work slightly better when productivity norms are high, though the evidence is not very conclusive.

Roberts and Bradley's (1988) study of a school superintendent who became a commissioner, but who was not able to enjoy the status of a charismatic leader in the latter role, is relevant in the present context since situational factors may have been responsible for her failure to 'transfer' her charisma. The authors' analysis suggests that she failed to replicate her charisma for two kinds of reason. One is that she failed to produce the kinds of effects that are a prerequisite for being seen as charismatic and hence attracting followers; thus, she was not seen as exceptional, she did not establish a relationship of mutual affection with others, her public addresses lost the vitality and linguistic flair associated with her speeches when superintendent, and she did not create a sense of collective energy among those with whom she worked. Second, a number of situational factors appear to account for the difference: the new situation confronting her was not one of crisis; she had much more limited authority because she was directly accountable to the governor; she was unable to create a coordinated team and personal affection towards herself because her eighteen-hour day gave her much less time to develop personal relationships with others.

The failure to give much attention to situational factors which moderate the effects of forms of leader behaviour associated with the New Leadership is surprising in view of the prominence of this form of analysis in leadership research in the recent past and in organizational behaviour research in general. The foregoing review of speculations and evidence prompts the following very general suggestions. First, leaders exhibiting the New Leadership probably find it easier to get their message across when situations are stressful or when there is considerable uncertainty. This suggests that proactive leaders, who seek to activate a vision which entails substantial change when the organization is not facing pressing difficulties, are likely to find it much more difficult to get support than when there is an acknowledgement of crisis. Jack Welch is a transformational leader who sought to inaugurate great change at GE at a time when the company was performing well (see Box 5.3). It may be that he sees himself as only partially successful because of the difficulty of effecting widespread change through the promotion of a new vision when conditions are favourable to the firm. It may also be that he is viewed as a tough boss because he has had to augment his transformational approach with great toughness in order to gain acceptance for his vision. Second, there is a possibility that when leaders are heavily constrained, their room for manoeuvre is adversely affected and that even the most impressive transformational or charismatic leader will be unable to lift people to the degree that the ideas presented in Chapter 5 anticipate. Thus, the foregoing review of the meagre literature on situational effects suggests that leaders in mechanistic organizations, leaders with little autonomy or with great restrictions on their time, and leaders who operate in environments with low performance expectations will find it difficult to produce the anticipated effects of the behaviour patterns associated with the New Leadership. It might be argued that the truly transformational or charismatic leader would be able to overcome these constraints. However, to view the leader as someone who can rise above or deflect constraints may equally risk vastly overstating the role of leadership in organizations and hence contribute to its romanticization.

The possibility of a drift to passivity

There is a risk that the emphasis in much of the New Leadership literature on senior leaders inaugurating large-scale change in line with a grand vision will breed passivity in many people who work in organizations. Tales of the dramatic transformations stimulated by people like Carlzon and Iacocca could engender a tendency to feel that leadership is all a matter of the dramatic interventions of free-wheeling CEOs. The suggestion that charisma is an important component of the process could exacerbate a belief that leadership is something that only exceptional individuals can exhibit, since charisma is often believed to imply a set of special qualities that certain people possess. A charismatic leader can be seen as empowering for his or her followers (see Chapter 3), but the association of leadership with exceptional individuals with grand visions may have a deleterious effect on the confidence of many individuals to exhibit leadership. As people's confidence in their capacity to provide leadership in the New Leadership mould diminishes, there may develop a tendency for passivity to emerge as individuals expect others to be able to exhibit leadership. Leadership could easily become something that is left to other people.

The quantitative research of writers like Bass, Kouzes and Posner, and Podsakoff et al. is less prone to this accusation for three main reasons. First, they emphasize many aspects of leader behaviour other than devising and implementing large visions. Second, their focus tends to be on individuals in putative leadership positions at all levels of the hierarchy and not just at the top. Third, by treating such activities as devising a vision as a variable, rather than something that a leader does or does not do, they are much less open to the criticism of depicting this kind of activity as the preserve of a few special individuals. On the other hand, much of the literature on the New Leadership focuses on various high-profile leaders and on certain well-publicized incidents, so that it tends to be this sort of context that achieves prominence in the minds of many executives.

Change for change's sake

The New Leadership is widely associated with organizational transformation. As has been suggested above, the dramatic turnaround of failing organizations by transformational leaders has meant that in many people's minds, the New Leadership means instilling a new vision that will change the organization. Part of the problem is that a term like transformational leadership, while referring to the transformation by the leader of others, can easily be taken to imply *organizational* transformation, while charismatic leadership is typically associated with change and innovation. No one would want to decry the implicit message that organizations need to adapt to contemporary environmental conditions and that leadership is likely to play a prominent role in the process, but the emphasis on change should not be taken to imply that transforming organizations is the essence of leadership.

For one thing, it is not at all clear that transformation necessarily benefits the organization. A study of Finnish newspapers over the period 1771–1963 by Miner et al. (1990) suggests that transformation typically engenders failure due to the costs of change. Second, there may be broad periods during which radical change is unnecessary and hence counterproductive. On the basis of an examination of a large number of organizations, Tushman et al. (1986) have proposed that successful firms go through periods of relative stability, during which change is incremental (these are called periods of 'convergence'), but are capable of initiating wholesale change, which they call 'frame-breaking change' or 'reorientations' (Tushman and Romanelli, 1985), when environmental conditions and organizational performance deteriorate abruptly. However, when an organization is in the midst of a period of convergence and is performing well, frame-breaking change may have adverse effects. During periods of convergence, the role of the executive leadership team is to preserve the company's strategy and culture. Frame-breaking change is needed when performance is poor and/or when the environment has changed to the company's disadvantage.

There is clearly a delicate balance here, because Tushman et al. note that the most effective cases of frame-breaking change arise when executives foresee the need to instigate major change in order to deal with anticipated environmental threats or to take advantage of new opportunities. Such proactive change requires the injection of vision into the organization by a management team. It might be anticipated that transformational leadership is precisely the kind of approach that is likely to be required to effect such changes, although Tushman et al. do not use the term. However, transformational leadership, in Burns's (1978) sense of the term, may be equally appropriate to periods of convergence in which leaders are responsible for facilitating incremental change. Thus, there may be periods of a company's development which require transformational leadership but not organizational transformation (or at least not of the fundamental, system-wide kind).[3] Transformational leadership in this situation entails custody of the company's direction and its culture and values. To associate transformational leadership with radical change may be dangerous if senior executives come to feel that they are there to engage in organizational transformation since they may not take sufficient account of the stage of the company's development. There is a special risk of this happening with new, outside executives who want to make their presence felt and who, following the New Leadership literature, see their role as leaders as one of introducing fundamental change in line with their vision. Gabarro (1987) has noted from an examination of the process by which new managers take charge that in successful transitions the incoming manager goes through stages of learning, orienting to the new circumstances, and reflection before engaging in major change.[4] The research of Tushman et al. suggests that it is especially important to go through these initial stages in order to appreciate the phase of the organization's evolution. However, the overall thrust of this section is to suggest that if the New Leadership is too closely associated with radical organizational transformations, there is a risk that inappropriate actions may be undertaken if the situation does not warrant such change.

Commitment to the rational model

In Bryman (1986), it was observed that the bulk of leadership research was underpinned by a rational model, a perspective which implies a close connection between means and ends in organizational behaviour. Leaders are depicted as highly goal-directed and purposive in their behaviour, seeking to produce particular effects with their actions. In spite of the fact that the New Leadership is often portrayed as a paradigm shift, it could be argued that most theory and research associated with it is closely bound to the same rational model. Leaders are still characterized as engaging in certain types of behaviour to produce particular outcomes. This tendency reveals itself in the normative statements concerning how the implications of research findings about what constitutes effective leadership can be translated into programmes of action for leaders to learn.

It is not surprising that leadership research has retained this orientation, because its emphasis on generating 'applied' or at least 'applicable' knowledge has also been preserved. Yet there is ample evidence that the behaviour of managers is not governed by a consistent reference to organizational goals in the manner that the rational model would imply (Stewart, 1983). The suggestion that many organizations are 'organized anarchies' also appears to limit the applicability of the rational model. According to this idea, many organizations can be viewed more fruitfully as a collection of choices looking for problems, issues and feelings looking for decision situations in which they might be aired, solutions looking for issues to which they might be an answer, and decision-makers looking for work. (Cohen et al., 1972: 2)

The rational model's impression of organizational structures being synchronized to preordained goals and of decision-makers calculating the relative value of various feasible means for the realization of such goals recedes from view in a quite dramatic fashion. Organizational life appears more fluid and its constituents appear more uncoupled than the rational model allows. It is true, of course, as Cohen et al. recognize, that not all organizations are best described in such terms. However, the implications for leadership researchers of the kind of scenario that they present are many, in that it undermines the idea of leaders engaging in certain patterns of behaviour in order to achieve certain outcomes and even the notion that we should expect a connection between leader behaviour and outcomes.

Insights from the institutional model of organizations (Meyer and Rowan, 1977; Zucker, 1987), a perspective which departs from the rational model (Bryman, 1984; Scott, 1981), might provide useful insights into the ways in which leader behaviour is affected by external, normative pressures. The institutional model sees organizations as seeking to incorporate practices and structures that are valued within society in order to achieve legitimacy in the eyes of the external environment, and so to enhance survival. These incorporated practices and structures may have little impact on what actually goes on in the organization. This perspective could enlighten the reasons behind executives engaging in certain forms of leader behaviour. Within the context of the New Leadership, it might be expected that leaders will increasingly feel that they have to indicate that they are seeking to promote a new vision for the organization, perhaps in large part for external consumption. In other words, to be credible, it may be that many leaders are saying that they really do have a vision for the company, even though that vision may have limited implications for the organization. On the other hand, for outsiders and members of the organization, statements about vision may betoken effective leadership and may therefore possess powerful symbolic value. Attention to such issues can provide a useful antidote to the pervasive rational model in leadership theory and research.[5]

It is not being suggested here that the postulate of rationality is necessarily misguided. In fact, the conceptualization of charismatic leadership presented in Chapter 3 has very clear elements of rationality built into it. The chief point being made in this section is to suggest that a number of approaches to the study of organizations have come to question the validity and appropriateness of the rational model (Bryman, 1984), and that the deployment of approaches which are not wedded to the postulate of rationality may inform the New Leadership, which is itself undergirded by the rational model. There is a tendency for leadership theory and research to be rather sealed off from organization studies, and the consideration of a wider range of underlying models would allow the former to feed off the latter to a greater degree than occurs at the present. Moreover, if there is any credibility in the notion that we are gradually drifting into a new social order, the post-modern world, these observations about the postulate of rationality will have particular weight. Post-modernism, both as an approach to the understanding of cultural and social phenomena and as a set of observations of an emergent societal form, is inimical to the theme of rationality as it is conventionally conceptualized. Thus, from within organization studies (of which the study of leadership in organizations is arguably a part) and from without, the citadel of rationality is under siege (see, for example, Clegg, 1990). Leadership theorists and researchers would do well to reflect on the implications of such themes, if only perhaps to be in a position to say that they have tried to take them seriously but to little effect.

Charismatic leadership in business organizations

Charismatic leadership has been a key focus in this book, so that after an evaluation of the New Leadership in general, it seems appropriate to return to this point of reference. It is clear that the New Leadership writers vary in their views about the importance of charisma. For writers like Biggart (1989), Conger (1989), House (1977) and Nadler and Tushman (1990) it represents a vital route to effective leadership; for Bass (1985) it is an important ingredient of transformational leadership which in turn is a source of exceptional performance; but for writers like Bennis and Nanus (1985), Kotter (1990) and Tichy and Devanna (1990) charisma is not regarded as an important aspect of effective leadership. One of the chief reasons for the rejection of charisma by this third group of writers is that they often identify it as a rare quality that only certain individuals exhibit by virtue of innate capacity or ability. However, while it is not inappropriate to regard charisma as rare, as the discussion in Chapter 3 suggests, it is unacceptable to depict it as reflecting a cluster of personal characteristics or abilities. Instead, charisma has to be viewed as a type of relationship between leader and led which is the outcome of a process which has been described as the social formation of charisma. Followers are as implicated in the social formation of charisma as the leaders themselves. It is the followers who must recognize and validate the leader's charisma and they often play an important role in spreading his/her mission or vision. In other words, it seems that some writers dismiss the application of charisma to the business setting on the basis of a highly dubious view that it is an individual trait.

Does this mean that the writers who emphasize charismatic leadership have correctly interpreted the nature of charisma and hence have hit on a key to effective leadership? None of the writers who have been encountered in Chapters 5 and 6 depicts charismatic leadership as an iterative process in the manner outlined in Figure 3.2. In treating charismatic leadership in terms of an attribution, whereby certain forms of behaviour tend to produce a perception of charisma by others, Conger (1989) comes closest to viewing charisma as a process, but his approach is perhaps a little too inclined to a simple model in which leader behaviour produces an attribution of charisma which in turn engenders certain follower responses. Moreover, the notion of charismatic leadership as a social relationship is not very developed in the model. In particular, it is not always very clear from Conger's work and that of a number of other examinations of charismatic leadership in business settings what members of an organization personally derive from such leadership. In Chapter 3 it was suggested that there may be merit in viewing charismatic leadership as a social relationship that pivots on an exchange in which power is a prominent resource. But the discussions of charismatic leadership in business organizations seem to display the tendency of the older approaches to leadership theory and research covered in Chapter 1 to present the leader as seeking to influence others in a certain direction, implying a one-way relationship rather than the reciprocal relationship implied by the portrayal of charismatic leadership as an exchange. As a result, the typical approach to the examination of charismatic leadership in business organizations seems to comprise many vestiges of traditional approaches to leadership and represents a much more static account of its nature than is implied by the evidence examined in Chapter 3. It might be argued that the difference can be attributed to the contrast between charismatic leadership in the highly formal organizational milieu of the business firm and its manifestation in other contexts, like religious movements. For example, the fact of pre-existing hierarchical arrangements in the former (and their absence or virtual absence in the latter) means that the charismatic leader in business and other formal organizations is almost bound to be conceptualized as someone who has the job of influencing others to perform in a goal-directed way. Such an argument could be taken to imply that the notion of charismatic leadership does not translate to business organizations as readily as some writers have thought. Before taking such a position, we need more in-depth and longitudinal investigations of the processes by which charismatic leadership is built up in business settings.

However, a more fundamental issue is the question of whether the leaders who are usually regarded as charismatic deserve this designation. Most writers view the charismatic leader as someone who has a vision or mission and who is able to produce high levels of personal loyalty and commitment to his or her goals. This conception is broadly consistent with Weber. An exception would be Howell and Frost's (1989) study which is really just concerned with the behaviour of individuals exhibiting a charismatic 'style'. There is no indication that the actresses concerned successfully created the personal loyalty and commitment that is a feature of the relationship between charismatic leaders and followers. Instead, experimental subjects' 'adjustment to the leader', which encapsulates such notions as quality of relationship with the leader and personal commitment and loyalty to the leader, was treated as a dependent variable. In fact, charismatic leaders typically fared better than considerate and structuring leaders in terms of this variable. However, if personal loyalty and commitment to the leader's vision are features of charismatic leadership, it is difficult to see how they can also be effects, as they are in this experiment.

The ingredient that is most frequently absent from most of the conceptions of charismatic leadership in business settings is the notion that the charismatic leader is perceived as exceptional and extraordinary. This is an essential aspect of charisma (see, for example, the quotations from Weber on pp. 24 and 25). It is precisely because charismatic leaders are viewed as exceptional that they command devotion. But in the writings on charismatic leaders in business there is rarely a great deal of attention given to this point. Instead, there tends to be an emphasis upon the leader's vision and the kinds of behaviour that produce loyalty and devotion. In Bass's measurement of charisma, as noted on p. 130, there seem to be only two items that reflect the idea that the charismatic leader is perceived to be exceptional. Also, the very fact that charisma is treated in his research as a variable implies that organizations are replete with individuals who are believed to be exceptional, albeit in different degrees. This seems an unlikely scenario; indeed, if it were true then it might be argued that if there are so many exceptional leaders, they cannot really be so exceptional! It seems much more likely that the combination of a clear vision plus a belief in the leader's exceptional qualities plus a high level of devotion to him or her is actually quite rare, or at least less common than implied by the measurement of charisma. These three minimal attributes of charisma, which follow the working definition presented on p. 41, are unlikely to be as frequently encountered as Bass implies. This is not to say that he has not uncovered an important aspect of effective leader behaviour, since 'charisma' is consistently associated with indicators of effectiveness. The question that is being raised here is how far it can validly be regarded as an operational definition of charisma.

The notion of the charismatic leader as exceptional is almost entirely absent from Howell and Frost's laboratory experiment. It is also largely missing from House's (1977) theory, mainly because he defines charismatic leadership in terms of its effects, rather than in terms of how the charismatic leader is perceived. A problem with this strategy is that it is not inconceivable that leaders who are not charismatic can have the same kinds of effect. Being perceived as extraordinary is barely mentioned in Nadler and Tushman's (1990) account of the reasons for the effects of charismatic leaders. In Conger's (1989) research, creating a sense of being extraordinary is a feature of stage three in the building of charismatic leadership and is a major source of the leader's power over others. This sense of being exceptional is created by charismatic leaders 'through their prior successes, personal talents, and persuasive skills, through unconventional behavior, and through shared values' (1989: 94–5). It is a means of gaining followers' trust in the ability of the leader to bring off the vision that he or she has presented. This is much closer to the Weberian notion, but for Weber the sense of extraordinariness belonged to the initial basis on which the leader attracts a following. The charismatic leaders who were the focus for Chapters 3 and 4 had managed to fashion an image of themselves as extraordinary, and it was this that led to their charisma. Two more examples can be cited. Gonzalez has remarked about Castro: 'Once Fidel had proven himself as an extraordinary leader, much of the Cuban populace appeared prepared to grant him virtually unlimited powers in fashioning a new order' (1974: 95). Or we could take the charismatic leader Irakau (1920?–75), of Manam Island in New Guinea, who achieved considerable support for his vision of change. Lutkehaus writes that because 'of his demonstrated success with business, he was someone whom many believed must surely have access to a greater-than-human source of power' (1990: 251). It is not behaviour *per se* that leads to the attribution of charisma, but the extent to which the prospective charismatic leader is able to create a belief that he or she is exceptional, and startling success often has an important role in this process.

Thus, while there are some affinities between Weber and the recent writings on charisma in business settings, the element of extraordinariness is either side-stepped or handled somewhat differently. Some of the reason for this lack of certainty may be due to unease about the suggestion that only individuals who are perceived as exceptional can accomplish great feats. It has already been noted that one of the reasons that charisma is dismissed by some New Leadership writers is that there is some disquiet about the idea that truly effective leadership is only available to those individuals with special gifts. Such a view would seem to imply that most leaders are very mundane and uninteresting; this is not an especially attractive self-image for the many hard-working individuals who are responsible for making organizations successful. Accordingly, many New Leadership writers prefer a conception of effective leadership that does not tie it so tightly to a sense of extraordinariness.

On the other hand, there are certainly leaders who fit the vision plus extraordinary plus devotion combination of minimal requirements. Of the leaders encountered in the previous chapters, Mary Kay Ash, Burr, Iacocca and Jobs could be adequately described as charismatic. They all had visions (though this is somewhat unclear in Iacocca's case). They all enjoyed the devotion of large sectors of their respective organizations. They were all seen as exceptional: Ash for overcoming personal adversity; Burr for getting a daring vision off the ground so rapidly; Iacocca for being a mastermind behind the Mustang when at Ford and for turning Chrysler around; and Jobs for building a massive corporation while still young. Welch and Sculley are not seen as exceptional and do not create devotion among members of their organization, so that it is not surprising that they are rarely viewed as charismatic.

Kanter (1977) gives a graphic account of 'the most noted charismatic leader' at Indsco, a pseudonym for a company where she carried out her research:

> I heard about the devotion that he inspired at many different levels of the organization and from many different kinds of people: 'If we had him still with us, he'd shoot from the hip and say, "Do it". We'd all fall over ourselves to do it, no matter whether it was logical or not. Unfortunately, he's gone [he died prematurely]; but where this thing might be were he still here! . . .' It was assumed that he could do anything, that no problem would be as bad if he were in charge. His rise to the top

and the power he consolidated once he got there, was based almost entirely on one extraordinary risk: he took over a very unproductive plant and turned it around, staking his career on the outcome. (1977: 179)

This vignette lends support to Conger's (1989) suggestion that risk-taking may be a powerful cause of the attribution of charisma. However, it also demonstrates the sense of Bennis and Nanus's (1985) comment that charisma is a consequence of success rather than a cause of it, and in like fashion we can say that being perceived as extraordinary is a necessary attribute of the charismatic leader.

Vision and charismatic leaders

Up to now, the term 'vision' has been used without question in the context of both charismatic and the New Leadership. It is easily assumed that it is the equivalent of mission and vision in the sense in which Weber employed the terms. However, caution is required here for the following reasons. First, it is often not easy to see what is visionary about the visions that are often referred to in the New Leadership literature. Often, there is little to distinguish leaders' visions from kindred terms like strategy. In the case of Jobs, the term seems warranted because he was concerned at Apple to transform people's lives through computers, but many 'visions' seem to involve little more than aiming to create a more competitive and entrepreneurial company by reducing bureaucracy and decentralizing operations (often making a substantial proportion of the work force redundant in the process). This approach lies at the base of Carlzon's and Welch's visions for their respective companies, although it is only the first of these who is regarded as charismatic (for example, Conger, 1989). It is not surprising that it tends to be those leaders whose 'visions' are either innovative or deal with ultimate values (such as Jobs, Burr, Ash) who are typically regarded as charismatic. Leaders who adopt visions that are barely distinguishable from strategic intent or from broad aims and which lack innovativeness (for example, stereotyped proclamations about competitiveness, emphasis on quality or the customer) are creating visions in name only. Because leadership is increasingly associated with vision, for many leaders their broad aims are simply being dressed up as visions. In fact, the more visions are just stylized blueprints for change which are translated with minor changes from company to company, the less appropriate it is to designate them as visions and the less appropriate it is to regard their promulgation as leadership rather than management.

Routinization of charisma

One of the most suprising aspects of the growing interest in charismatic leadership is that there has been almost no attention paid to the routinization of charisma. As noted in Chapter 2, this was a prominent concern for Weber, and since most writers on charismatic leadership in business organizations take their lead from him, it might have been expected that routinization would loom fairly large in their thinking. Also, if charisma really is the fleeting phenomenon that Weber and many others describe it as being, questions of the succession of charismatic leaders and of how their charisma can be absorbed into structures would seem to be as important in business organizations as they are in religious and political movements. In spite of this, the major contributors to discussions of charismatic leadership give it virtually no space.

Conger and Kanungo (1987) speculate that if the routinization of charisma propels charismatic leaders into acting as administrators or managers (which they refer to as 'caretaker' and 'nudging' roles respectively), their charisma will wane. Conger (1989) raises the issue of succession, arguing that when the charismatic leader leaves or dies, it is difficult for successors to emerge because of the dedication to the leader. Rose (1989), for example, reports that when Jobs left Apple, many employees felt a sense of supreme loss and that the company's soul had been surrendered. The passage quoted on p. 167 about the loss of the charismatic leader at Indsco displays a comparable response. Similarly, speculation about who is to succeed Iacocca has been intense, both within the company and in the business press, for precisely the same kind of reason.

A further illustration of the problem of routinizing the charisma in the business world can be discerned in the difficulties at ICI that Denys Henderson experienced as a successor to John Harvey-Jones, who has often been depicted as a charismatic figure. Thomson has described the contrast in the following way:

> With his garish ties and mane of unruly hair, the ebullient Sir John was a brilliant publicist for the company. Neither Sir Denys's ties nor his personality are as striking. Many who work for him see him a grey man who has taken the fun and the flair out of ICI ... But the differences go deeper than that. 'Sir John had a vision for the company. Sir Denys is just lurching', comments one close observer of ICI. (1991: 11)

Thomson goes on to relay the deficiencies exhibited by Henderson relative to Harvey-Jones, as perceived by various observers: lack of imagination and flair; failure to inspire; punitiveness; and inability to enjoy the full support of his main board. Such observations were made with greater frequency in the wake of evidence that Hanson Trust was on the verge of a takeover bid for ICI in May 1991. Quite apart from the veracity of the comparisons, which cannot be divorced from the divergent economic climates in which the two men were chairmen of the company, an element in the comparisons must be that a charismatic leader is a very difficult act to follow. This would suggest that charismatic leadership in business is extremely difficult to routinize. If this is generally the case, then the charismatic leader in business may be something of a mixed blessing if a longer time perspective is taken.

However, the routinization of charisma also relates to the question of the development of structures which allow the leader's charisma to have some permanence, and this issue has received almost no attention. Conger and Kanungo's speculation suggests that charismatic leaders lose their personal appeal the more immersed they become in the structures which emerge with routinization. This view is largely consistent with the evidence presented in Chapter 4 of the present book. In a sense, Jobs attempted to routinize his charisma by investing the Macintosh division that he headed with a kind of missionary zeal which reflected the true Apple values, but his lack of interest and concern for wider issues of organization and control led to the company's difficulties and to the rift with Sculley. This suggests something of a cleft stick for charismatic leaders in business organizations: they may lose their charisma if they become embroiled in mundane matters of management and administration, but in a business environment a lack of concern for such issues when they hold prominent positions can be disastrous. A similar kind of point can probably be made in relation to Burr of People Express, while Iacocca recognizes that in perpetuating his personal image, he took his eye off what was needed to keep Chrysler successful (see Box 5.1).

It should be apparent that the ways in which charisma can be successfully routinized in business organizations is clearly in need of attention. This will need to take into account matters of succession, the development of organization structures which institutionalize charisma, and how the leader's mission or vision is codified through the organization's culture. The literature reviewed in Chapter 4 strongly implies that charisma will dissipate if not routinized (as Weber predicted), that such routinization needs to be undertaken sooner rather than later, and that from the point of view of retaining their personal charisma, charismatic leaders should be minimally involved in routine administration.

Disadvantages of charismatic leadership in business settings

Most of the discussion in the first main section of this chapter, 'An evaluation of the New Leadership', is relevant to an assessment of the literature on charismatic leadership: all of the points made there are germane to the theory and research on charisma in business organizations. In fact, some of the critical observations appear in even sharper relief in the context of charismatic leadership. For example, writers on charismatic leadership are especially prone to viewing it as chiefly manifested at the top of the organization. Conger, for example, writes that his 'model applies principally to the top management of an organization' (1989: 25).

Also, charismatic leaders are particularly inclined to obsessiveness about their vision and to using their persuasive powers to get others behind their dreams. Jobs was known as someone who emitted a 'reality-distortion field' among those around him, in that he held his views with such conviction that his depiction of reality was extremely difficult to push aside (Rose, 1989). A further example of obsession in a figure who at one point came very close to the image of a charismatic leader is provided by Michael Cimino.

The story of the making of *Heaven's Gate*, the motion picture that brought United Artists to its knees, is one that is rarely referred to in management texts in spite of the fact that a monumental failure such as this can teach us a great deal. The information for what follows derives from Steven Bach's (1985) account of the making of the film. Bach and David Field were production executives at United Artists, which had the misfortune to secure the contract for making *Heaven's Gate*. Essentially, this is the story of Michael Cimino, the film's director, and his relationships with the company. Are we implying, therefore, that Cimino is a charismatic figure? To some extent, he was regarded with the kind of awe that we have seen in the charismatic leaders that have been discussed in this book. At the time that the deal with him was signed by UA, it was anticipated (accurately) that Cimino was on the verge of a major critical and commercial success with *The Deer Hunter*. This acclaim in a relatively young director invested him with the feel of stardom with which charisma in the movie business is sometimes associated (Dyer, 1979) and therefore with charismatic authority within the industry. Also, he was a man with a vision: that the story of the Johnson County War, which was based on a true incident, involving the illegal reaction of cattle barons in Wyoming to a surge of settlers, could provide the vehicle for a western of epic stature and of great artistic merit. He had spent many years dreaming about making the film, and in 1978 UA gave him the opportunity to do so. Cimino was viewed as possessing the characteristics of energy and enthusiasm (Bach, 1985: 154), which are often attributed to charismatic individuals. Because of the aura that surrounded him, UA was particularly keen to secure his services and to see off competitors for the film. Evidently, the company was too keen. He was allowed considerable latitude over the budget and, even though he was not able to secure the stars that he had originally claimed to seek (such as Jane Fonda or Diane Keaton for the lead female role), he was able to push through his preferred alternatives (such as then unknown French actress Isabelle Huppert). UA's enthusiasm for a Cimino film led to various departments of the company committing time and energy to various aspects of the project before it had been formally agreed.

What then follows is a story of massively growing costs in tandem with an accelerating time overrun. These problems were apparent at a very early stage. It was discovered that Cimino's personal expenses were colossal, while extras were paid for four hours travelling in an eight-hour day, often at double or even triple time in order to ensure that shooting took place at the correct time of the day. The time consumed by travel was due to Cimino's intransigence over location; only an inaccessible section of Montana would do. Rather than draw the project to a close, the production heads, Field and Bach, agreed to keep it going and to increase the budget. However, after the first six days of shooting, the film was five days behind and had produced one-and-a-half minutes of usable material at a cost of $900,000. UA sought to assert budgetary control and on various occasions considered both abandoning the film and even sacking Cimino. For his part, Cimino became more and more aloof – refusing to cooperate with UA officials and huffily threatening to take the film to another company. Matters got worse and it became apparent that the company was facing a total cost of $43.4 million, 600 per cent more than had been initially proposed. New budgets and a new schedule were prepared to contain the situation. However, two further problems manifested themselves. First, a former reporter who had secured a job as an extra exposed the extravagance of the film, and also the rapidly rising toll of injuries to people working on the film and to animals. This adverse publicity proved very significant. Second, it became increasingly apparent that the film was going to be far too long. Bach wanted the film to be no longer than two-and-a-half hours, to which Cimino was strongly resistant. However, UA executives were quite unprepared for the length at the first screening – five hours and twenty-five minutes. Cimino was forced to cut it and got it down to three hours and thirty-nine minutes. During the editing period he refused steadfastly to cooperate with the publicity department. When the film received its first showing, the critics' response was almost unprecedentedly dreadful – 'unqualified disaster' in the words of one critic. Cimino asked for the film to be 'pulled' to re-edit it. This was agreed to, much to the chagrin of people like Bach who had allowed themselves to believe that they had seen the end of the film. Cimino cut it to two-and-a-half hours, but the response was still dreadful. People refused to see a film that had received such a calamitously awful response from the critics. For their part, the critics were almost certainly responding only in part to the film itself: they were responding much more to the flagrant misuse of money and to some infelicitous remarks made by Cimino after *The Deer Hunter*. In the end, the film was removed from distribution and written off at a total cost of $44 million. As a direct result of *Heaven's Gate*, the company president and Bach lost their jobs and the company was taken over by MGM.

   What do we learn from this catalogue of disasters? We can see in sharp relief the problems that charismatic individuals can engender. We see in particular an arrogance about their special abilities that leads easily to folly. We also see the limitations of the possession of a vision: it can rapidly become an unyielding obsession over which the individual has no control. Moreover, Cimino was not the chief executive of a company; he was someone in nominal charge of a project in an inherently project-based industry. It could be that we perceive in this example the problems associated with having charismatic individuals in different locations in a company, in that they can easily get out of hand without some control. Bach and Field as production executives were there to oversee what was going on, but Cimino was allowed an excessively free hand to do as he wanted with both time and money at a very early stage in production, so that the rot had set in soon after the film had got under way. Of course, the response to this implication is that you should not stifle creativity and initiative, but the problem here was that until UA firmly called a halt to Cimino's excesses, he had not really needed to worry about suffering the consequences of his own actions because the company kept on adjusting their horizons. This tendency was due to a number of factors. First, particularly in the initial stages, UA were so pleased to have secured Cimino that he was allowed considerable leeway. Second, Bach and others displayed the tendency to allow their commitment to poor decisions or lines of action to escalate (Staw, 1976). Third, the early projections of cost overrun did not seem excessive compared with some films in the early 1980s. Fourth, like all managers who oversee a project, Bach and Field had other activities for which they were responsible, in this case a portfolio of other films competing for their attention. As a result, Cimino's excesses, even when they were highly apparent, could not be accorded full attention. Finally, the company was in the midst of a number of successes, like *Manhattan*, which mitigated the feeling of panic that could easily have overwhelmed them.

The story of *Heaven's Gate* also reminds us that charisma is not always something that can benefit an organization and that the charismatic individual is not always able to transfer his or her talents from one situation to another. Moreover, when vision becomes unshakeable obsession, the potential for catastrophe may not be far away. It also suggests that charismatic leaders may come to recognize the power that they can exert by virtue of the awe and reverence with which they are regarded and to use that power as a means of getting their own way regardless of the views of others.

The rhetorical strategies of charismatic leaders may also prove to be their undoing. They can employ the communication skills that they cultivate in order to present images which have tremendous power to persuade. However, this very capacity is one which runs the risk of leading others in directions that they would otherwise have not dreamed of going. To illustrate this penchant for spellbinding oratory, Jobs's speech at a meeting in October 1983 of 750 Apple sales representatives, executives and other employees is worth examining:

> It is 1958. IBM passes up the chance to buy a young, fledgling company that has just invented a new technology called Xerography. Two years later, Xerox is born and IBM has been kicking itself ever since. It is ten years later . . . Digital Equipment Corporation and others invent the minicomputer [but IBM dismisses the technology and DEC becomes a major corporation] . . . It is now ten years later . . . Apple, a young company on the West Coast, invents the Apple II, the first personal computer as we know it today. IBM dismisses the personal computer as too small to do serious computing and therefore insignificant to its business. It is now . . . 1981 [cheers are bellowed out as everyone in the audience knows that this is the year that IBM entered the personal computer market and the noise continues as Jobs tells the story, but has to raise his hand to quieten the audience] . . . It is now 1984. It appears IBM wants it all. Apple is perceived to be the only hope to offer IBM a run for its money. Dealers, initially welcoming IBM with open arms, now fear an IBM-dominated and -controlled future. They are increasingly turning back to Apple as the only force that can ensure their future freedom. IBM wants it all and is aiming its guns on the last obstacle to industry control, Apple. Will Big Blue dominate the entire computer industry, the computer age? Was George Orwell right? [pandemonium breaks out as the audience shrieks 'no' and then a giant screen descends showing an advertisement for *1984* and Jobs continues] On January 24, Apple Computer will introduce Macintosh and then you will see why 1984 won't be like *1984*. [this last remark was followed by hysteria lasting for many minutes][6]

It is difficult not to be impressed by such a bravura performance with its construction of a black and white world in which the baddies (IBM) are the enemies of freedom and technological progress. But such mesmerizing performances have the capacity to take people along and to detract from fundamentals, which in the case of Apple amounted to technological and delivery problems with its saviour – the Macintosh – and internal organizational difficulties. Moreover, Butcher (1988) has suggested that one of Jobs's problems was that he failed to take the potential threat from IBM seriously. Perhaps his rhetoric meant that others did not take IBM seriously either.

Over and above such possible problems, charismatic leaders often have a tendency towards authoritarianism, as can be seen in the case of individuals like 'Moses' Berg or Nkrumah. It is also evident in Burr's style as People Express paid the price of excessively rapid early growth, and in Cimino's lack of concern for the views of others. The same is true of Jobs who, according to Sculley,

> wouldn't hesitate to call their work 'a piece of shit' and throw it back at them in an angry rage. Their faces would grow numb, until they could gather just enough energy to move to a chair, sit down, and start again. (1987: 229)

This kind of behaviour can be as demotivating and disempowering as the oratorical performances can be motivating and empowering.

There are great dangers in drawing general conclusions about the limitations of charismatic leaders from such apparent extremes as Cimino, Burr and Jobs. In fact, writers on charisma outside the business sphere have long been aware of the limitations of charismatic leaders (see Newman, 1983; Rutan and Rice, 1981). Charismatic leaders can be despotic, mercurial, self-serving, obsessive, masters of illusion, and ultimately destructive of others. On the other hand, as we have seen time and time again, they and their followers can achieve amazing things. Further, since charismatic leaders are difficult acts to follow, their successors may experience great difficulty in following in their footsteps. But of all the forms of the New Leadership, charismatic leadership is the one where it is difficult to envisage how organizations populated with a large number of people who exhibit it could survive for long. The scenario of an organization brimming with charismatic leaders is one of chaos. It is no wonder, therefore, that most of the major examples that have been encountered relate to senior figures in business organizations.

Overview

The general sense of this final chapter has been one of critique. However, it may appear destructive to nip in the bud the developments that have been described in the previous two chapters since they are at a relatively early stage in their development. Instead of closing on a negative note, some of the main lessons and contributions that can be gleaned from the New Leadership will be briefly reviewed, including some insights that can be extracted from considerations of charismatic leadership.

• There should be no excuse any more for treating leadership and management as synonyms. They refer to different types of activity. However, there is some reason to feel uneasy about the tendency (sometimes implicit, other times explicit) among some writers to denigrate management. There is also reason to feel that a leadership versus management contrast is better than a leader versus manager contrast, since the latter comparison can easily imply that leaders and managers are different types of people, an inference that is not warranted by the existing evidence.

- Vision is an important, if not essential, component of the leadership of organizations and often of divisions within organizations. It gives direction, helps people to know where they fit in, and can enhance the motivation and sense of empowerment of members of an organization. There is a risk that vision is coming to be viewed as a panacea and that it is becoming an overworked term, but infusing an organization and its members with values and a sense of purpose will usually be better than having a rudderless body of people.

- The emphasis upon vision has brought to the fore the degree to which the instilling of values is a vital aspect of leadership, especially at the level of the senior executive. This element is almost entirely absent from the literature that was reviewed in Chapter 1, though the importance of leadership as the inculcation of values to give purpose to the organization was voiced by earlier writers (most notably, Selznick, 1957) but was given little attention in the bulk of theory and research. As a result, the role of the leader in maintaining an organization's culture or in changing it to implement a change of direction dictated by a new vision is an important contribution of the New Leadership writers. The need for culture change as a route to bringing a vision to fruition can be discerned in a number of the leaders that have been encountered, such as Akers, Carlzon, Sabin and the school superintendent.

- Vision is nothing unless it is properly communicated. This can be achieved through leaders themselves acting as personifications of their visions and by proper attention to the rhetorical strategies by which vision is communicated. The literature on the ways in which charismatic leaders present their visionary pretensions is especially important in the latter connection. Equally, the leader needs to establish an organizational framework which will facilitate the accomplishment of the vision.

- Leadership can be a route to the empowerment of others. This theme rarely appeared in the literature covered in Chapter 1, except in the rather restricted context of the examination of participative leadership. The notion of leadership as a means of empowerment goes further in that participative leadership is only one aspect of the process. Rather, empowerment is seen in the New Leadership as deriving from the involvement of members of the organization through the leader's vision and through strategies, which are often part of the vision, which seek to push autonomy and responsibility downwards, as in the cases of Sabin and Welch. However, it has been observed that the precise mechanism through which empowerment occurs is often understated.

- Leaders must be trusted and seen as having personal integrity. Without the achievement of these attributes, leaders cannot command loyalty. To some executives this may sound like going soft on employees, but without loyalty and commitment people will put into their work only that which is necessary. Such trust and personal integrity can be created by behaving consistently and honestly and by demonstrating personal commitment to the organization and the vision.

- The leader does not usually work alone. The New Leadership literature has brought out the contribution of teams that are convinced by the vision and who are prepared to spread the word and to provide support for the leader's vision and the means for achieving it. Such individuals function in a manner similar to the followers of charismatic leaders who were encountered in Chapters 3 and 4. However, while recognizing the importance of supporters of the leader's cause, the literature perhaps does not give sufficient credit to teams and often exaggerates the role of individual leaders.

- The New Leadership literature has been much more sensitive to the older approaches to the impact of the environment on leaders and their behaviour. This aspect is particularly evident in the qualitative case studies of leaders, which have demonstrated the importance of keeping a watchful eye on the environment for organizational effectiveness. The difference between the old and the New Leadership in this regard is partly to do with their different levels of analysis, in that the environment has a less direct impact on leaders at the lower echelons of organizations who generally provided the focus for the traditional approaches that were covered in Chapter 1.

- Linked to the previous point is a further contribution of the New Leadership: it has brought to the surface greater concern for the leadership *of* organizations than its predecessors.

- The New Leadership has shown a concern with the practical implications of its ideas and findings. Therefore, writers have been very quick to explore the applicability of their ideas and to devise ways of developing New Leadership principles in leaders. On the other hand, it could be argued that leadership theory and research in the past has been too preoccupied with applied issues, and that a period of basic research on New Leadership ideas would have been beneficial.

- When the leader is as near to being a charismatic leader as can be achieved in the business setting, it is crucial to recognize that he or she may not have a penchant for mundane administration and organization. Rather than bemoan the limitations of the charismatic leader, it may be better to ensure that such areas of work are being covered by others.

- The emphasis upon charismatic leadership has given followers (or subordinates as they are usually referred to in leadership theory) a much more prominent role than they traditionally enjoy in the theory and research examined in Chapter 1. The recognition that charisma is in the eye of the beholder has brought them much more to the surface. However, it has been argued that a perspective on charismatic leadership could and should go further in making followers central.

- Finally, Bass's research has shown that charisma is an important component of effective leadership, but it is only one facet. Some misgivings about the conceptualization and measurement of charisma in his scheme were voiced, but there is little doubt that his framework and the MLQ have produced an impressive set of findings.

These points are very general, but they call attention to the very real contributions of the New Leadership. In order to take the approach further, it will be necessary to attend to a number of issues.

- More studies are needed which draw on failures of the kind of leadership that the New Leadership literature extols. It is hard to believe that they do not exist in greater profusion than is sometimes implied by many writers.
- A longer time perspective is necessary to establish the effectiveness of New Leadership practices. Currently, the literature and the mythology emphasize very immediate benefits, but, as the follow-up by Tichy and Devanna (1990) implies, the advantages may be somewhat short-lived.
- The relative absence of any situational analysis of the New Leadership practices must be remedied. Past experience of leadership and organizational research suggests that it is unlikely that we really have discovered a 'one best way'.
- There is too much attention to leader behaviour and too little interest in what people who work in organizations want and expect from leaders. Kouzes and Posner (1987) are an exception in that many of their ideas about leadership were grounded in survey evidence on what people look for in leaders. But such issues require further exploration, possibly employing more sensitive, qualitative styles of data collection.
- It has been pointed out on a number of occasions in this book that the average manager or supervisor may find it difficult to see how the New Leadership applies to them. With the exception of the quantitative studies of writers like Bass, and Howell and Frost, the emphasis always seems to be upon top leaders. We keep on being told by the New Leadership writers that in fact they are not solely concerned with top leaders, but they consistently employ illustrations of notable figures in the business world. The general applicability of New Leadership ideas throughout the organization must be demonstrated far more than is currently the case.
- An implicit theme in the theory and research emanating from the New Leadership is that leaders *do* make a difference in organizations. On the other hand, quantitative studies of the effects of changes in top leaders have been highly inconsistent and have failed to provide a clear picture (see, for example, Bryman, 1986, 194–7; Day and Lord, 1988; Thomas, 1988). Some resolution of the rather contrasting implications of the two sets of literature is required.
- At a methodological level, I would like to see many more case studies of leadership conducted by social scientists. Case study evidence of New Leadership is far too geared either to what people like Iacocca, Carlzon and Sculley say about their achievements (or perhaps what others say about less accessible figures like Jobs and Welch) or to interviews with prominent figures (for example, Bennis and Nanus, 1985; Tichy and Devanna, 1990).

Detailed qualitative case studies of leadership in action may provide an additional layer of understanding to that which we already have. Where charismatic leadership is the focus (and perhaps in the case of other forms of the New Leadership also), the process whereby the social relationship is built up needs detailed study.

• Finally, by and large the New Leadership still operates within the framework of a rational model, so it could be argued that it is not as different from the kinds of approach covered in Chapter 1 as is sometimes believed. This means that the study of leadership in organizations still displays the tendency to operate largely in isolation from wider developments in organization theory and beyond. As the postulate of rationality is increasingly assailed from within organization theory (such as the organized anarchy and institutional approaches) and from further afield (in particular, post-modernist themes), leadership theorists, and proponents of the New Leadership in particular, will need to re-examine core assumptions and perhaps to construe their domain of study in more radically new ways. This is not to suggest that it will be necessary to jettison the theme of rationality altogether; indeed, the conception of charismatic leadership that was propounded in Chapter 3 of this book has very strong overtones of rationality. Rather, the point being made is that the notion that a leader engages in certain types of behaviour simply as a means to certain ends, which underpins the bulk of leadership theory and research, should be explored in conjunction with approaches in which this postulate of rationality is less prominent.

Notes

1 This suggestion is consistent with the 'romanticization' notion that was introduced in Chapter 6.

2 Price, a senior manager with Hewlett-Packard, has remarked that books like Peters and Waterman (1982) are more appealing to executives than much organizational research because they examine the factors that contribute to successful management, even though they 'may not be accurate' (1985: 131).

3 Hinings and Greenwood (1988), by contrast, directly associate transformational leadership with reorientations, whereas transactional leadership is portrayed as appropriate to organizations imbued with inertia. The view being presented in the present book is that this sort of association of transformational leadership with organizational transformation may underestimate the relevance of such leadership during periods of convergence (to use Tushman et al.'s term) and may create an impression that New Leadership is all to do with radical change in organizations.

4 By a successful transition is simply meant one in which the new manager 'establishes mastery and influence in a new assignment' (Gabarro, 1987: 6).

5 Biggart and Hamilton (1987) have proposed an institutional approach to leadership which has some affinities with the general ideas proposed here.

6 This passage has been put together from two sources: Rose (1989: 130–1) and Sculley (1987: 250–1).

References

Abse, D.W. and Ulman, R.B. (1977) 'Charismatic political leadership and collective regression', in R.S. Robins (ed.), *Psychopathology and Political Leadership*. New Orleans: Tulane University Press.

Ake, C. (1966) 'Charismatic legitimation and political integration', *Comparative Studies in Society and History*, 9: 1–13.

Albrow, M. (1990) *Max Weber's Construction of Social Theory*. London: Macmillan.

Al-Gattan, A.-R.A. (1985) 'Test of the path-goal theory of leadership in the multinational domain', *Group and Organization Studies*, 10: 429–45.

Apter, D.E. (1955) *The Gold Coast in Transition*. Princeton: Princeton University Press.

Apter, D.E. (1968) 'Nkrumah, charisma, and the coup', *Daedalus*, 97: 757–92.

Atkinson, J.M. (1984) *Our Masters' Voices: the Language and Body Language of Politics*. London: Methuen.

Avolio, B.J. and Gibbons, T.C. (1988) 'Developing transformational leaders: a life span approach', in J.A. Conger and R.N. Kanungo (eds), *Charismatic Leadership: the Elusive Factor in Organizational Effectiveness*. San Francisco: Jossey-Bass.

Avolio, B.J., Waldman, D.A. and Einstein, W.O. (1988) 'Transformational leadership in a management game simulation', *Group and Organization Studies*, 13: 59–80.

Avolio, B.J. and Yammarino, F.J. (1990) 'Operationalizing charismatic leadership using a levels-of-analysis framework', *Leadership Quarterly*, 1: 193–208.

Bach, S. (1985) *Final Cut: Dreams and Disaster in the Making of Heaven's Gate*. London: Cape.

Baehr, P. (1987) '"Caesarism" in the politics and sociology of Max Weber'. PhD thesis, University of Leicester.

Baehr, P. (1990) 'The "masses" in Weber's political sociology', *Economy and Society*, 19: 242–65.

Barker, E. (1987) 'Quo vadis? The Unification Church', in D.G. Bromley and P.E. Hammond (eds), *The Future of the New Religious Movements*. Macon, GA: Mercer University Press.

Barker, E. (1989) *New Religious Movements: a Practical Introduction*. London: HMSO.

Barnes, D.F. (1978) 'Charisma and religious leadership: an historical analysis', *Journal for the Scientific Study of Religion*, 17: 1–18.

Bass, B.M. (1981) *Stogdill's Handbook of Leadership*. New York: Free Press.

Bass, B.M. (1985) *Leadership and Performance Beyond Expectations*. New York: Free Press.

Bass, B.M. (1990a) *Bass and Stogdill's Handbook of Leadership: Theory, Research and Managerial Applications*, 3rd edn. New York: Free Press.

Bass, B.M. (1990b) 'From transactional to transformational leadership: learning to share the vision', *Organizational Dynamics*, 18: 19–31.

Bass, B.M. (1990c) 'Editorial: toward a meeting of minds', *Leadership Quarterly*, 1.

Bass, B.M. and Avolio, B.J. (1989) 'Potential biases in leadership measures: how prototypes, leniency, and general satisfaction relate to ratings and rankings of transformational and transactional leadership constructs', *Educational and Psychological Measurement*, 49: 509–27.

Bass, B.M. and Avolio, B.J. (1990a) 'The implications of transactional and transformational leadership for individual, team, and organizational development', *Research in Organizational Change and Development*, 4: 231–72.

Bass, B.M. and Avolio, B.J. (1990b) 'Developing transformational leadership: 1992 and beyond', *Journal of European Industrial Training*, 14: 21–7.

Beckford, J.A. (1972) 'The embryonic stage of a religious sect's development: the Jehovah's Witnesses', in M. Hill (ed.), *A Sociological Yearbook of Religion in Britain 5*. London: SCM Press.

Beckford, J.A. (1985) *Cult Controversies: the Societal Response to New Religious Movements*. London: Tavistock.

Beetham, D. (1974) *Max Weber and the Theory of Modern Politics*. London: George Allen & Unwin.

Bell, D. (1966) 'Sociodicy: a guide to modern usage', *American Scholar*, 35: 696–714.

Bendix, R. (1986) 'Reflections on charismatic leadership', in R.M. Glassman and W.H. Swatos (eds), *Charisma, History and Social Structure*. New York: Greenwood Press.

Bennis, W.G. (1976) *The Unconscious Conspiracy: Why Leaders Can't Lead*. New York: AMACOM.

Bennis, W.G. (1989) *On Becoming a Leader*. Reading, MA: Addison-Wesley.

Bennis, W.G. and Nanus, B. (1985) *Leaders: the Strategies for Taking Charge*. New York: Harper & Row.

Bensman, J. and Givant, M. (1975) 'Charisma and modernity: the use and abuse of a concept', *Social Research*, 42: 570–614.

Berger, A.L. (1986) 'Hasidism and Moonism: charisma in the counterculture', in R.M. Glassman and W.H. Swatos (eds), *Charisma, History and Social Structure*. New York: Greenwood Press.

Berger, P.L. (1963) 'Charisma and religious innovation: the social location of Israelite prophecy', *American Sociological Review*, 28: 940–50.

Berlew, D.E. (1974) 'Leadership and organizational excitement', *California Management Review*, 17: 21–30.

Betts, P., Taylor, R. and Tait, N. (1991) 'British Airways and SAS act to cut costs', *Financial Times*, 26 January: 22.

Biggart, N.W. (1989) *Charismatic Capitalism: Direct Selling Organizations in America*. Chicago: University of Chicago Press.

Biggart, N.W. and Hamilton, G.G. (1987) 'An institutional theory of leadership', *Journal of Applied Behavioral Science*, 23: 429–41.

Birmingham, D. (1990) *Kwame Nkrumah*. London: Sphere.

Boal, K.B. and Bryson, J.M. (1987) 'Charismatic leadership: a phenomenological and structural approach', in J.G. Hunt et al. (eds.), *Emerging Leadership Vistas*. Lexington: D.C. Heath.

Bolman, L.G. and Deal, T.E. (1991) *Reframing Organizations: Artistry, Choice, and Leadership*. San Francisco: Jossey-Bass.

Bosman, J. (1987) 'Persuasive effects of political metaphors', *Metaphor and Symbolic Activity*, 2: 97–113.

Bowers, D.G. and Seashore, S.E. (1966) 'Predicting organizational effectiveness with a four-factor theory of leadership', *Administrative Science Quarterly*, 11: 238–63.

Brearley, M. (1985) *The Art of Captaincy*. London: Hodder & Stoughton.

Brenner, L. (1988) 'Concepts of *Tarīqa* in West Africa: the case of the Qādiriyya', in D.B. Cruise O'Brien and C. Coulon (eds), *Charisma and Brotherhood in African Islam*. Oxford: Clarendon Press.

Bromley, D.G. and Shupe, A.D. (1979) *The Moonies in America*. Beverly Hills: Sage.

Brown, P. (1981) *Society and the Holy in Late Antiquity*. Berkeley: University of California Press.

Broyles, J.A. (1964) *The John Birch Society: Anatomy of a Protest*. Boston: Beacon.

Bryman, A. (1984) 'Organization studies and the concept of rationality', *Journal of Management Studies*, 21: 391–408.

Bryman, A. (1986) *Leadership and Organizations*. London: Routledge & Kegan Paul.

Bryman, A. (1987) 'The generalizability of implicit leadership theory', *Journal of Social Psychology*, 127: 129–41.

Bryman, A. (1988) *Quantity and Quality in Social Research*. London: Allen & Unwin.

Bryman, A. (1989) 'Leadership and culture in organizations', *Public Money and Management*, 9: 35–41.

Bull, P.E. (1986) 'The use of hand gestures in political speeches', *Journal of Language and Social Psychology*, 5: 103–18.

Burns, J.M. (1978) *Leadership*. New York: Harper & Row.

Burns, T. and Stalker, G.M. (1961) *The Management of Innovation*. London: Tavistock.

Butcher, L. (1988) *Accidental Millionaire: the Rise and Fall of Steve Jobs of Apple Computer*. New York: Paragon.

Butterfield, A.D. (1987) 'Chapter 2 commentary: welcome back charisma', in J.G. Hunt et al. (eds), *Emerging Leadership Vistas*. Lexington: D.C. Heath.

Byrne, J.A. (1985) 'Up, up and away?', *Business Week*, 25 November: 58–65.

Carlin, J. (1990) 'Freed to live up to his legend', *The Independent* 12 February: 19.

Carlzon, J. (1987) *Moments of Truth*. New York: Ballinger.

Carson, C. (1987) 'Martin Luther King, Jr.: charismatic leadership in a mass struggle', *Journal of American History*, 74: 448–54.

Cell, C.P. (1974) 'Charismatic heads of state: the social context', *Behavioral Science Research*, 4: 255–305.

Child, J. and Smith, C. (1987) 'The context and process of organizational transformation – Cadbury Limited in its sector', *Journal of Management Studies*, 24: 565–93.

Chittenden, M. and Roy, A. (1990) 'King musical revives its dream', *The Sunday Times*, 18 March: A28.

Clark, B.R. (1972) 'The organizational saga in higher education', *Administrative Science Quarterly*, 17: 178–84.

Clegg, S. (1990) *Modern Organizations: Organization Studies in the Postmodern World*. London: Sage.

Cohen, D.L. (1972) 'The concept of charisma and the analysis of leadership', *Political Studies*, 20: 299–305.

Cohen, M.D., March, J.G. and Olsen, J.P. (1972) 'A garbage can model of organizational choice', *Administrative Science Quarterly*, 17: 1–25.

Conger, J.A. (1989) *The Charismatic Leader: Behind the Mystique of Exceptional Leadership*. San Francisco: Jossey-Bass.

Conger, J.A. and Kanungo, R.N. (1987) 'Towards a behavioral theory of charismatic leadership in organizational settings', *Academy of Management Review*, 12: 637–47.

Conger, J.A. and Kanungo, R.N. (1988) 'Behavioral dimensions of charismatic leadership', in J.A. Conger and R.N. Kanungo (eds), *Charismatic Leadership: the Elusive Factor in Organizational Effectiveness*. San Francisco: Jossey-Bass.

Constantin, F. (1988) 'Charisma and the crisis of power in East Africa', in D.B. Cruise O'Brien and C. Coulon (eds), *Charisma and Brotherhood in African Islam*. Oxford: Clarendon Press.

Cruise O'Brien, D.B. (1988) 'Introduction', in D.B. Cruise O'Brien and C. Coulon (eds), *Charisma and Brotherhood in African Islam*. Oxford: Clarendon Press.

Cummings, L.L. (1975) 'Assessing the Graen/Cashman model and comparing it with other approaches', in J.G. Hunt and L.L. Larson (eds), *Leadership Frontiers*. Kent, Ohio: Kent State University Press.

Dansereau, F., Cashman, J. and Graen, G. (1973) 'Instrumentality theory and equity theory as complementary approaches to predicting the relationship of leadership to turnover among managers', *Organizational Behavior and Human Performance*, 10: 184–200.

Dansereau, F., Graen, G. and Haga, W.J. (1975) 'A vertical dyad linkage approach to leadership within formal organizations', *Organizational Behavior and Human Performance*, 13: 46–78.

Day, D.V. and Lord, R.G. (1988) 'Executive leadership and organizational performance: suggestions for a new theory and methodology', *Journal of Management*, 14: 453–64.

Day, P.J. (1980) 'Charismatic leadership in the small organization', *Human Organization*, 39: 50–8.

Dekmejian, R.H. and Wyszomirski, M.J. (1972) 'Charismatic leadership in Islam: the Mahdi of Sudan', *Comparative Studies in Society and History*, 14: 193–214.

Denison, D.R. (1990) *Corporate Culture and Organizational Effectiveness*. New York: Wiley.

Dessler, G. and Valenzi, E.R. (1977) 'Initiation of structure and subordinate satisfaction: a path analysis test of path-goal theory', *Academy of Management Journal*, 20: 251–9.

Dienesch, R.M. and Liden, R.C. (1986) 'Leader–member exchange model of leadership: a critique and further development', *Academy of Management Review*, 11: 618–34.

Dow, T.E. (1968) 'The role of charisma in modern African development', *Social Forces*, 46: 328–38.

Dow, T.E. (1969) 'The theory of charisma', *Sociological Quarterly*, 10: 306–18.

Downton, J.V. (1973) *Rebel Leadership: Commitment and Charisma in the Revolutionary Process*. New York: Free Press.

Drachkovitch, M.M. (1964) 'Succession and the charismatic leader in Yugoslavia', *Journal of International Affairs*, 18: 54–66.

Dreyfack, K. (1985) 'Why Beatrice had to dump Dutt', *Business Week*, 19 August: 20–1.

Dreyfuss, J. (1989) 'Reinventing IBM', *Fortune*, 14 August: 20–7.

Dubin, R. (1979) 'Metaphors of leadership: an overview', in J.G. Hunt and L.L. Larson (eds), *Crosscurrents in Leadership*. Carbondale, IL: Southern Illinois University Press.

Dubofsky, M. and Van Tine, W. (1977) *John L. Lewis: a Biography*. New York: Quadrangle.

Dunn, R. (1990) 'Mandela myth fades amid carnage', *The Sunday Times*, 26 August: 17.

Dyer, R. (1979) *Stars*. London: British Film Institute.

Edelman, M. (1988) *Constructing the Political Spectacle*. Chicago: University of Chicago Press.

Ehrlich, S.B., Meindl, J.R. and Viellieu, B. (1990) 'The charismatic appeal of a transformational leader: an empirical case study of a small, high-technology contractor', *Leadership Quarterly*, 1: 229–48.

Entelis, M.P. (1975) 'Nasser's Egypt: the failure of charismatic leadership', *Orbis*, 18: 451–64.

Etzioni, A.E. (1975) *A Comparative Analysis of Complex Organizations*, rev. edn (1st edn 1961). New York: Free Press.

Euden, J. (1990) 'The god who sank in the west', *The Independent*, 24 January: 19.

Fairclough, A. (1990) *Martin Luther King*. London: Sphere.

Fiedler, F.E. (1967) *A Theory of Leadership Effectiveness*. New York: McGraw-Hill.

Fiedler, F.E. and House, R.J. (1988) 'Leadership theory and research: a report of progress', in C.L. Cooper and I. Robertson (eds), *International Review of Industrial and Organizational Psychology*. New York: Wiley.

Filley, A.C., House, R.J. and Kerr, S. (1976) *Management Process and Organizational Behavior*. Glenview, IL: Scott, Foresman.

Fine, G.A. (1982) 'The Manson Family: the folklore traditions of a small group', *Journal of the Folklore Institute*, 19: 47–60.

Fisher, B.M. and Edwards, J.E. (1988) 'Consideration and initiating structure and their relationships with leader effectiveness: a meta-analysis', *Best Papers Proceedings, Academy of Management*, Anaheim, CA (cited in Bass, 1990a).

Fleishman, E.A., Harris, E.F. and Burtt, H.E. (1955) *Leadership and Supervision in Industry*. Columbus: Ohio State University, Bureau of Educational Research.

Foley, M. (1990) 'Presidential leadership and the presidency', in J. Hogan (ed.), *The Reagan Years: the Record in Presidential Leadership*. Manchester: Manchester University Press.

Freud, S. (1955) *Group Psychology and the Analysis of the Ego*. London: Hogarth Press.

Friedland, W.H. (1964) 'For a sociological concept of charisma', *Social Forces*, 43: 18–26.

Friedman, H.S., Prince, L.M., Riggio, R.E. and DiMatteo, M.R. (1980) 'Understanding and assessing nonverbal expressiveness', *Journal of Personality and Social Psychology*, 39: 333–51.

Friedrich, C.J. (1961) 'Political leadership and the problem of charismatic power', *Journal of Politics*, 23: 3–24.

Gabarro, J.J. (1987) *The Dynamics of Taking Charge*. Boston: Harvard University Press.

Galanter, M. (1981) 'Sociobiology and informal social controls of drinking: findings from two religious sects', *Journal of Studies of Alcohol*, 42: 64–79.

Galanter, M. (1982) 'Charismatic religious sects and psychiatry: an overview', *American Journal of Psychiatry*, 139: 1539–48.

Geertz, C. (1983) 'Centers, kings, and charisma: reflections of the symbolics of power', in C. Geertz, *Local Knowledge: Further Essays in Interpretive Anthropology*. New York: Basic Books.

Gibb, C.A. (1947) 'The principles and traits of leadership', *Journal of Abnormal and Social Psychology*, 42: 267–84.

Gibb, C.A. (1969) 'Leadership', in G. Lindzey and E. Aronson (eds), *The Handbook of Social Psychology*, vol. 4. Reading, MA: Addison-Wesley.

Gilsenan, M. (1973) *Saint and Sufi in Modern Egypt*. Oxford: Clarendon Press.

Gioia, D. and Sims, H.P. (1985) 'On avoiding the influence of implicit leadership theories in leader behavior descriptions', *Educational and Psychological Measurement*, 45: 217–32.

Gluck, F.W. (1984) 'Vision and leadership', *Interfaces*, 14: 10–18.

Gonzalez, E. (1974) *Cuba under Castro: the Limits of Charisma*. Boston: Houghton Mifflin.

Graen, G. and Cashman, J.F. (1975) 'A role making model of leadership in formal organizations: a developmental approach', in J.G. Hunt and L.L. Larson (eds), *Leadership Frontiers*, Carbondale, IL: Southern Illinois University Press.

Greene, C.N. (1975) 'The reciprocal nature of influence between leader and subordinate', *Journal of Applied Psychology*, 60: 187–93.

Greene, C.N. (1979) 'Questions of causation in the path-goal theory of leadership', *Academy of Management Journal*, 22: 22–41.

Greiner, L.E. and Bhambri, A. (1989) 'New CEO intervention and dynamics of deliberate strategic change', *Strategic Management Journal*, 10: 67–86.

Griffin, R.W. (1980) 'Relationships among individual, task design, and leader behavior variables', *Academy of Management Journal*, 23: 665–83.

Guilliat, R. (1991) 'Apple blossom time', *Business World*, 31 March: 30–6.

Hackman, R.J. (1984) 'The transition that hasn't happened', in J.R. Kimberly and R.E. Quinn (eds), *New Futures: the Challenge of Managing Corporate Transitions*. Homewood, IL: Dow-Jones-Irwin.

Haley, P. (1980) 'Rudolph Sohm on charisma', *Journal of Religion*, 60: 185–97.

Halpin, A.W. (1957) 'The observed leader behavior and ideal leader behavior of aircraft commanders and school superintendents', in R.M. Stogdill and A.E. Coons (eds), *Leader Behavior: Its Description and Measurement*. Columbus: Ohio State University, Bureau of Business Research.

Halpin, A.W. and Winer, B.J. (1957) 'A factorial study of the leader behavior descriptions', in R.M. Stogdill, and A.E. Coons (eds), *Leader Behavior: Its Description and Measurement*. Columbus: Ohio State University, Bureau of Business Research.

Hamer, D.A. (1978) 'Gladstone: the making of a political myth', *Victorian Studies*: 29–50.

Harré, R. (1972) *The Philosophies of Science*. Oxford: Oxford University Press.

Harrison, J.F.C. (1979) *The Second Coming: Popular Millenarianism 1780–1850*. London: Routledge & Kegan Paul.

Harvey-Jones, J. (1991) 'Managing change without a revolution', *Management Week*, no. 4: 35.

Hater, J.J. and Bass, B.M. (1988) 'Superiors' evaluations and subordinates' perceptions of transformational and transactional leadership', *Journal of Applied Psychology*, 73: 695–702.

Hegarty, S. (1991) 'Paul Sabin: bringing local government in from the cold', *Management Week*, no. 5: 66–70.

Hersey, P. and Blanchard, K.H. (1977) *Management of Organizational Behavior*, 3rd edn (1st edn 1969). Englewood Cliffs: Prentice-Hall.

Hickman, C.R. (1990) *Mind of a Manager, Soul of a Leader*. New York: Wiley.

Hinings, C.R. and Greenwood, R. (1988) *The Dynamics of Strategic Change*. Oxford: Basil Blackwell.

Hogan, R., Raskin, R. and Fazzini, D. (1990) 'How charisma cloaks incompetence', *Personnel Journal*, 69: 72–6.

Hollander, E.P. and Julian, J.W. (1978a) 'Studies in leader legitimacy, influence, and innovation', in L. Berkowitz (ed.), *Group Processes*. New York: Academic Press.

Hollander, E.P. and Julian, J.W. (1978b) 'A further look at leader legitimacy, influence, and innovation', in L. Berkowitz (ed.), *Group Processes*. New York: Academic Press.

Horowitz, I.L. (1972) *Three Worlds of Development*, 2nd edn (1st edn 1966). New York: Oxford University Press.

House, R.J. (1973) 'A path-goal theory of leadership effectiveness', in E.A. Fleishman and J.G. Hunt (eds), *Current Development in the Study of Leadership*. Carbondale, IL: Southern Illinois University Press.

House, R.J. (1977) 'A 1976 theory of charismatic leadership', in J.G. Hunt and L.L. Larson (eds), *Leadership: the Cutting Edge*. Carbondale, IL: Southern Illinois University Press.

House, R.J. and Baetz, M.L. (1979) 'Leadership: some empirical generalizations and new research directions', *Research in Organizational Behavior*, 1: 341–423.

House, R.J. and Dessler, G. (1974) 'The path-goal theory of leadership: some *post hoc* and *a priori* tests', in J.G. Hunt and L.L. Larson (eds), *Contingency Approaches to Leadership*. Carbondale, IL: Southern Illinois University Press.

House, R.J. and Mitchell, T.R. (1974) 'Path-goal theory of leadership', *Journal of Contemporary Business*, 3: 81–97.

House, R.J., Spangler, W.D. and Woycke, J. (1990) 'Personality and charisma in the U.S. presidency: a psychological theory of leader effectiveness', unpublished paper.

House, R.J. Woycke, J. and Fodor, E.M. (1988) 'Charismatic and noncharismatic leaders: differences in behavior and effectiveness', in J.A. Conger and R.N. Kanungo (eds), *Charismatic Leadership: the Elusive Factor in Organizational Effectiveness*. San Francisco: Jossey-Bass.

Howell, J.M. (1988) 'Two faces of charisma: socialized and personalized leadership in organizations', in J.A. Conger and R.N. Kanungo (eds), *Charismatic Leadership: the Elusive Factor in Organizational Effectiveness*. San Francisco: Josscy-Bass.

Howell, J.M. and Frost, P.J. (1989) 'A laboratory study of charismatic leadership', *Organizational Behavior and Human Decision Processes*, 43: 243–69.

Howell, J.M. and Higgins, C.A. (1990a) 'Champions of technological innovation', *Administrative Science Quarterly*, 35: 317–41.

Howell, J.M. and Higgins, C.A. (1990b) 'Leadership behaviors, influence tactics, and career experiences of champions of technological innovation', *Leadership Quarterly*, 1: 249–64.

Hunt, J.G., Baliga, B.R., Dachler, H.P. and Schriesheim, C.A. (eds) (1987) *Emerging Leadership Vistas*. Lexington: D.C. Heath.

Hunt, J.G., Sekaran, U. and Schriesheim, C.A. (eds) (1982) *Leadership: Beyond Establishment Views*. Carbondale, IL: Southern Illinois University Press.

Iacocca, L. (1984) *Iacocca: an Autobiography*. New York: Bantam.

Indvik, J. (1986) 'Path-goal theory of leadership: a meta-analysis'. Paper presented at the Academy of Management Conference, Chicago.

Indvik, J. (1988) 'A more complete testing of path-goal theory'. Paper presented at the Academy of Management Conference, Anaheim.

Jacobs, J. (1987) 'Deconversion from religious movements: an analysis of charismatic bonding and spiritual commitment', *Journal for the Scientific Study of Religion*, 26: 294–308.

Jacobson, G. and Hillkirk, J. (1986) *Xerox: American Samurai*. New York: Collier.

Janis, I.L. (1972) *Victims of Groupthink*. Boston: Houghton Mifflin.

Johnson, D.P. (1979) 'Dilemmas of charismatic leadership: the case of the People's Temple', *Sociological Analysis*, 40: 315–23.

Judis, J.B. (1990) 'The guru who forgot what he said', *Business World*, 40–6.

Kahn, R.L. and Katz, D. (1953) 'Leadership practices in relation to productivity and morale', in D. Cartwright and A. Zander (eds), *Group Dynamics*. New York: Harper & Row.

Kanter, R.M. (1968) 'Commitment and social organization: a study of commitment mechanisms in utopian communities', *American Sociological Review*, 33: 499–517.

Kanter, R.M. (1972) *Commitment and Community*. Cambridge, MA: Harvard University Press.

Kanter, R.M. (1977) *Men and Women of the Corporation*. New York: Basic Books.

Kanter, R.M. (1979) 'Power failures in management circuits', *Harvard Business Review*, 57: 65–75.

Katerberg, R. and Hom, P.W. (1981) 'Effects of within-group and between-groups variation in leadership', *Journal of Applied Psychology*, 66: 218–23.

Katz, R. (1977) 'The influence of group conflict on leadership effectiveness', *Organizational Behavior and Human Performance*, 20: 265–86.

Keller, M. (1989) *Rude Awakening: the Rise, Fall, and Struggle for Recovery of General Motors*. New York: William Morrow.

Keller, R.T. (1989) 'A test of the path-goal theory of leadership with need for clarity as a moderator in research and development organizations', *Journal of Applied Psychology*, 74: 208–12.

Kerr, S., Schriesheim, C.A., Murphy, C.J. and Stogdill, R.M. (1974) 'Toward a contingency theory of leadership based upon the consideration and initiating structure literature', *Organizational Behavior and Human Performance*, 12: 62–82.

Kets de Vries, M.F.R. (1990) *Prisoners of Leadership*. New York: Wiley.

Kimmel, M. (1989) '"New prophets" and "old ideals": charisma and tradition in the Iranian revolution', *Social Compass*, 36: 493–510.

Kimmel, M. and Tavakol, R. (1986) 'Against Satan: charisma and tradition in Iran', in R.M. Glassman and W.H. Swatos (eds), *Charisma, History and Social Structure*. New York: Greenwood Press.

Kirkpatrick, S.A. and Locke, E.A. (1991) 'Leadership: do traits matter?', *The Executive*, 5: 48–60.

Korman, A.K. (1966) '"Consideration", "initiating structure", and organizational criteria – a review', *Personnel Psychology* 19: 349–61.

Kotter, J.P. (1988) *The Leadership Factor*. New York: Free Press.

Kotter, J.P. (1990) *A Force for Change: How Leadership Differs from Management*. New York: Free Press.

Kouzes, J.M. and Posner, B.Z. (1987) *The Leadership Challenge*. San Francisco: Jossey-Bass.

Kuhn, T.S. (1970) *The Structure of Scientific Revolutions*, 2nd edn (1st edn 1962). Chicago: University of Chicago Press.

Larson, L.L., Hunt, J.G., and Osborn, R.N. (1976) 'The great hi-hi leader behavior myth: a lesson from Occam's razor', *Academy of Management Journal*, 19: 628–41.

Last, M. (1988) 'Charisma and medicine in Northern Nigeria', in D.B. Cruise O'Brien and C. Coulon (eds), *Charisma and Brotherhood in African Islam*. Oxford: Clarendon Press.

Levinson, H. and Rosenthal, S. (1984) *CEO: Corporate Leadership in Action*. New York: Basic Books.

Lewis, K.W. and Kuhnert, P. (1987) 'Transactional and transformational leadership: a constructive/developmental analysis', *Academy of Management Review*, 12: 648–57.

Lewy, E. (1979) 'Historical charismatic leaders and mythical heroes', *Journal of Psychohistory*, 6: 377–92.

Lichfield, J. (1989) 'Still no charisma for "kid" Quayle', *The Independent*, 17 July: 9.

Lindholm, C. (1990) *Charisma*. Oxford: Basil Blackwell.

Ling, R. (1987) 'The production of synthetic charisma', *Journal of Political and Military Sociology*, 15: 157–70.

Loomis, C.J. (1989) 'IBM's big blues: a legend tries to remake itself', *Fortune*, 14 January: 34–41.

Lord, R.G., Binning, J.F., Rush, M.C. and Thomas, J.C. (1978) 'The effect of performance cues and leader behavior on questionnaire ratings of leader behavior', *Organizational Behavior and Human Performance*, 21: 27–39.

Lord, R.G., DeVader, C.L. and Alliger, G.M. (1986) 'A meta-analysis of the relation between personality traits and leadership perceptions: an application of validity generalization procedures', *Journal of Applied Psychology*, 71: 402–10.

Lowin, A. and Craig, C.R. (1968) 'The influence of performance on managerial style: an experimental object lesson in the ambiguity of correlational data', *Organizational Behavior and Human Performance*, 3: 440–58.

Luke, T. (1986) 'Televisual democracy and the politics of charisma', *Telos*, 70: 59–79.

Lutkehaus, N.C. (1990) 'From charismatic leader to anti-hero: the life and legacy of Irakau as cultural allegory', *Ethnology*, 29: 243–59.

Madsen, D. and Snow, P.G. (1983) 'The dispersion of charisma', *Comparative Political Studies*, 16: 337–62.

Madsen, D. and Snow, P.G. (1987) 'Recruitment contrasts in a divided charismatic movement', *American Political Science Review*, 81: 233–8.

Mann, R.D. (1959) 'A review of the relationship between personality and performance in small groups', *Psychological Bulletin*, 56: 241–70.

Martin, J. and Siehl, C. (1983) 'Organizational culture and counterculture: an uneasy symbiosis', *Organizational Dynamics*, 12: 52–64.

Maslow, A.H. (1943) 'A theory of human motivation', *Psychological Review*, 50: 370–96.

McClelland, D.C. (1975) *Power: the Inner Experience*. New York: Wiley.

Meindl, J.R. (1989) 'On leadership: an alternative to conventional wisdom'. Paper presented at the Fourth International Conference on Organizational Symbolism and Corporate Culture, INSEAD.

Meindl, J.R., Ehrlich, S.B. and Dukerich, J.M. (1985) 'The romance of leadership', *Administrative Science Quarterly*, 30: 78–102.

Meyer, J.W. and Rowan, B. (1977) 'Institutionalized organizations: formal structure as myth and ceremony', *American Journal of Sociology*, 83: 340–63.

Miller, D. (1990) *The Icarus Paradox*. New York: Harper Business.

Milne, H. (1990) 'Obituary: Bhagwan Shree Rajneesh', *The Independent*, 22 January: 12.

Miner, A.S., Amburgey, T.L. and Stearns, T.M. (1990) 'Interorganizational linkages and population dynamics: buffering and transformational shields', *Administrative Science Quarterly*, 35: 689–713.

Mitchell, T.R. (1973) 'Motivation and participation: an integration', *Academy of Management Journal*, 16: 670–9.

Mitchell, T.R. (1979) 'Organizational behavior', *Annual Review of Psychology*, 30: 243–81.

Mommsen, W.J. (1989) *The Political and Social Theory of Max Weber*. Cambridge: Polity.

Moore, T. (1988) 'Make-or-break time for General Motors', *Fortune*, 15 February: 14–26.

Morgan, G. (1988a) 'Teaching MBAs transformational thinking', in R.E. Quinn and K.S. Cameron (eds), *Paradox and Transformation: Toward a Theory of Change in Organization and Management*. Cambridge, MA: Ballinger.

Morgan, G. (1988b) *Riding the Waves of Change: Developing Managerial Competencies for a Turbulent World*. San Francisco: Jossey-Bass.

Morrison, A.M. (1982) 'Trying to bring GE to life', *Fortune*, 25 January: 50–7.

Morrison, A.M. (1984) 'Apple bites back', *Fortune*, 20 February: 56–62.

Murphy, J.T. (1988) 'The unheroic side of leadership: notes from the swamp', *Phi Delta Kappan*, 69: 654–9.

Nadler, D.A. and Tushman, M.L. (1989) 'What makes for magic leadership?', in W.E. Rosenbach and R.L. Taylor (eds), *Contemporary Issues in Leadership*. Boulder: Westview.

Nadler, D.A. and Tushman, M.L. (1990) 'Beyond the charismatic leader: leadership and organizational change', *California Management Review*, 32: 77–97.

Naftulin, D.H., Ware, J.E. and Donnelly, F.A. (1973) 'The Doctor Fox lecture: a paradigm of educational seduction', *Journal of Medical Education*, 48: 630–5.

Nelson, G.K. (1969) *Spiritualism and Society*. London: Routledge & Kegan Paul.

Newman, R.G. (1983) 'Thoughts on superstars of charisma: pipers in our midst', *American Journal of Orthopsychiatry*, 53: 201–8.

Nyomarkay, J. (1967) *Charisma and Factionalism in the Nazi Party*. Minneapolis: University of Minnesota Press.

Nystrom, P.C. (1978) 'Managers and the hi-hi leader myth', *Academy of Management Journal*, 21: 325–31.

Oberg, W. (1972) 'Charisma, commitment, and contemporary organization theory', *MSU Business Topics*, 20: 18–32.

Oldham, G.R. (1976) 'The motivational strategies used by supervisors: relationships to effectiveness indicators', *Organizational Behavior and Human Performance*, 15: 66–86.

Olin, S.C. (1980) 'The Oneida Community and the instability of charismatic authority', *Journal of American History*, 67: 285–300.

Oomen, T.K. (1967) 'Charisma, social structure and social change', *Comparative Studies in Society and History*, 10: 85–99.

Palmer, S.J. (1988) 'Charisma and abdication: a study of the leadership of Bhagwan Shree Rajneesh', *Sociological Analysis*, 49: 119–35.

Perinbanayagam, R.S. (1971) 'The dialectic of charisma', *Sociological Quarterly*, 12: 387–402.

Peters, T. (1987) *Thriving on Chaos*. New York: Knopf.

Peters, T. and Austin, N. (1985) *A Passion for Excellence*. New York: Random House.

Peters, T. and Waterman, R.H. (1982) *In Search of Excellence: Lessons from America's Best-Run Companies*. New York: Harper & Row.

Peterson, M.F., Phillips, R.L. and Duran, C.A. (1989) 'A comparison of Japanese performance-maintenance measures with U.S. leadership scales', *Psychologia*, 32: 58–70.

Podsakoff, P.M., MacKenzie, S.B., Moorman, R.H. and Fetter, R. (1990) 'Transformational leader behaviors and their effects on followers' trust in leader, satisfaction, and organizational citizenship behaviors', *Leadership Quarterly*, 1: 107–42.

Podsakoff, P.M., Todor, W.D., Grover, R.A. and Huber, V.L. (1984) 'Situational moderators of leader reward and punishment behaviors: fact or fiction?', *Organizational Behavior and Human Performance*, 34: 21–63.

Posner, B.Z. and Kouzes, J.M. (1990) 'Leadership practices: an alternative to the psychological perspective', in K.E. Clark and M.B. Clark (eds), *Measures of Leadership*, West Orange, NJ: Leadership Library of America.

Potts, M. (1984) 'GE: changing a corporate culture', *Washington Post*, 23 September: G1, G10–G11.

Price, R.L. (1985) 'A consumer's view of organizational literature', in L.L. Cummings and P.J. Frost (eds), *Publishing in the Organizational Sciences*. Homewood, IL: Irwin.

Puffer, S.M. (1990) 'Attributions of charismatic leadership: the impact of decision style, outcome, and observer characteristics', *Leadership Quarterly*, 1: 177–92.

Quinn, R.E. (1988) *Beyond Rational Management*. San Francisco: Jossey-Bass.

Ralston, H. (1989) 'The construction of authority in the Christian Ashram movement', *Archives de Sciences Sociales des Religions*, 67: 53–75.

Reich, R.B. (1987) 'Entrepreneurship reconsidered: the team as hero', *Harvard Business Review*, 65: 77–83.

Rhodes, L. (1984) 'That daring young man and his flying machines', *Inc.*, January, 42 52.

Robbins, T. (1988) *Cults, Converts and Charisma*. London: Sage.

Roberts, N.C. (1985) 'Transforming leadership: a process of collective action', *Human Relations*, 38: 1023–46.

Roberts, N.C. and Bradley, R.T. (1988) 'Limits of charisma', in J.A. Conger and R.N. Kanungo (eds), *Charismatic Leadership: the Elusive Factor in Organizational Effectiveness*. San Francisco: Jossey-Bass.

Robinson, J.C. (1988) 'Mao after death: charisma and political legitimacy', *Asian Survey*, 28: 353–68.

Rochford, E.B. (1985) *Hare Krishna in America*. New Brunswick: Rutgers University Press.

Rose, F. (1989) *West of Eden: the End of Innocence at Apple Computer*. London: Business Books.

Rosenbach, W.E. and Hayman, S. (1989) 'Absentee charismatic leadership: Khomeini, Gandhi, and Mandela', in W.E. Rosenbach and R.L. Taylor (eds), *Contemporary Issues in Leadership*. Boulder: Westview.

Rotter, J.B. (1966) 'Generalized expectancies for internal versus external control of reinforcement', *Psychological Monographs*, 80, no. 609.

Runciman, W.G. (1963) 'Charismatic legitimation and one-party rule in Ghana', *Archives Européennes de Sociologie*, 4: 148–63.

Rush, M.D., Thomas, J.C. and Lord, R.G. (1977) 'Implicit leadership theory: a potential threat to the internal validity of leader behavior questionnaires', *Organizational Behavior and Human Performance*, 20: 93–110.

Rutan, J.S. and Rice, C.A. (1981) 'The charismatic leader: asset or liability?', *Psychotherapy: Theory, Research and Practice*, 18: 487–92.

Salaman, G. (1977) 'An historical discontinuity: from charisma to routinization', *Human Relations*, 30: 373–88.

Sashkin, M. (1986) 'True vision in leadership', *Training and Development Journal*, 40, 58–61.

Sashkin, M. (1988) 'The visionary leader', in J.A. Conger and R.N. Kanungo (eds), *Charismatic Leadership: the Elusive Factor in Organizational Effectiveness*. San Francisco: Jossey-Bass.

Sashkin, M. and Burke, W.W. (1990) 'Understanding and assessing organizational leadership', in K.E. Clark and M.B. Clark (eds), *Measures of Leadership*. West Orange, NJ: Leadership Library of America.

Schram, S.R. (1967) 'Mao Tse-Tung as a charismatic leader', *Asian Survey*, 7: 383–8.

Schriesheim, C.A. and DeNisi, A.S. (1981) 'Task dimensions of the effects of instrumental leadership: a two-sample replicated test of path-goal leadership theory', *Journal of Applied Psychology*, 66: 589–97.

Schriesheim, C.A. and Kerr, S. (1974) 'Theories and measures of leadership', in J.G. Hunt and

L.L. Larson (eds), *Leadership: the Cutting Edge*, Carbondale, IL: Southern Illinois University Press.

Schriesheim, C.A., Kinicki, A.J. and Schriesheim, J.F. (1979) 'The effect of leniency on leader behavior descriptions', *Organizational Behavior and Human Performance*, 23: 1–29.

Schriesheim, C.A. and Murphy, C.J. (1976), 'Relationships between leader behavior and subordinate satisfaction and performance: a test of some situational moderators', *Journal of Applied Psychology*, 61: 634–41.

Schriesheim, C.A. and von Glinow, M.A. (1977) 'Tests of the path-goal theory of leadership: a theoretical and empirical analysis', *Academy of Management Journal*, 20: 398–405.

Schriesheim, J.F. (1980) 'The social context of leader–subordinate relations: an investigation of the effects of group cohesiveness', *Journal of Applied Psychology*, 65: 183–94.

Schriesheim, J.F. and Schriesheim, C.A. (1980) 'A test of the path-goal theory of leadership and some suggested directions for future research', *Personnel Psychology*, 33: 349–70.

Schuler, R.S. (1976), 'Participation with supervisor and subordinate authoritarianism: a path-goal reconciliation', *Administrative Science Quarterly*, 21: 320–5.

Schwartz, B. (1990) 'The reconstruction of Abraham Lincoln', in D. Middleton and D. Edwards (eds), *Collective Remembering*. London: Sage.

Schweitzer, A. (1984) *The Age of Charisma*. Chicago: Nelson-Hall.

Scott, W.R. (1981) *Organizations: Rational, Natural and Open Systems*. Englewood Cliffs, NJ: Prentice-Hall.

Sculley, J. (1987) *Odyssey: Pepsi to Apple*. New York: Harper & Row (page references in the text refer to the 1989 Fontana paperback edition).

Seltzer, J., Numerof, R.E. and Bass, B.M. (1989) 'Transformational leadership: is it a source of more burnout and stress?', *Journal of Health and Human Resource Administration*, 12: 174–85.

Selznick, P. (1943) 'An approach to a theory of bureaucracy', *American Sociological Review*, 8: 47–54.

Selznick, P. (1957) *Leadership in Administration*. New York: Harper & Row.

Sherman, S.P. (1989) 'The mind of Jack Welch', *Fortune*, 27 March: 37–44.

Shils, E. (1958) 'The concentration and dispersion of charisma: their bearing on economic policy in underdeveloped countries', *World Politics*, 11: 1–19.

Shils, E. (1965) 'Charisma, order, and status', *American Sociological Review*, 30: 199–213.

Shils, E. (1968) 'Charisma', in D. Sills (ed.), *International Encyclopedia of the Social Sciences*, vol. 2. London: Macmillan.

Simonton, D.K. (1988) 'Presidential style: personality, biography, and performance', *Journal of Personality and Social Psychology*, 55: 928–36.

Singer, M.S. (1985) 'Transformational vs transactional leadership: a study of New Zealand company managers', *Psychological Reports*, 57: 143–6.

Singer, M.S. and Singer, A.E. (1990) 'Situational constraints on transformational versus transactional leadership behavior, subordinates' leadership preference, and satisfaction', *Journal of Social Psychology*, 130: 385–96.

Skinner, E.P. (1988) 'Sankara and the Burkinabé revolution: charisma and power, local and external dimensions', *Journal of Modern African Studies*, 26: 437–55.

Smith, P.B. and Peterson, M.F. (1988) *Leadership, Organizations and Culture*. London: Sage.

Snow, D.A., Rochford, E.B., Worden, S.K. and Benford, R.D. (1986) 'Frame alignment processes, micromobilization, and movement participation', *American Sociological Review*, 51: 464–81.

Sohm, R. (1882) *Kirchenrecht*, 2 vols. Leipzig: Duncker & Humblot.

Southwell, P. (1982) *Prophecy*. London: Hodder & Stoughton.

Stark, W. (1965) 'The routinization of charisma: a consideration of Catholicism', *Sociological Analysis*, 26: 203–11.

Staw, B.M. (1976) 'Knee-deep in the big muddy: a study of escalating commitment to a chosen course of action', *Organizational Behavior and Human Performance*, 16: 27–44.

Staw, B.M. and Ross, J. (1987) 'Knowing when to pull the plug', *Harvard Business Review*, 65: 68–74.

Stewart, G. (1974) 'Charisma and integration: an eighteenth-century North American case', *Comparative Studies in Society and History*, 16: 138–49.

Stewart, R. (1983) 'Managerial behaviour: how research has changed the traditional picture', in M.J. Earl (ed.), *Perspectives on Management*. Oxford: Oxford University Press.

Stewart, T.A. (1991) 'GE keeps those ideas coming', *Fortune*, 12 August: 19–25.

Stinson, J.E. and Johnson, T.W. (1975) 'The path-goal theory of leadership: a partial test and suggested refinement', *Academy of Management Journal*, 18: 242–52.

Stogdill, R.M. (1948) 'Personal factors associated with leadership: a survey of the literature', *Journal of Psychology*, 25: 35–71.

Stogdill, R.M. (1963) *Manual for the Leader Behavior Description Questionnaire – Form XII*. Columbus: Ohio State University, Bureau of Business Research.

Stogdill, R.M. (1974) *Handbook of Leadership: a Survey of Theory and Research*. New York: Free Press.

Stone, D. (1982) 'The charismatic authority of Werner Erhard', in R. Wallis (ed.), *Millenialism and Charisma*. Belfast: Queen's University.

Swain, J. (1991) 'Mao mania revived by a party in crisis', *The Sunday Times*, 30 June: 19.

Swidler, A. (1979) *Organization Without Authority: Dilemmas of Social Control in Free Schools*. Cambridge, MA: Harvard University Press.

Tai, H.-T.H. (1983) *Millenarianism and Peasant Politics in Vietnam*. Cambridge, MA: Harvard University Press.

Taylor, A. (1991) 'Can Iacocca fix Chrysler – again?', *Fortune*, 8 April: 40–4.

Taylor, P. (1983) 'Beliefs are imperatives', *Financial Times*, 31 December: 15.

Theobald, R. (1975) *Charisma: Some Empirical Problems Reconsidered*. London: Polytechnic of Central London.

Theobald, R. (1978) 'A charisma too versatile?', *Archives Européennes de Sociologie*, 19: 192–200.

Theobald, R.E. (1980) 'The role of charisma in the development of social movements: Ellen G. White and the emergence of Seventh-Day Adventism', *Archives de Sciences Sociales des Religions*, 49: 83–100.

Thomas, A.B. (1988) 'Does leadership make a difference to organizational performance?', *Administrative Science Quarterly*, 33: 388–400.

Thompson, E.P. (1968) *The Making of the English Working Class*. Harmondsworth, Middx.: Penguin.

Thompson, J. and Heelas, P. (1986) *The Way of the Heart: the Rajneesh Movement*. Wellingborough, Northants.: Aquarian Press.

Thompson, V. (1963) *Modern Organization*. New York: Knopf.

Thomson, R. (1991) 'In search of missing chemistry', *The Independent on Sunday*, 28 April: 11.

Thorbeck, J. (1991) 'The turnaround value of values', *Harvard Business Review*, 69: 52–61.

Tichy N. and Charan, R. (1989) 'Speed, simplicity and self-confidence: an interview with Jack Welch', *Harvard Business Review*, 67: 112–20.

Tichy, N.M. and Devanna, M.A. (1990) *The Transformational Leader*, updated edn (1st edn 1986). New York: Wiley.

Toth, M.A. (1981) *The Theory of the Two Charismas*. Washington, DC: University Press of America.

Tracy, L. (1987) 'Consideration and initiating structure: are they basic dimensions of leader behavior?', *Social Behavior and Personality* 15: 21–33.

Trice, H.M. and Beyer, J.M. (1986) 'Charisma and its routinization in two social movement organizations', *Research in Organizational Behavior*, 8: 113–64.

Trice, H.M. and Beyer, J.M. (1990) 'Cultural leadership in organizations', *Organizational Science*, 1.

Turner, B.S. (1974) *Weber and Islam: a Critical Study*. London: Routledge & Kegan Paul.

Tushman, M.L., Newman, W.H. and Romanelli, E. (1986) 'Convergence and upheaval: managing the unsteady pace of organizational evolution', *California Management Review*, 29: 29–44.

Tushman, M.L. and Romanelli, E. (1985) 'Organizational evolution: a metamorphosis model of convergence and reorientation', *Research in Organizational Behavior*, 7: 171–222.

190 *Charisma and leadership in organizations*

Uttal, B. (1985) 'Behind the fall of Steve Jobs', *Fortune*, 5 August: 12–16.

Vroom, V.H. and Jago, A.G. (1988) *The New Leadership: Managing Participation in Organizations*. Englewood Cliffs, NJ: Prentice-Hall.

Vroom, V.H. and Yetton, P.W. (1973) *Leadership and Decision-Making*. Pittsburgh: University of Pittsburgh Press.

Wallis, R. (1982) 'Charisma, commitment and control in a new religious movement', in R. Wallis (ed.), *Millenialism and Charisma*. Belfast: Queen's University.

Wallis, R. (1984) *The Elementary Forms of the New Religious Life*. London: Routledge & Kegan Paul.

Wallis, R. and Bruce, S. (1986a) 'The social construction of charisma', in R. Wallis and S. Bruce, *Sociological Theory, Religion and Collective Action*. Belfast: Queen's University.

Wallis, R. and Bruce, S. (1986b) 'Charisma, tradition, Paisley and the prophets', in R. Wallis and S. Bruce, *Sociological Theory, Religion and Collective Action*. Belfast: Queen's University.

Warner, J. and Fagan, M. (1991) 'IBM aims for 14,000 redundancies', *The Independent*, 29 March: 23.

Weber, M. (1948) 'Politics as a vocation' (1921), in H.H. Gerth and C.W. Mills (eds), *From Max Weber: Essays in Sociology*. London: Routledge & Kegan Paul.

Weber, M. (1952) *Ancient Judaism* (1917–19), trans. H.H. Gerth and D. Martindale. Glencoe: Free Press.

Weber, M. (1968) *Economy and Society* (1925), 3 vols, eds G. Roth and C. Wittich. New York: Bedminster.

Westley, F.R. and Mintzberg, H. (1988) 'Profiles of strategic vision: Levesque and Iacocca', in J.A. Conger and R.N. Kanungo (eds), *Charismatic Leadership: the Elusive Factor in Organizational Effectiveness*. San Francisco: Jossey-Bass.

Westley, F.R. and Mintzberg, H. (1989) 'Visionary leadership and strategic management', *Strategic Management Journal*, 10: 17–32.

Whitaker, R. (1990) 'Kashmir's schoolboy leader', *The Independent Magazine*, 23 June: 18.

Whyte, W.F. (1943) *Street Corner Society*. Chicago: University of Chicago Press.

Whyte, W.F. and Whyte, K.K. (1988) *Making Mondragón: the Growth and Development of the Worker Cooperative Complex*. Ithaca, NY: ILR, Cornell University.

Wilby, P. (1989) 'MacGregor: carry on being boring', *The Independent*, 27 July: 19.

Willner, A.R. (1984) *The Spellbinders: Charismatic Political Leadership*. New Haven: Yale University Press.

Wilson, B.R. (1961) *Sects and Society*. London: Heinemann.

Wilson, B.R. (1975) *The Noble Savages: the Primitive Origins of Charisma and its Contemporary Survival*. Berkeley: University of California Press.

Woycke, J. (1990) 'Managing political modernization: charismatic leadership in the developing countries', in A.M. Jaeger and R.N. Kanungo (eds), *Management in Developing Countries*. London: Routledge.

Yammarino, F.J. and Bass, B.M. (1990a) 'Transformational leadership and multiple levels of analysis', *Human Relations*, 43: 975–95.

Yammarino, F.J. and Bass, B.M. (1990b) 'Long-term forecasting of transformational leadership and its effects among naval officers: some preliminary findings', in K.E. Clark and M.B. Clark (eds), *Measures of Leadership*. West Orange, NJ: Leadership Library of America.

Zald, M.N. and Ash, R. (1966) 'Social movement organizations: growth, decay and change', *Social Forces*, 44: 327–41.

Zaleznik, A. (1977) 'Managers and leaders: are they different?' *Harvard Business Review*, 55: 67–78.

Zaleznik, A. (1983) 'The leadership gap', *The Washington Quarterly*, 6: 32–9.

Zaleznik, A. (1990) 'The leadership gap', *The Executive*, 4: 7–22.

Zucker, L.G. (1987) 'Institutional theories of organization', *Annual Review of Sociology*, 13: 443–64.

Author Index

Subject Index

Rutherford, Joseph, 75

Sabin, Paul, 150, 151, 153, 175
Salama ibn Hassan Salama, 54, 56–7, 74–5, 79, 82
Sankara, Thomas, 44
satisfaction with leader, as consequence of leader behaviour, 122, 127
Scandinavian Airlines (SAS), 109
Sculley, John, 105–6, 109, 152, 167, 170, 174, 177
selection of leaders, 4, 44
Seventh Day Adventism, 58, 81–2, 85
situational factors,
  charismatic leadership and, 50, 56, 89, 114n, 158
  leadership research and, 2, 3, 6–7, 157–8
Smith, Roger, 148
social formation of charisma, 37, 46, 47, 55, 56–69, 75, 93, 111, 118, 136, 164
  followers, role of, 57–8, 59, 60, 61, 62, 63
  mass media, role of, 66, 87
  myth and legend in, 62–3, 93, 120
  oratory, role of, 31, 47, 58, 60–2
  rationality in, 68–9, 178
  success, role of, 65–6, 118, 167
Southcott, Joanna, 47, 48, 58, 62, 63
Southcottians, 55
Spiritualism, 83
Stalin, Joseph, 30
style approach, 1, 3, 4–11, 157
Stylites, St. Simon, 47
Sufism, 50–1, 53, 54, 56–7, 58, 62
Sukarno, 42
supportive leadership, 12, 13, 16–17, 19, 20
symbolism in leadership, 36–7, 67, 93, 96, 99, 101, 137, 145, 147

task attributes, 13, 14, 15, 16, 17–18, 19–20, 21, 157
teams in organizations, 153–5
Thorbeck, John, 147
Tito, Josip Broz, 62
traditional authority, 27, 34, 40, 64, 70, 82; *see also* legitimate authority, types of,
training of leaders, 4, 107, 112, 119, 140–2, 146, 147
trait approach, 1, 2–4, 11, 20, 44, 112, 157
traits as situational factors, 12–13, 14–15, 17–18
transactional leadership
  concept of, 95–102, 107–8, 144, 145, 146, 158–9

dimensions of, 99–100, 131
  measurement of, 121–3
transformational leadership
  concept of, 91, 95–102, 107–8, 113, 121–36, 137, 142, 143, 144, 155, 157, 160, 161–2
  dimensions of, 98–9, 131
  as distinct from charismatic leadership, 104–7, 113, 134
  measurement of, 121–3, 128–9
  personal attributes and, 100–1, 134
  as romanticized leadership, 135–6, 143
  selection for, 141
  situational factors and, 129, 130, 158–9
  training for, 100, 101–2, 140–2
trust in the leader, 51–2, 88, 94, 99, 102, 117, 131–2, 137, 138, 147–8, 150, 166, 175

Unification Church, 44, 53, 77–8, 82
United Artists, 170–3
United Mineworkers, 87
United States presidents, studies of, 48, 49

vertical dyad linkage (VDL) approach, 8–9, 129–30
Vinoba Bhave, 55, 64
vision, 38, 39, 88, 90, 92, 99, 105, 106, 107, 109, 110, 111, 112, 113, 118, 122, 131, 132–3, 134, 141, 142, 143, 144, 148, 158, 159–60, 161, 163, 169, 171
  advantages of, 117, 136, 175
  communication of, 101, 110, 117, 133, 136–7, 138, 141, 145, 146–7, 148, 150, 151, 155, 175
  disadvantages of, 150–3, 172–4
  nature of, 97, 102, 103, 133, 136, 137, 138, 150, 153–4, 155–6, 166, 168
visionary leadership, 107–8, 113, 114n, 115, 144, 146–7, 155
voice of charismatic leaders, 47
Vroom-Yetton contingency model, 20

Welch, John F. (Jack), 107, 108, 109, 132, 133, 142, 143, 147, 150, 159, 167, 168, 175, 177
Welch, Robert, 76
White, Ellen, 58, 81–2
Williams, Art, 120

Xerox, 148, 173

zaddikim, 51, 71